Staple Inn, home of the Institute of Actuaries since 1887.

Of Staples' Inn, who knows the purpose or use?
Who are its members, and what do they do as such?

Anthony Trollope, *Can you Forgive her?*, 1867

Mind over data
AN ACTUARIAL HISTORY

Laurie Dennett

GRANTA EDITIONS

in association with
The Institute of Actuaries

© Institute of Actuaries 2004

Granta Editions is a wholly owned imprint of Book Production Consultants plc

A CIP catalogue record for this book is available from the British Library.
ISBN 1 85757 082 0

Designed by Peter Dolton.
Design, editorial and production in association with
Book Production Consultants plc, 25–27 High Street, Chesterton, Cambridge CB4 1ND,
United Kingdom.
Printed and bound in Singapore by Kyodo Printing Co (Singapore) Pte Ltd.

CONTENTS

The symbol (*) in the text denotes an entry in Appendix Three: Biographies

BACK in 2001, in an early phase of research for this book, I interviewed Dr Angus Macdonald of the Department of Actuarial Mathematics and Statistics at Heriot-Watt University in Edinburgh. At a point in our discussion he told me the story of how, after a recent all-day meeting at Staple Inn, he had visited one of the larger bookshops in Charing Cross Road and, out of curiosity, scanned the shelves for books about the actuarial profession. He found only one: *Life, Death and Money*, published in the Institute's 150th anniversary year, 1998.

The contrast with the many books devoted to the sister-profession of accountancy made an impact upon Dr Macdonald, and his story in turn made one upon me. In a sense the present book is the result of trying to find the answer to what I increasingly came to feel was a mystery. Why has the actuarial profession (one of the smallest, to be sure, with only 35,000 members world-wide), with its crucial importance to nearly everyone, been so comparatively unsung? The more I learned in the months that followed my meeting with Dr Macdonald, the more perplexing became the contrast between the importance of actuaries and their work and the amount known about the profession by people outside it – my friends, for instance, many of whom are professional people themselves.

Both *Life, Death and Money* and the impressive 1998 touring exhibition 'Modelling the Future' have helped to make the actuarial profession better known and understood here in the United Kingdom, where it first came into being. In commissioning the present book, the Institute of Actuaries wanted to bring its own history up to date, summarising the period from 1848 to 1948 that had been covered by a previous author, Reginald Simmonds, as the context from which the history of the past half-century has emerged. It was felt that such an account, contemporary and as far as possible non-technical, would be of use to future newly qualified actuaries and of interest to the wider public. This latter aim became my own to a far greater degree than I ever imagined it would – it will please me as much as it will any actuary to find *Mind over Data* in the bookshops of Charing Cross Road, helping to right the balance among the studies of the various professions. My admiration for this smallest among them has grown along with the book, thanks both to my research and to acquaintance with so many members of the Institute. I hope they will find here a fair reflection of the past they have been part of, and that newly quali-fied actuaries will gain a sense of the professional community stretching back in time as well as forward into the future.

Many people have contributed to making the aim a reality. I should like to thank the more than thirty members of the Institute of Actuaries and the Faculty of Actuaries who gave me the benefit of their time and experience, and in many cases their hospitality, as interview subjects – and Dennis Gilley in particular, who provided me with useful printed material and kindly answered many questions as they arose. Members of the Steering Group – Roger Corley, Gordon Bayley, Paul Thornton, Chris Lewin, Howard Webb, Frank Guaschi and Alex McKinnell – have each commented constructively on the manuscript in its entirety, and many others on specific parts of it. I am grateful to them all for their enthusiasm and encouragement, not to mention their patience. The advice and assistance to the group provided by Book Production Consultants – Stephanie Zarach, Sue Gray, Peter Dolton, Jo'e Coleby and Jenny Knight – has been much appreciated. The staff of the Institute's Library, headed by Sally Grover, has been unfailingly courteous and helpful. If I had the power to award a 'Gold Medal', as the Institute does from time to time, it would go to one member of that staff, David Raymont, whose research support and practical assistance have been given so generously at every stage. It seems fitting that the title of the book is his.

Laurie Dennett,
December 2003

Recruitment material produced by the Institute between 1948 and the present charts the broadening and increasing sophistication of the target audience.

Present at this 1898 gathering of Fellows of the Institute of Actuaries were fifteen past or future Presidents, and nine Presidents of the Faculty.

1 Thomas Emley YOUNG, BA
2 Thomas Bond SPRAGUE, MA, LL.D, FFA, FSS, FRSE
3 David DEUCHAR, FFA FRSE
4 Marcus Nathan ADLER, MA
5 James TERRY
6 Augustus HENDRIKS, FSS
7 James CHISHOLM, FFA
8 Gordon DOUGLAS, FFA
9 Thomas WALLACE, FFA
10 Archibald DAY
11 Joseph Alfred ARCHER
12 Hubert ANSELL
13 George Stephen CRISFORD
14 James SORLEY, FFA, CA, FRSE
15 Francis Ernest COLENSO, MA
16 James MEIKLE, FFA
17 George KING, FIA
18 Phillip Lewin NEWMAN, BA
19 Sir Henry HARBEN
20 Henry Walsingham ANDRAS
21 Henry COCKBURN, FIA

22 Arthur Francis BURRIDGE
23 Herbert Cecil THISELTON, FFA
24 William HUGHES
25 Henry William MANLY
26 Geoffrey MARKS
27 Frank Bertrand WYATT
28 Louis Michael SIMON
29 Niel Ballingal GUNN, FFA
30 Charles STEVENS
31 William L. LEMON
32 William Joseph Hutchings WHITTALL
33 Frederick SCHOOLING
34 William SUTTON, MA
35 Arthur Hutcheson BAILEY, FSS
36 Thomas Charles DEWEY
37 James Heron DUNCAN
38 George William BERRIDGE
39 Edwin JUSTICAN, FSS
40 Arthur SMITHER
41 John George PRIESTLEY
42 John DUNCAN
43 Alfred Barton ADLARD
44 Arthur PEARSON
45 Andrew Hugh TURNBULL, FFA
46 Ernest WOODS
47 Harris Charter Lindon SAUNDERS, FRAS
48 Griffith DAVIES
49 Thomas Gans ACKLAND, FSS

50 Arthur George HEMMING, FSS
51 Frederick HENDRIKS, FSS
52 Willis BROWNE
53 Frederick BELL
54 Ernest COLQUHOUN
55 Spencer Campbell THOMSON, BA, FFA
56 Stanley DAY
57 George Francis HARDY
58 Kenneth William ELDER
59 Harry Ethelston NIGHTINGALE
60 John MOODY-STUART, FFA
61 Arthur Gregory ALLEN
62 John Mayhew ALLEN
63 Owen KENTISH
64 Herbert FOOT, BA
65 Rowland Hill FELLOWS, FSS
66 James Robert HART
67 John William MILNER
68 John Norman LEWIS, FFA
69 Arthur Wyndham TARN
70 Herbert Archer THOMSON, BA
71 Arthur Ernest MOLYNEUX
72 David Alexander BUMSTED
73 Robert CROSS
74 Thomas KYD, FFA
75 William Hancock ALDCROFT
76 William Anderson HUTCHESON, FFA
77 William Smith ANDERSON

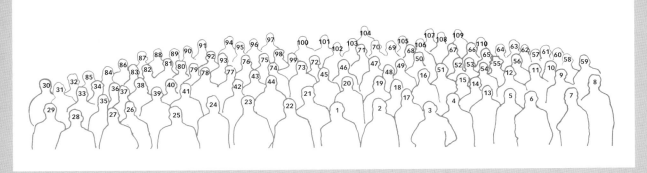

78 Henry Phillip CALDERON	**89** James Douglas WATSON	**100** Frederick Timothy Mason BYERS
79 John Bell TENNANT	**90** Samuel George WARNER	**101** Frederick Wesley FULFORD
80 Arthur Rhys BARRAND	**91** George James LIDSTONE	**102** William Abernethy SIM, FFA
81 Arthur Digby BESANT, BA	**92** Arthur Harold CLARKE	**103** William Pritchard PULLEY
82 Alexander G. MACKENZIE, FFA	**93** Edward Robert STRAKER	**104** Lancelot Andrewes WINTLE
83 William HUTTON, FFA	**94** Henry James BAKER	**105** Harry BEARMAN
84 Archibald HEWAT, FFA, FSS	**95** William Peyton PHELPS, MA	**106** G. E. MAY
85 William Henry TYNDALL, FSS, FRMetS	**96** Louis STAHLSCHMIDT	**107** Joseph Flack MORAN
86 Edward Arthur RUSHER, FSS	**97** Arnold Stoughton HARRIS, MA	**108** Joseph BURN
87 Alfred Charles THORNE	**98** Ernest Charles THOMAS	**109** Joseph Howard BARNES, FSS
88 John McDONALD	**99** James CHATHAM, FFA, FSS	**110** Willie Oscar NASH

PICTURE ACKNOWLEDGEMENTS

Pictures and photographs © Institute of Actuaries, except as follows, by kind permission:

The Actuaries Club 24, 43, 108; © Association of British Insurers 30; Continuous Mortality Investigation Bureau 69; Crown copyright 2000, First [Earlier] Edition published 1984 (Ogden tables) (Crown copyright material is reproduced with the permission of the Controller of HMSO and the Queen's Printer for Scotland) 120; The Denarius Club 91; Laurie Dennett 3; Peter Farr 147; © Financial Times 68 (photography by Alan Bird/Axiom Design Partnership); Lucy Fox, for the descendant family and executors of the estate of the late Sir Michael Ogden 120; Frank Guaschi 74; Executors for the Henriques family (descendant family of Benjamin Gompertz) 11; © Satoshi Kambayashi 19, 53; Eric Lander, created by Runaway Technology Inc. using PhotoMosaic by Robert Silvers from original artwork by Darryl Leja, courtesy of the Whitehead Institute for Biomedical Research 159; Lloyd's of London 127; © Nigel Luckhurst, Cambridge University, Centre of Mathematical Sciences 174; © National Library of Wales 5; © NOAA Photo Library, NOAA Central Library, OAR/ERL/ National Severe Storms Laboratory (NSSL) 76; Paul Sanderson cartoon © SIAS/ The Actuary 153; © Science Museum/Science & Society Picture Library 63, 64, 65; © SIAS/The Actuary 137, 167; Colin Stewart 74; © The Times, London/NI Syndication Ltd 67, 72, 130 (130 photography by Alan Bird/Axiom Design Partnership); Worshipful Company of Actuaries 99.

With additional thanks to Lewis Photos Ltd for new photography of Institute artefacts.

All efforts have been made to contact copyright holders, but if any have been inadvertently overlooked, the Institute of Actuaries will be pleased to make the necessary arrangement at the earliest opportunity.

CHAPTER ONE

The battle for the middle ground – and the growth of a profession

WHILE actuarial science has a longer history, the emergence of the *profession* of actuary was an intrinsic part of the establishment of life assurance on scientific principles in the mid-eighteenth century. Until then, assurances on lives had been effected in a variety of ways, mainly with individual underwriters prepared to take on short-term risks of, say, a year at a time. There were also tontine schemes and the societies formed to provide specific groups of people with a means of saving against the eventualities of sickness and burial. The earliest life insurance companies, such as the Amicable of 1706 and the London Assurance and the Royal Exchange, both founded in 1720, offered significant improvements, while the Scottish Ministers' Widows Fund of 1743 is said to have been the first actuarially based pension fund. The formation of the Society for Equitable Assurances on Lives and Survivorships in 1762 marked a turning point. The 'Old Equitable', as it later came to be known, was a mutual society (that is, one which is owned by its policyholders, rather than by shareholders). It was the first society to set level annual premiums varying according to the age at entry of the policy-holder, thus enabling the build-up of a fund as the risk of mortality increased. The mathematical calculations that made this long-term life assurance possible were supplied by James Dodson, based on mortality tables constructed from deaths in London between 1728 and 1750. Dodson died a few years before the founding of the Equitable, but he is usually acknowledged as the father of modern life insurance.

The Equitable not only introduced the concept of setting premium levels according to the risks presented by various ages, but coincidentally supplied a name for the officer who came to assume responsibility for such calculations. The word 'actuary' appears in the Equitable's deed of settlement, composed by the company's prime mover Edward Rowe Mores, a keen antiquarian. Much has been written about the antecedents and original meaning of the name 'actuary'. It is usually held to derive from the Latin *actuarius*, the scribe or notary who recorded the debates and decisions of the Roman Senate. There is, however, something more to its etymology. The word was originally an adjective (*actuarius, actuaria, actuarium*), meaning 'fast' or 'agile'. By the process of transference, over time it became a noun denoting anything particularly rapid, such as the fast ships carrying passengers rather than cargo: *actuaria navis*, the 'fast ship', became the *actuaria*, the equivalent of an 'express'. Similarly, among the many clerks belonging to the Roman civil service, the scribe especially trained for speedy writing came to be called *actuarius scriba* – and in due course simply *actuarius*, the classical equivalent of the nineteenth-century Hansard writer or short-hand clerk.[1] This was the sense the word retained in the context of the medieval church courts. Some members of the profession even in its earliest days blamed the choice of this unfamiliar name for the public's difficulty in understanding what it was and did. Some still do.

The Equitable's actuary, however, was far removed from both his modern namesake and his Roman one. He was not required to be particularly speedy, but only 'to attend daily, Sundays excepted …' to receive proposals, and 'in a fair and clerk-like hand, method, and manner, keep and write all such books as the future occasions of the Society shall require', including, of course, the contracts made with policyholders. This sounds rather like the job of a company secretary and, indeed, the duties which later became the province of the actuary were for some years handled by Mores and the other directors. Since the first four of the company's so-called actuaries were not trained in mathematics, this may have been no more than prudent. The fifth, William Morgan, was a mathematician with medical training and an interest in mortality investigation. He was the first to assume tasks that were properly actuarial, such as calculating premiums, valuing the liabilities and deciding on the distribution of surplus as 'bonus'. Joining the Equitable in 1774, he remained with the company until 1830 – an extraordinarily long period of service and influence. Not only did he unite the title of actuary with responsibilities requiring mathematical expertise and an understanding of mortality rates, but he applied theoretical solutions to practical business problems in a way characteristic of the modern actuary.[2]

Morgan had the advantage of being the nephew of another prominent figure in the annals of actuarial history, Dr Richard Price, who devised the famous Northampton life tables.[3] These were adopted by Morgan as the basis for the Equitable's premium calculations and widely used by other companies until well into the next century. Price's tables were based on a very small sample of lives, and contained other errors which only became apparent some time later. The tables' underestimate of life expectancy led the Equitable to charge premiums for life assurance that were too high, so that the company inadvertently benefited. The National Debt Office, on the other hand, adopted the Northampton tables in 1808 on Morgan's advice as the basis for the sale of life annuities, and slowly and steadily began to lose money.

Until the beginning of the nineteenth century the Equitable and a few other offices had the life assurance field to themselves. Then, under the pressures of a growing population and a rapidly expanding economy, the number of life assurance companies began to increase. Between 1800, when there were six offices, and 1830, by which time there were thirty-eight, the meaning and use of the title of 'Actuary' and the responsibilities carried out by the officer who bore it varied widely. In some of the older life offices, the 'Registrar',

'Secretary' or 'Life Accountant' performed the actuarial function, while in others, the 'Actuary' did. The Scottish offices tended to use the term 'Manager'. Many of the new offices sought the cachet of appearing long established by following the Equitable's precedent and appointing 'Actuaries', but these often lacked mathematical training and were really only superior clerks. There were also men who had worked their way up through the ranks of their respective offices. The proliferation of offices created a somewhat self-conscious disparity between, on one hand, the more experienced officers, often mathematically trained, who might be called 'Actuary' or some other title, and the newer appointments, who might claim the title but lack the training.

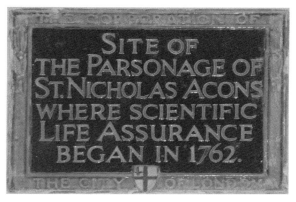

Having survived the assaults of war and modernisation, this plaque has been mounted on a wall in Nicholas Lane in the City of London, near the site of the Equitable Assurance Society's first office.

Naturally, the experienced men inspired by mathematics – well known to one another through membership of learned institutions such as the Royal Society, and convinced that the study of mortality and probability was a means to social improvement – were more sensitive to discrepancies in standards. These were the men whose spheres of influence transcended their positions – whatever their titles – in the life offices. They acted as consultants to other institutions, from the friendly societies that insured the working classes of the industrial districts[4] to parliamentary committees. Some wrote books that became standard works. Besides the seven editions of Price's *Observations on Reversionary Payments* and the two editions of Morgan's *The Doctrine of Annuities and Assurances on Lives and Survivorships*, surveys such as Francis Baily's *Doctrine* of 1813 and the *Treatise* of 1815 written by Joshua Milne (the compiler of another famous set of mortality tables, the 'Carlisle') provided the rudiments of training for the next generation.

In 1819, reference was first made to actuaries in an Act of Parliament and thus both the word and the function acquired a measure of official recognition. The Friendly Societies' Act,[5] arising out of concern about the stability and honesty of some of these institutions, required that each have its table of benefits confirmed by a judge, prior to which it was to be approved by two

persons 'known to be professional Actuaries or persons skilled in calculation'. Unfortunately, as the Committee set up in 1825 to investigate the working of the 1819 Act discovered, 'the Bench have been satisfied with the
signatures of petty schoolmasters and accountants whose opinion upon the
probability of sickness, and the duration of life, is not to be depended upon'.
Among the witnesses called by this Committee were William Morgan, Joshua
Milne, John Finlaison and several others practising as actuaries. Finlaison was
the Actuary of the National Debt Office, a post created in 1821 to which he had
been appointed on the strength of having reorganised the vast and hitherto
chaotic records of the Admiralty. In the course of doing this he had created
pension funds for the widows and orphans of several categories of naval
employee, and set up friendly societies to administer them.

Shortly after taking up his post Finlaison advised the Government that
grave losses of some £8,000 a week were being sustained on the sale of life
annuities calculated according to the outdated Northampton tables. He compiled new tables showing that the average duration of human life had
increased over the previous century, and that there were important differences
between male and female mortality. These conclusions were only accepted
after much resistance, but in due course Finlaison was vindicated and in 1829
the sale of life annuities was re-established on the sound basis he provided.[6]
Finlaison was the successor to William Morgan in impressing upon both government and public that the value of actuarial calculations was not confined to
the individual lives covered by the life offices. It was in keeping with his prestige as actuary to a variety of government bodies, long before the formal creation of the position of Government Actuary, that he would be elected the first
President of the Institute of Actuaries. But this is to advance too far: the founding of the Institute was still twenty years in the future, though circumstances
were ripening for its creation.

Between 1819 and 1830 references to 'Actuaries' continued to appear in
legislation, and the title, linked to the performance of calculations relating to
life assurance and requiring a degree of mathematical skill, came to be generally accepted, at least in English life offices. In Scottish offices the title of
'Manager' persisted, possibly because 'Actuary' was already in common use in
relation to savings banks. It is interesting to observe that in Edinburgh an
informal discussion group known as the Association of Managers of Life
Offices of Scotland was formed in 1833. Following its expansion to include
offices outside Edinburgh, it became the Associated Scottish Life Offices in
1841, and 'the first insurance trade association in the world'.[7] Scottish over-
tures to some of the prominent English actuaries, encouraging the formation
of a similar body in London, at this stage came to nothing.

The fact was that in England matters were less well advanced and less
harmonious, due to the growing number of life offices – by 1840 there
would be 100 of them, some of dubious status. Charles Babbage, inventor of

the calculating device known as the 'difference engine' and an actuary of note, identified one source of disunity when he wrote in 1836 in his *Comparative View of the Various Institutions for the Assurance of Lives* that, regarding actuaries, 'the degree of knowledge possessed by persons so situated at the different institutions, is exceedingly various ... from the most superficial acquirements, derived merely from the routine of an office, up to the most profound knowledge of the subject'.[8]

The second quarter of the nineteenth century was a period of growing self-consciousness on the part of established professions such as medicine and law, and of emerging ones such as engineering, surveying and accountancy. It also saw the formation of many scholarly and investigative societies aimed at social improvement. The Royal Statistical Society, to which a number of practising actuaries belonged, dates from 1834, and it would be strange if the idea of establishing a forum for actuarial concerns did not suggest itself to some of them. There is fragmentary evidence to suggest that a group of London life office actuaries met regularly on a friendly basis in one another's homes from the late 1820s onward.[9] Foremost among them was the Welsh autodidact Griffith Davies, who had already done much to encourage the study of calculation as a summer tutor to Merchant Taylors' School and had been eased by William Morgan into an actuary's post at the Guardian.[10] Other names, some brought to life by anecdote, emerge from the account of these pre-Institute years written by another member of the group, J. J. Downes of the Economic. Here are the brilliant Jewish mathematician Benjamin Gompertz, for whom Nathan Rothschild founded the Alliance when the discriminatory practices of the day denied him a post else-

GRIFFITH DAVIES.

The mathematician Griffith Davies (1788–1855) overcame poverty to educate himself to become the first actuary of the Guardian Assurance Company and a leading figure in the formation of the Institute.

where; Charles Ansell of the Atlas, known as 'the Bishop'; Barker Woolhouse, as outstanding a violinist as he was mathematician; and the urbane and kindly Charles Jellicoe of the Eagle, one of the forerunners of the Eagle Star.

The first concerted effort on the part of English actuaries seems to have been the preparation, in about 1837, of a petition to the House of Commons, requesting the publication of the data upon which Finlaison's new Government Annuitants' Tables were based. Finlaison apparently derided the signatories as 'the Forty Thieves' even though the attached names numbered forty-two;[11] the petition was never sent. A more straightforward attempt to put life business on sturdier foundations was made in 1838, when a Committee was formed to collect and arrange the mortality records of seventeen of the largest life offices. This resulted in the publication, paid for by subscriptions from fifty-eight life companies, of the *Seventeen Offices Experience* in 1843. The 'Experience Committee' was never formally disbanded, so that in 1846 – when the Scottish offices, led by William Thomson, sought support from their English counterparts 'to promote upon sound principles the great objects of that scientific occupation in which they were all engaged'[12] – it was this body that they approached. But deliberations on the English side were cautious and it was not until a further Scottish overture, early in 1848, that the Experience Committee convened a meeting at the offices of the Standard Life Assurance in King William Street in the City, on 15 April. Even then, the Committee (chaired by Griffith Davies) claimed to be merely testing the waters, and a sub-committee was appointed to produce a Report on how best to proceed.

These preliminary steps have been described more fully in R. C. Simmonds's *The Institute of Actuaries 1848–1948*. What emerges from that account is the wide separation between the fraternity representing the older offices and the majority, drawn from the newer companies. The former wished only to adopt the Scottish model of an 'Association of Managers', rather than finding themselves outnumbered by men unknown to them, as members of a 'College of Actuaries' – the suggestion of Peter Hardy, the actuary of the London Assurance. This attitude was partially justified: the life assurance field was as yet poorly controlled by legislation, despite (or, as is sometimes alleged, thanks to) the Joint Stock Companies' Act of 1844. Shaky companies and unscrupulous practices were rife, and scarcely a week passed without the revelation of some new scandal by the *Post Magazine and Insurance Monitor*. But however understandable the position of the 'old guard', in narrowly seeking to preserve the standards set by the few, they ignored the challenge of raising them for the many. They may have believed that actuarial experience was best acquired through being articled to an expert practitioner, as in the legal profession.[13] They may also have been protective of the consulting work, largely to friendly societies, which came to them through personal reputation. It was not surprising that on 10 June 1848, at a further meeting, the Report of the sub-committee recommended against 'the formation of a Society of any description' and proposed no future action other than the holding of 'occasional meetings'. This Report clearly did not express the will of those present, for when Peter Hardy moved the establishment of 'a scientific and practical Association amongst the Actuaries, Secretaries and Managers of the Life Assurance Societies of Great Britain', the motion was approved by a large majority of the sixty-six men present. Nonetheless, when a new Committee of fifteen was elected, it included some who had served on earlier Committees. Five members, among them Charles Jellicoe, Joseph Sylvester of the Equity and Law Life and Peter Hardy, were asked to prepare a draft constitution.[14]

Some of the men from the older offices stayed away from a third meeting, held on Saturday 8 July, but more than fifty others holding actuarial posts did attend, and voted into being 'The Institute of Actuaries of Great Britain and Ireland'. Its main objects were, as its constitution set out, firstly, 'the development and improvement of the mathematical theories upon which the practice of Life Assurance is based, and the collection and arrangement of data connected with the subjects of duration of life, health, and finance'; and, secondly, the education of the public in 'correct principles relating to subjects involving monetary considerations and the doctrine of probability'. Further clauses assumed for the Institute the responsibility for setting uniform standards of practice, raising the status of the profession, fostering investigation and debate, and founding a library. Membership as a Fellow was open to any actuary already employed in a registered British life office, while those engaged in actuarial work under other titles could become Associates. The Institute was to be governed by a President and a Council of sixteen, later twenty-two, then thirty, elected by the members from among the Fellows, and there were further measures dealing with discipline, administration and finance. Three Fellows were to be elected annually to examine candidates – in mathematical theory, vital statistics, computation and the construction of tables, and book-keeping – prior to granting them 'Certificates of Competency'. Among the first tutors appointed in 1849 was Joseph Sylvester, who later became the first Professor of Mathematics at Johns Hopkins University; among those who sat the first examinations in 1850 were future Institute Presidents Arthur Hutcheson Bailey and Archibald Day.

What the Institute needed most urgently was members. A letter about the formation, accompanied by a copy of the constitution, was sent to every prospective member in the country, allowing six weeks in which to claim enrolment. Subscriptions were set at £3.3s for Fellows and £2.2s for Associates. A modicum of publicity was obtained *gratis* through the good offices of the *Post Magazine*. By the time of the first meeting in October, ninety-four Fellows and thirty-seven Associates had joined. Referring to the disgruntled coterie that still held aloof, but from which there had already been a few defections, the *Post Magazine* had observed in July that:

*It could scarcely be expected that the members of the Old Committee, whose report
and suggestions were so unceremoniously set aside, would readily apply to join an
Institute the necessity of which they thought did not exist. But the fact of no one else
entertaining this opinion but themselves, is we believe gradually working its way
and they are gradually and wisely adding their names to the list of the enrolled.*[15]

By the October meeting, at which (since Griffith Davies's poor health precluded his accepting) John Finlaison was elected the Institute's first President, this optimistic forecast was shown to be premature. The 'Old Committee' of thirteen influential actuaries remained obdurate in its hostility to the upstart, and – on seeing that the Institute was gaining, rather than losing, adherents –

on 4 November met at the Atlas, of which Charles Ansell was actuary, to consider what best to do. The result of its deliberations was the Actuaries' Club, launched on 18 November – the formal expression of the rivalry that would colour the next thirty-six years. The Actuaries' Club was never much more than a dining club and forum for the discussion of points of practice, though its members regarded it as superior to the Institute on account of their own prestige as chief officers of some of the leading companies. This attitude was in striking contrast to that voiced by Charles Jellicoe of the Institute, who expressed himself incapable of believing that the split would last long. For all to be well,

John Finlaison, President of the Institute of Actuaries from its formation in 1848 until 1869. From 1809 to 1822 he had been Keeper of the Admiralty records and from 1822 to 1851 he was Actuary of the National Debt.

they had only to be true to themselves, to work together for the common end, to lose sight of any little selfish considerations, to entertain a due respect for the claims of each member of the body and especially for that younger portion of it which stood most in need of friendly counsel and assistance.[16]

In January 1849, and again in January 1851, Finlaison wrote to the members of the Actuaries' Club inviting them in the most gracious terms to join the Institute as Fellows and partners in building up the actuarial profession, but all refused.

The Institute was now poised to embark on the pursuit of the objects for which it had been formed, but first it had to resolve the practical matter of a base from which to operate. Its early meetings were held at the offices of the Guardian and the Statistical Society, since at this stage it had no funds. In January 1849, the Institute agreed a modest rent with the Family Endowment Society for office space on the second floor 12 Chatham Place, Blackfriars, overlooking the Thames, and remained there until the autumn of 1852. During 1852 the possibility was explored of sharing the premises belonging to the Statistical Society, with which the Institute maintained close relations, due to similar fields of interest and a significantly overlapping membership. This was readily agreed, and the Institute moved on 1 October to 12 St James's Square, where it would remain until 1874.

Once the Institute had a headquarters and a venue for meetings, it could begin to build a sense of cohesion among the members. This was done primarily through monthly 'Sessional Meetings' (advertised in quality newspapers such as *The Times* as well as in the *Post Magazine*) at which papers on some aspect of actuarial mathematics or practice were presented and discussed. The first few annual general meetings, with formal dinners afterwards at the Richmond Hotel, gave Charles Jellicoe the chance to set out his vision of the Institute's future, in which not only insurance, but 'the cognate subjects of taxation, currency, finance, and political economy generally, should receive their fullest development'. From 1850 the Institute elected Honorary Members, such as the great statistician Dr William Farr, and Augustus De Morgan who taught actuarial mathematics at University College London. The Library rapidly became a reality: the standard books and tools of reference were bought, and author-members donated copies of their own works. Most important of all, the *Assurance Magazine* began its long career in September 1850, with Jellicoe as editor. From 1852 it was known as the *Assurance Magazine and Journal of the Institute of Actuaries*,[17] but from the beginning, by – among other things – reproducing the papers given at sessional meetings, it performed the vital functions of keeping the members abreast of current actuarial work in a way that few men had time to do on their own account.

The 1850s, the years when the Institute was still finding its feet, were dominated by a second schism. This time it was effected by the Scottish members, who comprised about a third of the whole membership. A perceived lack of fairness in representation on the Council and the desire for a Scottish 'Section' were matters first raised in 1853, and too fundamental to be easily resolved. Painful discussions dragged on until the spring of 1855, when the seven Scottish members of Council and a further twenty-four Scottish members resigned from the Institute, to be followed by forty-one more in the autumn. On 4 January 1856, the Faculty of Actuaries was established in Edinburgh. The breach was deeply felt in London, and although the two actuarial bodies agreed to collaborate in future, the secession damaged not only the morale of the Institute, but its finances, provoking a deficit that required some ingenuity on the part of Council to overcome.[18]

The Institute was left leaner, if less ebullient, and Council even more imbued with a sense of occupying a middle ground free of particular or geographical interests, and an almost missionary conviction that this ground had to be maintained and extended on behalf of the new profession, still in the process of coalescing. The inherent difficulty was that the term 'actuary' was still so elastic. It was unfortunate that the Institute's financial needs following the Scottish secession would perpetuate this particular problem, since one means of allaying the shortfall was the admission as Fellows, from 1857, of men deemed to possess the *status* of actuary, without requiring them to obtain a Certificate of Competency. This set off a vigorous internal debate about the definition of an actuary that threatened to create further division. It also put paid, due to opposition from the Actuaries' Club, to early hopes of obtaining a Royal Charter for the Institute.

Gradually the Institute took on an aspect of permanence, and recovered its balance financially. While Council members and tutors were, of course, unpaid (examiners received an honorarium from 1869), a minimal staff – consisting of an assistant secretary, a clerk and a messenger – was taken on. Council set up Standing Committees to deal with ongoing concerns, and subscription income just managed to keep pace with the demands on the funds. The need for education and standards had been one of the main reasons behind the formation of the Institute, and had been addressed almost at once. The examinations leading to the Certificate of Competency evolved from two papers in 1849 to three 'Parts' (the first two of three papers each and the third of six), each Part requiring a minimum of a year's study. The first-year examination was offered in 1851, the second in 1853 and the third in 1855, and no candidate was allowed to sit the final Part unless he had five years' life office experience. By 1860 the syllabus was undergoing the first of its many revisions, but even then the dearth of candidates coupled with poor pass rates convinced the Institute of 'the urgent necessity that exists for affording to students some guidance in preparing for the examination'. The remedy took some time to effect. C. D. Higham later recalled that:

Reading for the examinations in those days was very different …, for, except that in 1871 a tutor and class were set up for the second [year] there were no tutors and no classes and it was necessary to grope about for the information that had to be obtained.[19]

Those already possessing honours degrees in mathematics were spared the rigours of the first-year examination, but from 1882 those who were not had cause to be grateful to William Sutton, who produced a textbook on life annuities, assurances and interest for 'preliminary' students; the second-year, or 'intermediate', students had to wait until 1887 for a textbook.

The life of the Institute settled into an annual round of sessional meetings and examinations. Council was ever vigilant for means by which the Institute could contribute to scientific advance, and was soon awarding prizes for original work – the Messenger (for essays by Associates) from 1858, the Brown (named for Samuel Brown, President of the Institute 1867–70, for 'an Essay on some subject of Political or Social Economy') from 1870. A dining club, the Institute of Actuaries Club, was founded in 1856, along the lines of a college dining club. Council conceived of the Institute as, among other things, a learned society, and in 1870 joined a mixed bag of societies that included the Statistical Society and associations dedicated to meteorology, anthropology, social science and photography in seeking government support for more dignified accommodation. This initiative came to nothing,[20] however, and the Institute moved with the Statistical Society to the Principal's House, King's College, Strand, in 1874, remaining there until both associations moved to 9 Adelphi Terrace in 1884. From its beginnings the Institute exchanged its journal with other societies, and was represented at meetings of the British

Association and at international statistical congresses. As for projects, the importance of the collection of mortality data for the life assurance industry and the whole field of vital statistics could scarcely be overstated. During the 1850s an attempt was made to collect the experience of the life offices for persons living abroad, but although fifty-two offices participated, the sampling was small and little could be deduced from it. In 1862 Council embarked on a far larger undertaking by attempting to collect and combine the experience of all British life companies. This immense project took five years and the resulting tables were published under the supervision of Peter Gray ('that extraordinary man who, with all his actuarial attainments, was never one of the craft, but a Manchester warehouseman'[21]) in 1872. Known as the 'Hm (Healthy Males) Tables', they were the fruits of the 'first of the really important investigations' and provided a standard tool that remained in use for the next thirty years.[22]

Dramatic incidents are relatively few during these decades. Such human interest as there is in looking back over the period is supplied, rather, by the giants of the profession who belonged to the Institute during its first half-century. Besides monumental figures such as John Finlaison, Griffith Davies and Benjamin Gompertz, there were William Makeham, who carried Gompertz's 'law of mortality' further as 'Makeham's Formula', Barker Woolhouse and Thomas Bond Sprague – all pioneers in the field of mortality investigation and the graduation of mortality tables, and all of whom would merit further attention if space allowed.

In the rising area of pensions and annuities, the names of Ralph Price Hardy (son of Peter), Henry Manly and George King were prominent. Hardy was a man of outstanding analytical judgement, who had trained under Jellicoe at the Eagle but also built up a large private practice among friendly societies and commercial interests. As the author of many original studies published in the *Journal*, Manly was credited by his contemporaries with having virtually created the mathematics of the earliest group pension funds. King, whose vast contribution to the profession would be acknowledged by the award of the Institute's first Gold Medal in 1927, was the author of the Institute's 'intermediate' textbook, which became the 'Bible' of actuarial students for thirty-five years and was widely used abroad in translation. In investment, Arthur Hutcheson Bailey established the 'Canons' that would dominate the field for eighty years. On his election in 1880, he became the first President to deliver an Address; the pronouncement that 'An actuary must be a mathematician,

Benjamin Gompertz (1779–1865), an outstanding mathematician, was the first actuary of the Alliance Assurance office and later its chief officer. In 1825 he formulated an important law of mortality that was later modified by William Makeham. He was made an Honorary Fellow of the Institute in 1855.

but a mere mathematician will be a very incompetent actuary' at once became part of the lore of the profession. As all-round practitioners, Samuel Brown, Archibald Day, Thomas Young and William Hughes each commanded great respect. Most of these men served the Institute as tutors and examiners, members of Council or Presidents, and some filled all of these roles.

Thomas Bond Sprague was an especially commanding figure. While he apparently claimed that the Institute and the profession owed most to Charles Jellicoe, who became its second President on the death of John Finlaison in 1860, later authorities have awarded this palm to Sprague for the qualities of leadership that partnered his achievements in almost every area of actuarial

George King exemplified the ideal of service that helped to build up the profession – acting as tutor and examiner, producing the earliest textbook on life contingencies, and editing the *Journal* from 1896 to 1905. He received the Institute's first Gold Medal in 1927.

work.[23] He was actuary, successively, to the Liverpool and London and the Equity and Law Life before moving to Edinburgh as actuary to the Scottish Equitable in 1873. He was the only man to be elected President of both the Institute and the Faculty; he succeeded Jellicoe as editor of the *Journal* in 1867 and for the next sixteen years wielded immense influence through its pages. He also wrote numerous valuable articles for it – the earliest in 1856, the last in 1897. Part of his contribution to the preparation of the Institute of Actuaries Life Tables – the Hm Tables' official name – was concerned with a system of actuarial notation for general use which at the end of the century would be adopted internationally. He placed great emphasis on actuarial education, and encouraged a professional openness which he called 'publicity' (which today would probably be called 'transparency', a by-product of responsible self-regulation) or 'the practice for actuaries to work in the light of day, and to explain fully their processes, and the reasons which influence them'[24] as opposed to the attitudes of earlier days when senior actuaries jealously guarded their data and methods. This more generous approach he attributed to the influence of the Institute's leading members.

Two further circumstances in Sprague's lengthy career merit particular mention since he acted as the spokesman of the profession at the time they occurred. Even before the failure of the Albert life office in 1869, public concern had been centred on the life assurance industry, and in the run-up to the Life Assurance Act of 1870 the Council of the Institute, and Sprague in particular, sought to secure the right balance between safeguarding the public and allowing the life companies a necessary freedom of manoeuvre. Sprague was firmly opposed to government control of the life assurance companies, and his watchword – and that of Council – became 'Liberty with Publicity' (later on,

'Freedom with Publicity'): in other words, no interference from the state, but the publication by each company of detailed information that would enable outside actuaries to form a true picture of the real position of the business.[25] This general principle duly came to underlie the Act, and the life assurance legislation that superseded it in 1909.

Secondly, Sprague was President of the Institute when at last, thirty-six years after its formation, it obtained a Royal Charter in 1884. It had been not only a lengthy but an undignified struggle. The Life Assurance Act of 1870, in requiring that life office calculations be entrusted to an actuary, had again touched off a debate about who might justifiably claim to be one. The Institute had sought to make common cause with the Actuaries' Club in the hope of obtaining a mention of the Certificate of Competency in the Act, but this idea had foundered on the old ill-will. (The Faculty, on the other hand, fully representative of Scottish actuaries, had obtained its Royal Charter in 1868.)

But Sprague's Presidency marked the turning point in the Institute's relations with the Actuaries' Club. Formal application for a Charter was made in the summer of 1882, soon after his election. There followed two years during which the Institute, guided by Sprague, countered the successive allegations made by the Club to the Privy Council and the Board of Trade.[26] William Sutton (a later President of the Institute), who was actuary to the Registrar of Friendly Societies and coincidentally to the Board of Trade, had drafted the Charter and the Institute's Bye-laws, and very likely clarified the situation behind the scenes. The Royal Charter, amounting to official recognition that professional standing had been achieved, was granted on 29 July 1884. Soon

Thomas Bond Sprague, President from 1882 to 1886, coordinated the successful appeal for the Royal Charter and the healing of the breach with the Actuaries' Club. He bore the distinction of also becoming President of the Faculty, and was a powerful spokesman for the actuarial profession.

after, peace was finally made between the Institute and the Actuaries' Club. Each gave the other a dinner, the fifteen diehards of the Club – now well advanced in years – were made Fellows of the Institute; Sprague and the President of the Institute of Actuaries Club, the dining club of the Institute (at that time Archibald Day, one of the first Fellows to qualify under the examination system established in 1850) were elected to the Club. The profession in England was at last united and could speak with a single voice. For a time there existed a duplication of dining clubs, but in 1899 the Actuaries' Club (which had been retained as a social entity) absorbed the Institute of Actuaries Club. The Actuaries' Club remains the senior of the many actuarial dining clubs in both age and prestige.

Only a few years after being granted the Charter, the Institute had the great good fortune to be offered accommodation at Staple Inn. For centuries this

The Royal Charter granted to the Institute of Actuaries on 29 July 1884 changed its official status from, in the words of the then President, Thomas Sprague, 'a private scientific society' to 'a professional body'.

striking building had presented an overhanging late-medieval façade to one of London's busiest streets. The visitor who passed through its arched entrance found himself in a leafy courtyard surrounded by the restrained architectural harmony of the eighteenth century. The complex of buildings, parts of which were in a shocking state of decay, was bought at auction by the Prudential Assurance Company, which stood opposite in High Holborn and had several Fellows of the Institute on its staff. The Prudential employed Alfred (later Sir Alfred) Waterhouse to restore Staple Inn, and invited the Institute to become one of the first tenants. The Institute acquired in Staple Inn Hall an evocative setting for its Council and sessional meetings, and in a panelled anteroom the perfect space for the steadily growing Library. By 1888 there were two honorary Librarians, and in 1892 S. H. Jarvis – the embodiment of the Institute to students between the wars – joined as an assistant clerk.

The 1890s saw the Institute collaborating with the Faculty in organising the Om (Ordinary Males) Investigation of Assured Lives and the Oa (Ordinary Annuitants) Experience of Annuitants, beginning in 1893. The data collected from the life offices covered the period from 1863 to 1892, and the project itself, immense in scope and painstaking in execution, was not concluded until 1905. The published result ran to many volumes of tables, the sale of which benefited the Institute and the Faculty equally. The graduation of the most important of these tables was done by George Francis (later Sir George) Hardy, who in a series of Reports was the first to bring to the attention of his colleagues the methods of curve-fitting devised by Professsor Karl Pearson at University College London.[27]

The Institute had long been in touch with prominent actuaries in other countries, particularly in France, Belgium and the United States. The 1st International Congress of Actuaries was held in Brussels in 1895, and the 2nd in London in 1898 so as to coincide with the Institute's Jubilee celebrations. (It was at this congress that the actuarial notation known as 'Universal' was adopted, although it would be revised in 1927.) To those few men who had witnessed the whole span of Institute history, this must have been a particularly satisfying occasion. A new generation of outstanding actuaries was on the rise during the 1890s: George Hardy was the most revered of the tutors, but among those who qualified during that decade and carried forward the ideals of the first half-century were George Lidstone (who qualified in 1892 at the exceptionally young age of 21), Digby Besant and Ralph Todhunter (three of the five founders of a new dining club, the Gallio, in 1903, the others being Archer Thomson and James Watson); William Phelps; and George (later Lord) May and Joseph (later Sir Joseph) Burn, who became major figures in the Prudential. Slightly younger was William (later Sir William) Palin Elderton, who became, in the course of a 48-year career with the Equitable, one of the foremost actuaries of the twentieth century and another champion of the application of Pearsonian statistical methods to actuarial work. George Hardy had the distinction of being invited, while President of the Institute from 1908 to 1910, to advise on the proposed National Insurance scheme introduced in 1911, and thus earned increased recognition for the profession as well as

Staple Inn in 1887, following its purchase by the Prudential Assurance Company and its restoration by the well-known architect Alfred (later Sir Alfred) Waterhouse.

personal honours.[28] By then it had become the norm for the Institute to be approached for advice by the Exchequer, by government departments and parliamentary committees, and it was regularly consulted on the National Census. In 1917 the position of Government Actuary was created, its first holder being Sir Alfred Watson, chief actuary to the National Health Insurance Joint Committee from 1912; in 1919 the Government Actuary's Department was established as a separate department within the Civil Service. (Sir Alfred Watson was the grandson of Reuben Watson, whose firm, R. Watson & Sons, founded in 1878, was the largest and most senior of the handful of consulting actuarial firms before the First World War.)

The prestige of the profession was steadily increasing, as was the scope for actuaries to contribute in areas other than life assurance. According to the Institute *Year Book* – earlier issues of which would contain a useful backward glance at the evolution of the profession – this had much to do with 'the development in the national consciousness of the idea of communal provision against certain risks which, while they threaten all classes, are of particular significance in relation to the wage-earning and salaried classes of the community'.[29] Instances of the application of this idea were to be found not only in the Old Age Pension Act 1908 and the National Insurance Act 1911, but in the growing number of superannuation schemes, employers' pension plans and widows' pension arrangements, the organisation of which all required actuarial assistance. It was common practice for actuaries employed by the life offices to act at the same time as consultants to friendly societies, private pension funds and the like. As a professional body (and emphatically *not* a trade association) the Institute as a rule was not concerned with commercial relationships unless – as in a mere handful of cases – they violated the unwritten code of professional conduct. The kind of incident that provoked a stiff letter from the Institute included unseemly behaviour on the part of Fellows (probably less on account of anything scandalous than for having advertised their services in a newspaper), and the affront of unqualified persons setting themselves up as actuaries, whether or not they compounded the insult by claiming Fellowship of the Institute. Sometimes the Institute took legal action. In 1906, for example, an injunction was obtained against a so-called 'Institute of Accountants' whose members were calling themselves 'FIA (Lond.)' and 'AIA (Lond.)'.[30]

The education offered by the Institute was the focus of constant attention in the years before the First World War: the syllabus was revised in 1892, 1898 and 1908; the new examinations were designated 'Parts I', 'II' and 'III', and a Board of Examiners was appointed in 1907 to oversee the examinations and ensure consistency. Some of the texts produced before the war became classics: Lidstone's *Short Collection of Actuarial Tables*, Todhunter's *Compound Interest*, Elderton's *Frequency Curves and Correlation* and Burn's *Stock Exchange Investments* among them. The Institute of Actuaries' Students' Society (the idea of Steuart Macnaghten, later a President of the Faculty) was founded in 1910 to assist junior members to prepare for their examinations, but additionally, as a forum for the presentation of papers, it gave them a chance to gain confidence and experience in debate.

The coming of war naturally disrupted the studies of most would-be actuaries. By 1915 the monthly sessional meetings, and by 1916 the examinations, had been suspended for want of numbers and were not resumed until 1919, following which the examinations were held half-yearly for a time to help the returning men to catch up. In 1919, too, the Institute's Gold Medal was established, to commemorate actuarial work of outstanding merit and benefit to the profession. Following the direct appeal of Geoffrey Marks in his

Presidential Address on 16 December 1918, the way was opened for the admission of women to membership of the Institute. It took a few years for normal functioning to resume after the enervating experience of war, but in 1923 the idea of a facility for ongoing research into mortality rates using assurance data, first voiced in 1912 by William Elderton and R. C. Fippard (the latter died at Gallipoli in 1915), was revived by the Institute and Faculty together as the Continuous Mortality Investigation (CMI) Bureau. H. E. Melville and H. J. P. Oakley were associated with Elderton in overturning the methodology of decades in favour of ways that lost nothing of accuracy in being speedier and permitting continuous investigation.[31] Closer collaboration with the Faculty on matters of mutual interest continued during the 1920s, although the hope of establishing common examinations was not realised at that time. It is interesting to note that the Faculty offered a course leading to an examination in investment at this point, whereas the Institute did not. The Institute's syllabus underwent yet more revision in 1923 as efforts were made to accommodate an expanding field of knowledge and the changing demands of post-war society.

Geoffrey Marks recognised the challenge of the post-war panorama, and had great confidence in the ability of actuaries to meet it if training in statistics, economics and finance could be added to the syllabus. Actuaries with such training could be regarded as 'scientific financiers', and given the qualities of 'mother wit, energy, originality, tact, insight, courage, and enterprise' there were no limits to their prospects.[32] Marks was ahead of his time, but his ideas struck a sympathetic chord in an actuarial student called Fred Menzler who qualified in 1919. At a Special General Meeting on 26 October 1925, he presented a paper that stated the challenge more directly. The subject was 'The future of the actuarial profession' with some remarks about extending its scope. It seemed to him that few people had much grasp of what an actuary was or did. But whereas the profession had been in the vanguard of applied science in the nineteenth century, Menzler considered that it had not kept abreast of more recent advances, especially in the field of statistics. Despite the controversies occasioned by some branches of this subject, Menzler held that statistics was part of the territory where actuaries should feel particularly at home. He pointed out the rightful place of the profession, in a society increasingly dependent upon statistics, as 'the only body of professional statisticians', and the value of bringing appropriate statistical methods to the problems currently arising in industry, public administration and commerce – the 'wider fields' that awaited individual members of the profession.

These remarks were purposefully controversial and touched off passionate debate. The areas that Menzler invited actuaries to claim as their own were at some remove from the life insurance offices that were the usual sphere of most actuaries, but their role in these was also presented as falling short of what actuaries could and should contribute to the field of life assurance. The problem here was two-fold: firstly, more specialised training was needed if actuaries were to be fit for managerial posts in the life offices, or for employment in the 'wider fields'; and secondly, actuaries were bound by rules of professional etiquette that forbade them to advertise or otherwise promote their professional services. The post-war narrowing of employment opportunities in the life offices made the prospects for younger actuaries a matter of practical importance. An equal priority was the Institute's responsibility for fostering contact with less specialised associations, and in positioning the profession in the public mind.

Menzler's paper moved Council to appoint a Committee to look into the situation he had outlined. Its Report appeared in the *Journal* in February 1926, and recommended that a number of the ideas expressed a few months earlier be put into effect. Most important was the creation of a permanent Committee called, appropriately, 'The Scope of the Profession Committee'. It was given the tasks of maintaining contact with similar institutions, keeping informed of new legislation so that the profession could offer assistance or opinions quickly when appropriate, and publicising the affairs of the Institute. An Appointments Board was set up along the lines of the one in operation at Cambridge University. The education of the public about the nature of actuarial work was undertaken in a variety of ways. The *Institute of Actuaries Year Book* with Fred Menzler as editor has already been mentioned. An Annual Dinner was instituted – with Winston Churchill, then Chancellor of the Exchequer, as guest of honour at the first one in October 1926.[33] Existing contacts with foreign associations – in Belgium, the United States and Canada – were augmented by friendly visits to and from Scandinavian actuaries and close relationships, including the hosting of students, with newly founded actuarial bodies in India, Mexico and other countries. The first International Congress to be held in London since 1898 was in fact the eighth such gathering, and brought actuaries from all over the world to the congenial setting of Staple Inn in 1927. Sir Joseph Burn as President of the Institute greeted the members of a profession that was by now multi-racial and multi-lingual. Statistics and investment were targeted for special attention in yet another revision of the syllabus in 1928, and the amount of tuition available was increased. Between the wars there was a scarcity of tutors and examiners, so that almost as soon as a man qualified he was asked to take on what was really quite a substantial unpaid commitment. (Most performed it gladly and conscientiously, although there are reports that wives on occasion complained.) Finally, in 1936, following on from the classes given for some years by W. F. (Bill) Marples, a partner in the Liverpool-based consulting firm of Duncan C. Fraser, the Institute and the Faculty together formed the Actuarial Tuition Service (ATS), with the aim of offering more efficient and comprehensive tuition.

One of the period's more important developments – and one which owed nothing to Menzler's paper – was the formation of a Joint Committee for

Investment Research with the Faculty (on the latter's initiative) in 1929. This weekly survey of the price and yield indices for groups of ordinary stocks – other kinds of securities were treated monthly – operated on a subscription basis and was, in those pre-computer days, exceedingly time and labour intensive to compile. Known as the Actuaries' Investment Index, and later as the Actuaries' Share Index, it was the first attempt at providing comprehensive figures for investment analysis, and the precursor of today's FTSE listings, about which more will be said.

What was the Institute *like* in those years before the Second World War? Firstly, it was – and still is – so closely identified with Staple Inn that to any Fellow the two were synonymous. Dickens's description of the place in *The Mystery of Edwin Drood* was still perfectly accurate in the late 1930s. What it signified, to those who studied there and continued to participate in Institute life, is less easy to sum up. Charles Wood, in a Presidential Address delivered much later, in 1956, portrayed the ancient buildings bordering the tranquil courtyard off Holborn as the *alma mater* of those who had not been to Oxbridge, and a reminder of their golden years to those who had. The arrangement of space altered substantially over the years as needs dictated. In the 1930s (and for a

'... *given the qualities of "mother wit, energy, originality, tact, insight, courage, and enterprise", there was no limit to their prospects...*'

long time thereafter) the main entrance to the Institute was in the far south-west corner, where the entrance to the Hall now is. Once inside, the materials – stone, and dark, polished wood – spoke of timelessness and tradition: the venerable Hall, the whirring and striking of the gallery clock, the Library occupying every cranny and overflowing onto shelves in the corridor – all conspired to evoke a collegiate calm and a tacit respect for past accomplishment. Wood provides some telling social detail, such as the Institute's generous provision of hat-pegs, since 'in those days a professional man was inseparable from his hat'.[34] Council members and Institute staff were important too: men who 'expressed the personality of the Institute because of what they themselves had added to it; and conversely, because they had absorbed so much from the Institute and from Staple Inn'.[35] Among the people Wood recalls was:

Sydney Jarvis began 'a temporary engagement of a few weeks' in May 1892 and stayed until 1939, from 1902 as Assistant Secretary. He was a dedicated administrator and a master of tact and detail, revered by generations of actuaries.

a slim figure, neatly attired and precise in his movements. His name was Jarvis. He had two initials S.H. but no one was ever told what those initials stood for … To the young student, to the tutor, to the examiner, to the Council member, Jarvis was the fount of all information about the Institute. If you wanted to know something about the profession, you talked to Jarvis … if you wanted to borrow a volume of the Journal, *you talked to Jarvis … But the most important and vital purpose for which you would want to visit Jarvis was to hear the examination results. The names of the successful candidates were pinned to the bookcase in his room after the Council meeting at which they had been approved.*[36]

Sydney Harry Jarvis had been a fixture of the Institute since 1892 and retired only in 1939. His early duties had included lighting the gas jets in the Hall by means of a long pole on the nights of sessional meetings. These meetings, and those of the Students' Society, usually began at 6 pm and could go on until 9 or even later, depending on the length of the discussions that habitually followed the papers being presented. Meetings were preceded by a generous tea, and sometimes drawn to a close by the exit of the members of the dining clubs (of which by the 1930s there were half a dozen). As Wood recalls, the Institute was a place in which everyone knew everyone else: the actuarial profession was a small one and it was essential that most members of it took some active part in Institute life. The friendships formed while studying to qualify lasted through life. 'Employers changed, the place of work changed, but the link with the Institute continued … When qualification was achieved there was the link of service as a tutor, as an examiner, as the reader of a paper, as the

The ruins of Staple Inn Hall
following its destruction by a
flying bomb on 24 August 1944.

author of a text book or a member of a committee'.[37] All this suggests that the
Institute, although traditional in *mores*, was not particularly hierarchical; once
over the big hurdle of qualification, a young man was in the company of
equals, although the deference due to age and experience no doubt applied.
Tutoring and committee work were great levellers, and election to Council was
usually preceded by years of both, during which time a man became known for
his character as well as for his intellectual attainments. One says 'man' – and
there were 535 Fellows and 362 Associates by 1939[38] – but there were also 6
qualified women. The first of them, Dorothy Davis, was admitted in 1923 and
invited to open the debate at a sessional meeting in 1926, but the Institute and
the profession were to remain almost exclusively male for many years yet.

The coming of war in 1939 initially had much the same effect as in 1914, in
the sudden disappearance into the forces of Students and younger members,
but this time the dislocation was proportional to the far greater danger on the
home front. The staff of the Institute was offered safer accommodation across
the road at the Prudential, and the Library and the stained-glass windows in
the Hall were removed to safe custody. The decline in the numbers studying
for the examinations had a serious effect on Institute finances, especially those
of the ATS. From 1942 the examinations were suspended. Sessional meetings
continued to be held in the Hall, but in daylight hours owing to the difficulty
of blacking it out. Luckily there was no meeting on the evening of 24 August
1944, when a flying bomb landed in the Italian garden situated in the rear
courtyard. Staple Inn Hall, in which the Institute took such pride, was utterly

destroyed, along with 1 and 10 Staple Inn. This appalling event was made yet more poignant by the death in the blast of an elderly woman who had worked in the Inn for forty years.[39] News of the disaster brought messages of support to the Institute from the actuarial community around the world. Even before the end of the war the thought of rebuilding became a point of hope amidst all the uncertainty.

The loss of Staple Inn Hall was as much a psychological blow as a physical one: those who saw the great timbered roof lying in one piece on top of the ruins were at once moved and unnerved, as though the Institute's very identity had been reduced to rubble along with the scene of so much spirited debate and good fellowship. The Institute, however, was more than its Hall. Through the good offices of the Law Society, the Patent Agents, the Prudential and the Chartered Insurance Institute, sessional and Council meetings, as well as those of the Students' Society, continued to be held. The rest of Staple Inn survived the war unscathed, and with the return of Fellows and Students after 1945 came a gradual recovery of direction. Reconstruction would take time (the same was true of whole areas of London), but the Institute's more immediate task would be to assist the Student members returning from the forces to recover their momentum. Its centenary was now on the horizon, and this too provided a focus that carried members' thoughts beyond the end of the war to the resumption of peace and the links with the international actuarial community.

CHAPTER TWO

Rebuilding and renewal

O N 8 June 1945, the Institute of Actuaries held its ninety-eighth Annual General Meeting – not, of course, in the usual location, but some 100 metres away, in the Conference Hall of the Prudential Assurance Company on the other side of Holborn. It was the first occasion since 1887 that the AGM had taken place anywhere other than in Staple Inn Hall. 'Tonight, the Institute is homeless, but the rigour of our condition has been mitigated by the charity of friends'[1] was how Reginald Simmonds (*) put it, the 'friends' being the Prudential, which was housing the Library and the possessions salvaged from the bombed-out Hall, and the Chartered Insurance Institute, where Council continued to meet. When his term as President was over, Simmonds would write the history of the Institute's first century and allude movingly to Staple Inn Hall and what its loss represented to the Institute. On this occasion, with the war in the Far East not yet won, he set the disaster in perspective by contrasting it with the loss of thirty-five Institute members (one Fellow, three Associates and thirty-one Students) who had perished on active service.[2] Three elder statesmen of the profession, each of whom had served as President of the Institute, had died during the war: Henry Brown, Bill Phelps and Henry Oakley.

In the circumstances in which this AGM took place, with London devastated and the national economy exhausted, there seemed limited value in dwelling on the past, even to relish the Institute's now lengthy history. At this same gathering the 77-year-old Digby Besant (*) spoke proudly of his own links with its earliest days. Nominated in 1889 by the great Dr Sprague, who had been 'a youth of 18 and just about to go to Cambridge University when the Institute was founded' in 1848, Besant was now celebrating his fifty years as a Fellow, but his memories were of a world gone for ever.[3] Victory in Europe had

Bill Phillips's painting of 'Besant's Corner' of the dining-room of Kettner's Restaurant shows Digby Besant on 11 January 1954, his 85th birthday, just short of his 60th anniversary as a Fellow of the Institute. Sir Andrew Rowell (left) and Jim Pegler (right) share the occasion.

been won barely a month earlier and a General Election was a matter of weeks away. In the post-war world the Institute would have to be forward looking: to the immediate task of resuming its teaching function, and in the longer term to the actuarial profession's wider participation in society, in both its traditional areas and a variety of new ones.

These 'wider fields' were already prefigured by the important tasks undertaken by some actuaries during the war, and the role of others in planning what was to come after it. And yet, as Simmonds reminded his audience, 'Science itself is not enough. Even scientific progress will be halted if there is not the man who sees beyond' – meaning, in an actuarial context, 'beyond' the equation and the formula to the human realities represented by the numbers and symbols used in actuarial work. In the post-war period just beginning, the emerging conundrums posed by demographic change and the vast programme of legislation attendant on the creation of the Welfare State would pose the dominant challenges to the profession but, in time, not the only ones.

The immediate priority for the Council of the Institute was the resumption of training and examining the Students whose progress towards qualification had been interrupted by the war. The first examinations since 1942 were held in May 1945 and among those who wrote them were three former prisoners-of-war, recently released, and eleven others still on active service.[4] For a few years the examinations were held every six months, with the aim of speeding qualification time for the many, especially in India, who had managed to keep up their studies despite the war. In May 1950 annual examinations again became the norm (although the twice-yearly Entrance examination remained). The life offices were persuaded by the Institute, the Faculty and the Chartered

Insurance Institute to grant special leaves of absence to men returning from the war, on the assumption that making up for lost time would be almost impossible if this had to be done out of working hours – the worst-off had 'lost' seven years, and some now had wives and children to support. Tutor-supervised study facilities were organised by the Actuarial Tuition Service (ATS) at Staple Inn for such men on three half-days a week, beginning in the autumn of 1945. By then the Library had been removed from the basement of the Prudential and reassembled. Further streamlining was achieved by reducing the length of the 'Course of Reading', and extending the system by which credits could be gained for individual sections of Parts of the syllabus. These were interim measures, part of a reassessment of the education provided by the Institute that had taken place during the war and which would shortly be put into effect.

On the national level, the elation that marked the coming of peace was accompanied by the determination to build a better and more equal society. This universal sentiment, uniting the country and cutting across the traditional class divides, coloured the immediate post-war period. What is less often mentioned in studies of the time is the difficulty in readjusting to civilian life experienced by so many who had been in the Forces. It is a fair assumption that the average actuary or actuarial Student returning to his pre-war situation felt this sense of let-down as keenly as the next man. The Institute's Appointments Board, whose chairman was Harold Clough of the consulting firm of Bacon & Woodrow, helped returning actuaries to find suitable – and in some cases better – positions. Some chose to emigrate; those who tried to pick up where they had left off were perhaps encouraged by the stories that leaked out about the wartime accomplishments of senior – and some not so senior – members of the profession. Everyone knew that Sir William Elderton (*) (knighted in 1938) had served as Chief Statistical Adviser to the Ministry of War Transport and for this had recently received an unprecedented second knighthood. How many had heard that John Gunlake, a partner in R. Watson & Sons, had been Statistical Adviser to the Minister himself, and had seen history in the making at the Washington, Quebec, Cairo and Yalta Conferences? Bobbie Beard acted as Statistical Adviser to the Director of Air Equipment of the Fleet Air Arm, while Bill Phillips (whose work on binary calculation had made his reputation before the war) had secretly visited the University of Pennsylvania to view the prototype ENIAC computer. Fred Lloyd, a young would-be actuary halfway through his exams in 1942, was selected for operational research at Bomber Command and given the job of reducing the loss rate among Lancaster and Halifax bomber pilots.[5] As a member of an 'OR' Section attached to Fighter Command, Jack Plymen worked on radar systems, and helped to develop a special cine-camera aligned with a plane's gunsight so that fighter combat tactics could later be analysed. Sidney Townsend was plucked from an actuarial post at the Prudential by the War Office and spent the war in Whitehall, setting up the Statistical Sections around the country that produced dramatic savings in Forces expenditure. (Among the experts he recruited to man these sections were six fellow-actuaries.)[6] Jo Hamilton-Jones served as a meteorological officer with the Royal Navy on the Atlantic convoys and in the Far East. Leonard Hall, serving with the Royal Air Force in the same capacity, was torpedoed in mid-ocean, picked up by the offending U-boat and sent to the infamous Stalag Luft III prisoner-of-war camp, where he took part in what became known as 'the Great Escape'. (Those curious to know how an airman came to be torpedoed can read about his exploits in his *Stock's as Good as Money*, now in the Institute Library.) There were others, most of them Students, who experienced the 'wider fields' so often referred to, thanks to the War Office and intensive training in ballistics, electronics and engineering at the Military College of Science.

Reginald Simmonds, President 1944–46, also wrote a history of the Institute's first hundred years for the centenary celebrations in 1948.

Those who remained in their jobs had not been idle, either. Many of the Institute's most active members, serving on Council and on committees, were senior life office actuaries, and represented their offices on the committees of the Life Offices Association (LOA) or the Industrial Life Offices Association (ILOA). Such men, by the end of the war, had devoted countless committee hours to the consideration of the situation and future role of the insurance industry under the heightened State control that seemed certain to be implemented in the event of a Labour electoral victory after the war.

It was in this capacity, as members of an LOA committee back in 1942, that they had brought the views of their offices and of the actuarial profession to the notice of the Interdepartmental Committee on Social Insurance and Allied Services chaired by Sir William Beveridge. This Committee was set up to undertake a wide investigation into social conditions and to rationalise the system of benefits that had evolved since 1911. Its investigations thus included the friendly societies, the providers of life assurance and pensions, and the so-called 'approved societies', some of which were administered by the large life offices themselves, which provided piecemeal health benefits to more than half of the British population.

Initially the Joint Committee set up by the LOA and ASLO (the Associated Scottish Life Offices) had responded to the investigation by preparing a purely informative Memorandum on superannuation schemes. But Beveridge's 300-page Report, published in December 1942, was much more ambitious than had originally been envisaged. Fired by a crusading determination to eradicate the 'Five Giants' of Want, Disease, Ignorance, Squalor and Idleness, Beveridge produced a blueprint for a cradle-to-grave, flat-rate contributory system of social security that included family allowances and pensions, together with maternity, unemployment, sickness, workmen's compensation and funeral benefits. By January 1943 (by which time the Beveridge Report had been out a month and the short, popular version of it had sold more than 100,000 copies), the two life office associations had recorded in their minutes their apprehension at the Report's suggestion that 'the ordinary life assurance business of some offices should be transferred to a Public Board'[7] and were taking up the defensive position that they would be forced to maintain for the next seven years.

This is not to say that the LOA/ASLO Joint Committee, or the individual members of the Institute who were part of it, opposed the socially reforming temper of the times; only that as actuaries they were predisposed to enquire into how Beveridge's reforms were to be paid for, and what their long-term implications might be. Many actuaries, as individuals, may have had strong political allegiances, but the Institute itself was deliberately kept free of them, as its successive Councils considered proper for a professional body. At the three evening meetings organised by the Institute early in 1943 to discuss the Beveridge Report[8] the opinions expressed ranged over the whole political spectrum. Along with a variety of doubts about whether the plan was affordable came trepidation about encouraging people to abandon traditional self-reliance for dependence on the State. Despite the many criticisms raised from the economic, administrative and moral points of view, these actuarial gatherings accepted that there was a need for a coherent and comprehensive system of social provisions to replace the hodge podge of measures that had grown up since 1911. The war had shown the existing system to be gravely wanting, and restoring the pre-war *status quo* was not a humane or responsible option. Bob Kirton (*), in introducing the first evening's debate, stated the overriding argument very simply. Beveridge, he said, 'has done two things. He has put forward the principle that subsistence is the right of the citizen who is willing to work, and he has sketched out a plan to give effect to that principle.' The plan might be open to criticism and to adjustment, but Kirton concluded that the nation

must proceed to implement the principle, either by means of the Beveridge plan or otherwise, or for ever stand condemned for having lost a timely opportunity of taking a step in the evolution of the social order. And upon us actuaries rests the inescapable duty of helping to enlighten informed public opinion.[9]

But, as events would tell, the task was not to prove as simple as Kirton's summary of it. Reginald Simmonds called the Beveridge plan 'a sign of decency in a very evil age … a determination to do something that is really worthwhile', but pointed out that the dogmatic stance of its author 'had not made it easy for men of goodwill to accept his plan in its entirety'.[10] Only the best of wills and a genuine spirit of service could make the Report palatable to the actuaries of the life offices, whose scope looked likely to be restricted through State competition. The words of Leslie Brown of the Prudential would find their echo numerous times over the next sixty years, whenever pensions were debated in Staple Inn Hall:

the Report in effect proposes that this generation shall bear a certain burden, and at the same time promises that the next generation will undertake a very much greater burden for our benefit. What shall we say to our children when in due course they ask us why we committed them to this task, the equivalent of which in 1945 we are only partly willing to bear ourselves?[11]

Yet most of the objections were confined to the Report's actuarial considerations, or to the Bunyanesque rhetoric that clouded its underlying assumptions. The shorter, 'popular' version contained little that would help the layman to understand how the new arrangements would actually work. 'Much as we all agree with freedom from want', Frank Gardner asserted,

I think that Beveridge should not expect the public to understand in a few war-time weeks what he took years to think out … I do not see how the public can ever get any sort of digestible information on the functioning of this plan unless we as an Institute either provide it ourselves, or suggest publicly that it ought to be provided.

He went on to express the hope that 'when the Council considers whether any report of these proceedings should be issued or not, that aspect of the matter will be borne in mind'.[12]

It is interesting to observe that while Council did indeed order the printing of the Verbatim Report of the Discussions, it then sought to ensure that the document was not widely circulated. When copies were requested by the *Post Magazine* and the rest of the insurance press, permission to quote from or comment upon the debates was refused. When the Society of Actuaries in the United States conveyed a similar request, 200 copies were sent, but it was agreed to ask the Americans 'to make it clear to their members that the document must be regarded as confidential and to request them to see that no permission to quote the pamphlet or comment upon it is granted to the press'.[13] This was an instance when it would appear that fear of adopting a stance construed to be 'political' ensured that the important questions raised by actuaries received no wider notice. Perhaps, too, Council took the view that individual speakers might not wish their contributions to the debate to be widely aired.

While the war continued, and in the face of the overwhelming public endorsement the Beveridge Report received, little could have been done in any case to enlighten public opinion. The landslide victory that brought the Labour

Party to power in July 1945 saw the start of a programme of the nationalisation of key industries and the initiation of the social reforms masterminded by Beveridge. From September 1946 the LOA was closely involved, at the invitation of the Government Actuary (by then Sir George Maddex; Sir George Epps had retired in November 1944 and his successor Sir Percy Harvey died in August 1946) in facilitating the smooth transfer of existing pension schemes and funds to the new boards being set up to run the nationalised coal and railway industries.[14] Under the National Insurance Act of 1946, death benefit, up to now covered by the policies sold by the industrial life offices and the friendly societies, became a State provision, while the approved societies were absorbed into the new State social security system. There was nothing that could be done to save them, although the ILOA briefly sought to do so.[15]

The greater challenge came in 1948, with the prospect of the nationalisation of the entire life assurance industry. The Institute could not be seen to be politically motivated, nor motivated by the consideration of the effects of the proposed legislation upon its membership. More than 70 per cent of Institute members were employed in that industry, and the outcome was thus vitally important. The LOA, however, was a trade association and the strong overlap in membership between its Committee and the Council of the Institute meant that matters could be discussed and action taken by the one without compromising the other. Matters that might affect Institute members but that were deemed to be 'of a business nature' were automatically relegated to the LOA, while Council viewed the Institute's role purely as one of keeping its members informed of developments that might affect them (which it did mainly by circular).[16]

Officially, then, the Institute was at one remove from the battle for the life assurance industry that began in earnest early in 1948. By May the LOA was feeling (in the diplomatic wording of its minutes) the need of 'an organised system of distribution of news of life assurance matters, with the object of conveying to the public the suggestion that the Life Offices were doing useful work from the national point of view'.[17] This might seem a tepid response to a threat that was gaining momentum during the rest of the year, but the LOA's innately cautious cast of mind made a proactive and vigorous defence distasteful. Similarly, the fear of provoking further criticism of the industry on the grounds of seeking to protect its own interests led the LOA to choose repeatedly to wait on events and hope for the best.

By February 1949 the accusations being levelled at the life offices[18] finally prodded the LOA and the ASLO into action. A plan for publicising the issue was devised, and it was agreed to act in conjunction with, and under the direction of, the British Insurance Association (BIA). In the joint Memorandum prepared for circulation at the Labour Party Conference in May, the associations declared their motives non-political: 'their concern over the question of nationalisation arises from their belief that its effects would be gravely harmful not only to the interests of individual policyholders but to the community as a whole, involving the national economy itself'.[19] The Memorandum was to no avail: at the conference the National Executive of the Labour Party announced its plan to nationalise both the industrial and the ordinary business of the life offices.

Now defence plans were quickly launched under the overall direction of the BIA. The primary task was to remind or to inform insurance staffs, agents and the public of the valuable contribution of the life insurance industry to the nation's economic life, and of the reasons why it should remain independent of government control. The LOA's Special Committee, composed of senior actuaries, all members of the Institute and including John Bunford, Wilfred Perks, Harry Tappenden and Frank Gardner, met weekly. Hundreds of volunteer committees were established throughout the country. By July, 800,000 copies of a pamphlet setting out the facts and arguments had been distributed, and further leaflets were included in every renewal notice and every product circular sent out by the life offices. The BIA took space in sixty newspapers. Leading the anti-nationalisation crusade was Sir Frank Morgan, the General Manager of the Prudential, who travelled and spoke tirelessly on behalf of the threatened industry. The 65,000 life office agents carried resistance to the Government's proposal into every household in the country.

The strength of the opposition led the Government to modify its plan to one of 'mutualisation', but the life offices kept up their resistance, past the election of February 1950 – which saw the Labour majority reduced to just seventeen – and on through the year. In the end, economic woes eroded the public's support for Labour: the 'cheap money' era of the immediate post-war years had

The ILOA's opposition to the Labour Government's plan to nationalise the industrial insurance industry took many forms, including the leaflet in which this satirical cartoon appeared.

given way to one of gathering inflation, and in September 1949 the pound was devalued. With the Conservative electoral victory of October 1951 the spectre of nationalisation faded. The new Government rightly identified inflation as the enemy now, much to the relief of the actuarial profession, which was wrestling with its consequences.

The creation of the 'Welfare State' and the attendant drama of the anti-nationalisation campaign were the backdrop against which the day-to-day life of the Institute was carried on in the immediate post-war years. National reconstruction, at a time when every effort was geared to increasing exports, was a slow process, and similarly at Staple Inn it was a long time before the conditions for work and study were really conducive to either. While the Hall lay in ruins, the buildings surrounding the courtyard continued to be used. Rationing and shortages of everything from coal to paper affected the whole staff, but the unrelieved chill of the gatehouse over the archway leading to Holborn was a particular trial for those who studied there. When in the frigid winter of 1947 the Patent Agents in the adjacent Staple Inn Buildings made their Hall available for the examinations, the Students wore their overcoats while snow blew into the room and settled around their feet.[20]

But there was a new spirit abroad in the Institute, as in the country at large, and possibly deriving from that same zeal for post-war 'reconstruction' mentioned above. This new spirit was centred on the conviction that the actuary was in essence a mathematical statistician, but that the statistical side of his training had been neglected. Were this to be brought up to date, the actuary's training should fit him for a host of roles in the post-war world. The importance of statistics had been demonstrated in the First World War and had steadily increased during the interwar years. Statistics had become indispensable in fields such as administration and economic planning, but the application of statistical methods to actuarial problems, first raised in the Institute in the 'future of the profession' debate in the 1920s and championed by Sir William Elderton in the 1930s, had not found more than a niche in the syllabus by the time the Institute's examinations were put on hold in 1942. From 1943, the small coterie belonging to the Students' Society (which in time would give birth to both the 'Woolgatherers' Club' and the Statistical Study Group, and had a certain proportion of qualified members) was meeting weekly to discuss the likely prospects after the war, and especially the need for greater emphasis on statistics and economics in actuarial education.[21] Its aim came to be that of broadening and reforming actuarial training so as to bring the profession 'up to date' and enable actuaries to assume a wider range of professional responsibilities.

The Committee of the Students' Society took up this reforming objective in 1943. Out of its discussions came recommendations published in 1945 under the title *The Future of the Profession*, a fairly radical document in Institute terms. Based on a questionnaire replied to by more than three hundred Society members, it put forward some well-thought-out (though not unanimously agreed) proposals for reducing the average qualifying age of 28,[22] and securing a higher public profile for the profession through enhanced public relations and contact with the universities and other professional bodies. The core recommendations, however, concerned the need for more exposure to statistics and economics – the latter to include the more intensive study of investment – and to the novel area of 'mechanical computing' that was as yet little more than a cloud on the horizon. Statistics was distinguished from 'ordinary mathematics' in that it dealt 'not with rare exact quantities and with simple averages, but with those common everyday phenomena of which the mathematical essence is variability'.[23]

There was, perhaps naturally, a degree of initial resistance to the ideas set out by the Students' Society. The majority of actuaries worked in the traditional field of life assurance, and while acknowledging statistics as part of their equipment, were reluctant to see this newly fashionable specialism given such prominence, and the training which they themselves had received by implication made to seem somewhat outmoded. But the form and content of the Institute's examination system was already under discussion by Council at about the same time, and in June 1944 a sub-committee was set up under the chairmanship of Ernest (later Sir Ernest) Lever (*) to consider and report upon the existing arrangement 'from its widest aspect'. Its task was essentially that of updating something to which much care and thought had been devoted over a long period, keeping what was best while creating an educational structure that could adapt to the changing requirements of the future. The Lever Committee came rapidly to two conclusions which strongly influenced its subsequent recommendations: first, that the average time needed to qualify was, at eleven years, unacceptably long, and secondly, that among the younger members of the profession there existed a strong desire to extend its scope.[24]

The Lever Committee reported in November 1946 and it was at once apparent that considerable notice had been taken of the recommendations set out in *The Future of the Profession*. It had grappled with the possibility that the Institute might, for reasons of manpower and the need to preserve standards, be faced with the choice between limiting itself to the production of actuaries trained to fill the traditional roles in the life offices, the consulting practices and the Government Actuary's Department (GAD), or taking positive steps to promote the advance into wider fields. The Committee had concluded, however, that the training and examinations offered by the Institute should and could bridge these two channels.

En route to its recommendations the Committee dealt with a variety of perplexing questions. Basic to the whole educational process was the type of actuarial student recruited in the first place. The majority still came directly to actuarial study from school (although the number of graduates was growing) and all were assessed on mathematical aptitude and English in the searching Preliminary examination. The Committee changed little here except emphasis: the actuary needed other abilities besides the mathematical, and a 'broad educational and cultural background' was felt to be the necessary counter-weight to a strong mathematical bent.[25]

Nor could recruitment really be considered in isolation from the ideal the Institute should seek to produce. This, the Committee asserted, should be a man who was still young and enthusiastic enough when he qualified to make a contribution to the profession through research or teaching; one who was balanced in outlook, practical as well as scientific in his approach to problems, and realistic about his own capabilities and limitations. This was an admirable recipe, but the Committee considered that the existing mix of subjects and examinations lacked some ingredients while having an excess of others. The division of the syllabus into six Parts, each with several sections, was complex and daunting; the theoretical and severely mathematical approach of the early Parts was poor preparation for the abrupt change to a practical approach in the later ones, with the result that the progress of many Students ground to a halt at that point. The comparative lack of statistical and economic content was far from being the only cause for remedy.

The Committee's solution was the reorganisation of the material to be studied into four Parts, the examinations for the first three comprising the Associateship and the final one the Fellowship, and the commissioning of new textbooks across the board. The novelty lay in the 'progressive' approach which allocated the subjects in each of the first three Parts to a mathematical, a statistical or a financial group within which the development of the subject over three years could be clearly grasped. While the weight given to the mathematical group (finite differences, probability, life and other contingencies) was not reduced, some of its inessential detail was pruned. This and the better ordering of the material in general made it possible to give additional weight to the statistical group (statistics, mortality and other investigations, demography) and the financial group (compound interest, finance, investment, life interests, reversions). While it was estimated that some time could be saved through this restructuring, the real saving was to be made through the introduction of partial specialisation (or 'specialised emphasis') at Fellowship level. Here, the candidate had to pass groups of subjects relating to 'Life Offices – Ordinary and Industrial' and 'Friendly Societies, Pension Funds and Social Insurance Schemes' to a 'less advanced' standard, but only one of these groups, or 'Advanced Statistics' at 'more advanced' level.[26]

The introduction of this programme, it was hoped, would reduce qualification time to six or seven years. The Lever Committee seemed indeed to have resolved the issues raised by the Students' Society while allaying the inevitable fears about lowering standards, but it accepted that the 'Economic Background' was still inadequately covered, and that much remained to be done to effect liaison with other educational bodies proceeding along similar lines to the Institute. The Lever Report was considered and approved by Council at meetings on 13 and 20 May 1946 and its measures were scheduled to come into effect in 1949 – presumably so as not to create further upheaval in 1948, the year of the Institute's centenary. (In the event, because the anti-nationalisation campaign absorbed so much energy in 1949, the new measures were not effected until 1950.)

The fact that the Lever Committee had accepted much of the Students' Society's thinking as expressed in *The Future of the Profession* lent strength to the arm of the statistical enthusiasts, of whom Hilary Seal was the undeclared spokesman. Seal was elected to the Students' Society Committee in 1945 and took over as editor of the Society's *Journal* (*JSS*) in January 1946. The Statistical Study Group, of which he was the great protagonist, and the Economics Study Group under the aegis of Francis Bacon, date from about the same time. The content of the *Journal*, since its foundation in 1926, had catered to the examination needs of Students or to their need for information about topics of current actuarial interest. From January 1946 until he relinquished his post in April 1949, Seal used it as the fulcrum for a virtual crusade. 'Quite simply, Seal made a dramatic attempt to conduct a supporting apostolic campaign for the redemption of the actuarial outlook through mathematical statistics'[27] by filling the *Journal* with weighty articles which, some readers complained in unpublishable letters to the editor, they could not understand.[28] There were also complaints that such material was of no help in passing the examinations. One rearguard initiative was the publication in 1946 of *Random Muse*, which covered new ideas in a lighter vein than either the *JIA* or the *JSS*, but lasted little more than a year.

It was Seal himself who suggested a mock trial of the editor as a means of airing the contentious issue publicly. This 'interesting and significant episode' took place on 4 December 1947 in the Conference Hall of the Prudential. Court formalities were observed and the judge (Bill Phillips), barristers (Frank Spratling and Tom Suttie) and solicitors (Ronald Michaelson and George Ross Goobey) wore robes and wigs obtained from a theatrical costume outlet. Some 130 Students' Society members turned out to watch the fun as witnesses for the Prosecution and the Defence were called to give evidence. The audience, as an enlarged jury, was asked to vote. The numbers present caused the verdict for a time to be in doubt,[29] but it soon emerged that victory had gone to the protestors. Seal took his 'conviction' in good part and carried on as editor. Only from the vantage point of years was it possible to see that in essence he had been right in claiming, in his 'Apologia', that the Society's *Journal* had become the forum for post-graduate investigation now that its earlier function was filled by the ATS. The 'trial of Hilary Seal', a light-hearted incident in itself, served to illustrate the paradox that statistics, which had claimed the attention of some of the best actuarial minds since before the First World War, had up to now not received a corresponding degree of exposure in the Institute syllabus – yet expertise in this area was the prerequisite for entering the 'wider fields' that had captured younger actuarial imaginations for nearly as long. The Lever

Report did much to put this right: almost all of the material that gave rise to controversy in 1947 became 'Required Reading' under the new syllabus of 1950. The biennial Sir Alfred Watson Memorial Lectures, instituted in 1947, were devoted to 'extending the scope of the profession with particular reference to the interests of the younger members', and it is interesting to note the preponderance of statistical topics that lasted until the 1960s.[30]

After months of preparation, the celebration of the Institute's centenary in 1948 was a happy interlude in a period of otherwise unrelieved economic gloom and austerity. The Centenary Assembly, presided over by Sir Andrew Rowell (*) as President of the Institute, was attended by more than 400 Fellows and their wives, together with members of the Faculty and 109 actuaries from around the world, including the United States and Canada, Australia and India. For a week beginning on 21 June, the Institute hosted a series of working sessions at the Chartered Insurance Institute's building in Aldermanbury, which stood virtually alone amidst the devastation of that area of the City of London. In addition there were an exhibition on actuarial history, excursions around the City and to Windsor, and evening receptions[31] that testified to the victory of imagination over shortages and rationing regulations. In recognition of a century of leadership – and to replace items lost in 1944 – a number of the foreign actuarial associations presented the Institute with gifts, mainly articles of silver. The goodwill in evidence during the celebratory week was proof – if such were necessary – of how revered the Institute was by the international actuarial family, which by now (the Actuarial Society of India being the most recent member, having come into being in 1946) included some twenty-nine associations in twenty-six countries. A further cause for celebration was the news that the Prudential was now committed to rebuilding Staple Inn Hall. Plans that had been evolving since 1946, to which the Institute had been invited to contribute, would include reordered accommodation on four floors along the west side of the Inn. The Hall would be a near-perfect replica of the lost original.[32]

The Seal of the Institute, according to Thomas Young, President 1896–98, represents an adaptation of the classical mythological figures, the Fates. Atropos (centre), with her hourglass and scythe, signifies mortality (see R. Simmonds, *The Institute of Actuaries 1848–1948*, pp. 127–128).

The Institute's natural tendency to take stock on the occasion of its centenary revealed that in 1948 there were 630 Fellows of the Institute, some 404 in active practice in Britain; this was only 20 more than in 1939. The figure which gave rise to unease – and to the feeling that the implementation of the Lever Report could not come too soon – was the comparison between the 1,000 actuarial Students before the war and the current 790. Fears that the Institute might, under the revised syllabus, shortly be producing too many additions to the profession were balanced by the view that recent nationalisation and its consequences were creating a demand for actuaries. The life offices were expanding, and the need for qualified men to staff new branches at home and abroad was increasing. Of practising UK actuaries, 288 were employed in the insurance offices, as against 25 in consulting practice and 34 in the GAD.[33] The situations of those in the life offices and the GAD looked likely to remain secure, and – in the case of the GAD – offered the prospect of work that was increasingly prized as evaluation and planning got under way in the early years following the war. The situation of the consulting actuaries was less clear cut. These were either independent practitioners or members of professional partnerships, and a large proportion of their work consisted of advising and valuing the friendly societies. This was a connection that went back to the very beginnings of the profession with the legal requirement for the 'approval' of friendly society tables and rules that dated from 1819. Actuarial valuation of friendly societies became law in 1875. The first full-time independent consulting actuary – that is, one who was not also engaged in life office work – was Reuben Watson, from 1875 the Grand Master of the Independent Order of Oddfellows, Manchester Unity. In 1878 he began the individual valuation of some 3,500 of its lodges, and founded R. Watson & Sons on the sturdy foundation provided by this work. (He was made an honorary Associate of the Institute in 1888.) At that time there were about 13,250 registered friendly societies and registered branches of orders. By 1901 there were 23,500, but the coming of National Insurance legislation in 1911 and the consequent creation of the 'approved societies' reduced their number, and in 1939 there were about 19,500.[34]

The friendly societies were greatly affected by the advent of the National Insurance Act and the National Health Act, and not only they, but their actuarial advisers also, had been presented with some difficult problems. The higher rates of State benefit during sickness and greater contributions to the State scheme had forced the larger societies to revise their own contracts, while the smaller ones had experienced strong rates of lapse among members who could not afford to pay two sets of contributions, and a falling-off in new memberships. Without sufficient new members, a friendly society could not survive; its most likely eventual fate was dissolution, and the actuarial adviser of such a society was hence in a position of some delicacy. Sir George Maddex (*), President of the Institute 1948–50, considered that 'Every effort should be made by the professional adviser to assist his clients to adapt their benefits and their methods to the new era', recognising that instances involving a declining membership presented

a state of affairs in which it is more difficult for the actuary to give positive help but he is often in a position to give guidance, and dissolution should be a last resort … a transfer of engagements or a merging of small units may yet prove a practicable and desirable alternative.[35]

The decline of the societies, however, was an inevitable consequence of the creation of the Welfare State, and by the mid-1950s some seven thousand of them would have ceased to exist.

The change in the status of the friendly societies was, however, balanced by the proliferation of occupational pension schemes, and this had become a growth area for consulting actuaries. These schemes had been increasingly popular since the Finance Act of 1921 made them exempt from taxation in return for compliance with certain requirements that would ensure the emergence of taxable benefits. From about 1,000 in 1928, they had grown to over 3,000 by 1947, and now – at a time of full employment – employers were establishing them in ever-greater numbers: there would be more than 6,000 by 1956.[36] Many occupational schemes were managed by the life offices (and a number of life office actuaries, among them some of the most eminent men in the profession, still carried on the traditional custom of having private clients), but increasingly the larger commercial firms that were setting up new schemes sought the advice of the Institute in finding a qualified actuary. In 1948 this formed the subject of discussion between the Institute and the two largest consulting partnerships, R. Watson & Son of Reigate and the London firm of Bacon & Woodrow (formed by James Bacon and Guy Woodrow in 1919). Having decided that actuaries holding full-time appointments were unlikely to be persuaded to relinquish consulting work to members practising as consultants only, the parties left such recommendations to the President to share out equitably from a list of consultants that included the partnerships.[37]

This, however, was only an interim measure, and served to heighten the consulting actuaries' sense that their particular circumstances might require a specifically tailored solution. This awareness grew with the rise, in the late 1940s, of firms of insurance brokers unfettered by the Institute's professional code forbidding advertising, which quickly set about making the most of the vogue for employers' pension plans. The consulting actuaries, vastly outnumbered by the life office actuaries in any case, thus found their territory encroached upon from both sides. As they saw it, 'There was a great need for good, disinterested professional advice and a great need, too, to bring to the attention of the many employers wanting such advice the existence of independent consulting actuaries'.[38]

It took only the right occasion (the International Congress in Scheveningen, Holland, in June 1951) and a little encouragement (from Fred Menzler (*), by now President of the Institute) to inspire Geoffrey Heywood and Max Lander (*), both of the Liverpool firm of Duncan C. Fraser, and Ernest Lancashire of Watsons with the idea of forming an association of consulting actuaries. A meeting was soon held to agree its purpose and aims. These centred on raising the status of consulting actuaries and providing a focus for concerted effort so that they might bring a collective voice to bear when policy on matters such as pensions was being formulated at government level. (This was particularly important since the Millard Tucker Committee recently appointed to review the tax treatment of pension and superannuation schemes included a former Institute President but no consulting actuary.) Membership was to be restricted to those Fellows of the Institute and Faculty who were engaged professionally as full-time consulting actuaries.[39]

The Society of Consulting Actuaries came into being on 12 November 1951, with Victor Burrows (of Watsons) as its first Chairman. James Bacon, the senior partner of Bacon & Woodrow, and Reginald Maudling (*), senior partner of Watsons, were invited to become joint Presidents; Ernest Lancashire was elected Honorary Secretary and Geoffrey Heywood Honorary Treasurer. Somewhat to the surprise of the founders, there was strong opposition to the new entity from the Faculty, as it emerged that there were many part-time consultants in Scotland, and to a lesser degree from the Institute, where some senior actuaries viewed it as a rival professional body. The Society was induced to alter its name to the Association of Consulting Actuaries (ACA), but could not agree to modify its criterion for membership to include part-timers. It became an association of individual and full-time consulting FIAs, not of firms, and agreed to consult the Institute and the Faculty before taking any action involving the public. Even so (and despite the good offices of Fred Menzler), its formation was not 'approved' but merely 'noted' in the Institute's Council minutes; the Faculty also withheld its approval. It was an uneasy beginning, in that the need for the ACA was not accepted by the parent bodies. In the more open business climate of the 1950s, however, the continuance of the trends mentioned above, combined with the consulting actuary's professional independence and varied work, made consulting practice increasingly attractive to entrants to the profession. If being a consulting actuary was not quite like (as James Bacon is reputed to have told the newly qualified, newly recruited Ronald Abbott in 1946) 'sitting permanently on the edge of a volcano', neither was Sir Alfred Watson right when he declared back in 1911 (on selling his shares in R. Watson & Sons and handing over to Reginald Maudling, who became Senior Partner on 1 January 1912) that he 'saw no future in actuarial consultancy at all'.[40]

CHAPTER THREE

A challenging decade

CLAIMING a wider sphere of influence for the profession, without adopting partisan standpoints or compromising its independence, was the challenge taken up by the Institute during the 1950s. The effects of long-term economic and demographic change were fast becoming apparent to actuaries, if not to the general public. The Institute's traditional self-containment would gradually be put to the test as the decade wore on, and leading members of the profession became convinced that it had a duty to make known its views. It would be a long time, however, before it developed any regular and formal means by which its voice might be heard. Like most professional bodies at the time, it regarded 'public relations' with suspicion and not a little distaste ('the mere utterance of the words 'Public Relations Officer' is apt to cause some people to reach for, if not their revolver, then at least their economy axe' was how Fred Menzler put it, at the AGM in 1952). It would be another twenty years before the Institute set up any form of public relations outreach.[1] In the interval, the memorable instance in 1958 when the subject of national pensions stirred the Councils of the Institute and Faculty to issue and widely publicise a joint statement, was the first departure from the profession's habitual tendency to shun the spotlight. Today 'An Appeal to Statesmanship' seems mild, but in its day it was an Institute milestone and as such signalled a new attitude within the profession.

At Staple Inn, the Lever reforms were fully in place by 1951. The revised syllabus seemed to be having the desired effect, since by 1952 the number of Students registered with the Actuarial Tuition Service, at 937, was back to the pre-war level, with honours graduates comprising 40 per cent of the intake.[2] This probably resulted from the exemption from the Entrance examination afforded to graduates in mathematics, economics and statistics; formal links with London University, and in particular with the London School of Economics, would soon shorten the route to qualification for graduates whose courses had included statistical or other actuarial elements. It remained to be seen whether the new set of hurdles would allow the majority of candidates, who were employed full-time (usually by the life offices) to get round the course more quickly. Some offices allowed a certain amount of time off work for exam preparation, while others did not. If such concessions, where they existed, gave actuarial Students an elite status in their respective offices, they were expected to correspond to it by working to a more rigorous standard. As a 17-year-old employed by the Gresham Life, Frank Guaschi was gently reprimanded for leaving the office at 5 pm as the other staff did; it was understood that as an actuarial Student he would stay until all work was done.

Frederick Menzler, President 1950–52. This rather sombre photograph does not capture the intellectual vitality of a man who throughout his career encouraged actuaries to explore the 'wider fields' where their expertise could contribute to the advancement of society.

Courses for the four Parts were still taught predominantly (and if a Student preferred it, exclusively) by correspondence, but discussion classes were being held in some subjects in London and Edinburgh, and in some at certain centres abroad. A panel of appointed voluntary tutors led these groups and marked a battery of tests for the subjects of each Part, while a separate Board of Examiners devised and marked the examination papers. Many of the profession's best minds were also fine teachers – Bert Haycocks (*) and, later, Jack Dyson being outstanding examples – and played a generous part in educating the next generation of actuaries. If the reading lists were still weighted towards the actuarial classics, this category would continue to be steadily augmented through current research. Some tutors produced the texts on which lessons were based – such as Maurice Ogborn (*), who with Norman Coe wrote the first comprehensive textbook on life assurance applications. Others who contributed in this way were Michael Bizley, who wrote the textbook on probability; Norman Benz and Henry Tappenden, who produced the text on reversions and life interests; and Herbert Tetley who wrote a two-volume work on statistics. Peter Cox wrote the first textbook wholly dedicated to demography to be published in Britain. Reginald Crabbe and Cyril Poyser, the authors of *Pension, Widows' and Orphans' Funds*, published in 1953, brought the earlier treatment of the subject by Douglas Porteous up to date.

The fact that meetings were still being held in three different venues did not detract from what in retrospect would be seen as an outstanding period in the life of the Institute. It was a time of significant contributions to actuarial thought, produced by some of the most distinguished intellects and memorable personalities of the profession: Phillips, Pegler, Haynes, Kirton, Beard,

Perks, Redington, Bayley and a host of others. Most of their work was in the form of papers presented at one of the sessional meetings (usually six each year), followed by discussion. This was often of a quality consistent with the papers themselves. The comment of fellow-actuaries was frequently, but not always, made from notes prepared from prior reading of the paper, and distilled the essence of wider learning in a way that was a gift to the actuarial Students who crowded in to listen. Opposing points of view were sometimes debated with real fervour and an eloquence born of moral passion. The prospect of speaking in such august actuarial company, terrifying for first-timers, was on occasion made less so by the encouragement of more experienced men. Dennis Gilley recalls a paper about which,

Green though I was at that time, I fancied that I had something to say and, for the first time on such an occasion, prepared some remarks. … I found myself sitting next to Hosking-Taylor who observing the trembling hands in which my notes were clutched asked me kindly whether I intended to speak. Shyly I indicated that I might and went on shaking. Came a break in the flow of eminent speakers, Hosking-Taylor shot me a sideways glance and breathed 'Go on then'. I rose to my feet and being given the nod from the President, lurched in a haze to the lectern and launched forth.[3]

Many of the exceptional papers of the 1950s were written in response to an economic scenario never previously experienced, which presented actuaries with a succession of novel perplexities. The underlying problem was inflation, or the deterioration in the purchasing power of money. Inflation is a fact of economic life. Some increase of the money supply is, of course, necessary – to allow for the additional volume of goods and services in an expanding economy – but problems arise when the money supply expands beyond what is necessary to cover increased production. What was new was that since the war inflation had coincided with the high borrowings and low interest rates of the Government's 'cheap money' policy, intended to facilitate national reconstruction and rearmament. The devaluation of the pound in 1949 and a serious trade imbalance were additional economic woes besetting the country.

The effect of inflation on both the impulse to save, and on the value of existing savings in the form of life office investments and pensions, posed a grave problem for actuaries. Saving, defined by the economist Roy Harrod in an address to the Institute as 'carrying value forward through time',[4] was discouraged by inflation, yet paradoxically was one of the few means of bringing it under control. In the words of Frank Gardner,

if the actuary has to suffer the disappointment of seeing the practical outcome of his efforts diminished by inflation, he at least has the satisfaction of knowing that he is associated with thrift movements which, though they may not stop inflation, do much to retard it.[5]

A great deal of new business was in fact flooding into the life offices, but low interest rates meant that while liabilities in the form of long contracts were accumulating, asset values were not keeping pace with them. The question was thus how best to protect the value of assets from the ravages of inflation.

Despite its novel complications in the early 1950s, inflation had existed in simpler form for the previous half-century, apart from a prolonged period of deflation in the 1930s. Writing in 1927, amidst the rampant inflation that followed the First World War, Harold Raynes (*) had queried 'The place of ordinary stocks and shares in the investment of life assurance funds',[6] drawing from his comparison of the ordinary shares and the fixed-interest securities of nine categories of investments over the fifteen-year period between 1912 and 1927 the conclusion that – contrary to received opinion – the ordinary shares performed better, and hence that, in this period of currency depreciation, they would have been a good investment for at least a portion of the funds of a life office seeking to offset erosion. The life offices, of course, had to balance the higher risk attached to the return on ordinary shares against the hallowed investment criterion of security of capital. Ten years later, Raynes published another study along similar lines,[7] adding some new investment areas and extending his comparison over a 25-year period. Although in this paper the author was accused of not comparing like with like, it was plain, even in a period of such instability as the 1930s, that the selected ordinary shares had outperformed a list of fixed-interest stocks.

In considering the impetus given to inflation by the Second World War, it fell to Jim Pegler (*) in 1948 to bring up to date the actuarial principles on which the investment policy of a life office should be founded.[8] His revision of Bailey's canons for the investment of life office funds, which had broadly shaped investment policy since they were propounded in 1862,[9] led him to suggest four new principles to reflect the post-war investment climate. Where Bailey's overriding concern had been security of capital, Pegler's was the overall return from both capital and interest. From his view that life offices should invest so as to maximise long-term returns and spread investment risk, it followed that the re-evaluation of the place of ordinary shares in life office investment was an appropriate response to post-war conditions. His suggestion that offices should seek to orient their investment policy towards socially and economically desirable ends foreshadowed later calls for socially responsible investment. A year later Hugh Recknell, in a paper presented to the Faculty called 'Insurance against Inflation', examined the effects of continuing inflation on the proceeds of life policies, and queried whether it were possible to devise some means of lessening them. This could only be done by finding a measure for benefits which could vary with the value of money, and which could enable offices to cover their liabilities with similar assets. Recknell observed that there were 'many orthodoxies of today which started life as extreme heresies' and held that the revision of opinion regarding the suitability of ordinary shares as life office investments was certainly one of them. He concluded that, given that ordinary shares were 'investments in real things' and hence responsive to inflation, some link with ordinary shares was the only practicable means of achieving the desired protection.[10]

From the consideration of hedges against inflation, it was a relatively short step to the concept of 'matching' assets and liabilities over time and in terms of likely performance. This idea was not exactly new – something similar had been put forward by Tom Suttie in a paper written in 1944 entitled 'Equity in bonus distribution'.[11] Nonetheless, when it was developed and set out in two papers given within weeks of each other in 1952, it was recognised as being of great importance and the papers themselves became landmarks. The 'Financial structure of a life office', written jointly by Trevor Haynes and Bob Kirton for presentation to the Faculty, studied the principle of 'matched assets' in relation to stationary and increasing funds, operating under ideal and non-ideal conditions, to reach the conclusion that 'the essence of matching is to maintain the interest yield for the right future term, and the capital security at the right future date'.[12] Protection from inflation lay in holding medium or long-dated assets, according to the nature of the liabilities, and while the investor could choose to depart from the matched position, sufficient free reserves must be held to meet the losses that might arise in consequence.

Frank Redington took this a step further with his 'Review of the principles of life-office valuations'.[13] The question of whether a fund could be safeguarded against changes in interest rates had been informally discussed in an unpublished exchange of letters between Maurice Ogborn and Gordon Bayley in 1946.[14] This query, although not the main theme of Redington's paper, was answered affirmatively by the theory of 'immunization', which held that in certain simplified conditions, the most important of which is that the rate of interest be uniform for all the terms of security, the mean term of the value of the proceeds of the assets (their interest and capital together) must equal the mean term of the value of the liabilities. A fund which satisfied this criterion was defined as 'immunized' against changes in interest rates under these simplified conditions. It was held, also, that in theory a profit could arise through either a rise or a fall in the rate of interest, if the spread of the assets is broader than the spread of the liabilities. Redington's paper, still held today as 'part of the very thought processes of the profession',[15] brought about a shift in the thinking of the life office actuary. Rather than considering assets and liabilities

This photograph of Frank Redington dates from about 1950, when the theory of immunization was beginning to take shape in his mind.

in isolation from each other, there arose a new perspective that regarded them as interrelated. Immunization theory seemed to offer a way for life offices to 'ride out any storm which threatens in the economic air'.[16] Not all of Redington's colleagues were wholly in agreement with his ideas, however: 'A consistent system of investment and bonus distribution for a life office' presented in November 1952 by Gordon Bayley and Wilfred Perks[17] proposed, as an alternative to the full immunization of with-profits business, a two-tier system of immunizing benefits from past premiums only, called 'paid-up immunization', leaving benefits flowing from future premiums to their own (immunized) destiny as they are paid. The authors also introduced the modern concept of the 'reasonable expectations of policyholders' as a cornerstone of their approach, an idea which would resurface in the 1970s.

While dealing with the effects of interest rate changes was absorbing, as a subject for actuarial debate it was soon displaced by another conundrum. By 1954 ordinary share values were rising, and would go on rising for the next decade. No account of the Institute would be complete without mentioning the pioneering role of George Ross Goobey (*), when investment manager of the Imperial Tobacco pension fund, in persuading the trustees to invest in equities. Thus was born the investment phenomenon known as the 'cult of the equity' that saw numerous pension fund managers follow Ross Goobey's example[18]. The great benefit of investing in equities was that the higher returns financed the inflationary increases in salary-related benefits from occupational schemes and the discretionary increases given to pensions once in payment. The effect for life business was equally gratifying but did present the life offices with a new problem. Out of the annual surplus they declared reversionary bonuses determined according to duration and payable at death or maturity. Whilst capital values remained relatively stable these uniform bonus declarations were justified, but the substantial increase in capital values of equities in the later 1950s posed a problem of fairness that could not be rectified simply by awarding larger reversionary bonuses. The investments enjoying such favour had in fact been made in the past, with the funds contributed by older policyholders, and it seemed right, therefore, that they should receive a correspondingly larger share of the profits. Actuaries' minds were greatly exercised by how best to resolve this difficulty, and various ways were found to meet it. One formula was the special or 'terminal' bonus devised by Frank Redington for the Prudential, which later took its name from the fact that it was only calculated and paid on death or when a policy matured. These bonuses reflected the duration of the policy and current state of investment markets and were paid in addition to any reversionary bonus due.[19] Subsequently their calculation took a variety of forms, but the amounts could always be varied by the company – even abandoned – unlike reversionary bonuses, which were guaranteed additions once declared.

By 1955, the rebuilding of Staple Inn Hall, so long delayed, was nearing completion, and those guiding the Institute could envisage the day when once again its activities would be united under one roof. A sub-committee had been working closely with the Prudential and the contractors during the period of reconstruction. Improvements in the layout of 1 and 2 Staple Inn, together with the construction of a basement under the Hall and existing buildings, added another 4,000 square feet (370 square metres) to the nearly 6,000 (560) occupied by the Institute before the war. This was allocated to a new Library, lecture rooms,[20] and reception and service areas, in keeping with the Institute's educational function and the profession's need for a fully supported venue.

None of this interior construction was permitted to intrude upon the character of the historic Inn. The view of the courtyard from the gateway off High Holborn was as it had been from time immemorial. The Hall itself, subject to building restrictions, had been

reconstructed as nearly as possible to the original design. Old timber was procured to match what could be salvaged of the original roof. One truss – at the gallery end of the hall – was made from the original timber. New oak panelling was designed from a panelled room (c.1603) exhibited at the Victoria and Albert Museum. The stained glass windows were taken out of store and replaced in their original positions, giving colour and grace to the hall.[21]

Even the twisted remains of the old gallery clock, whose 'wheezy clatter' had punctuated every discourse given in the Hall until the fatal event of August 1944, had been restored. Until a further renovation in the 1990s the new clock would retain something of the original wheeze and clatter, and marked the hours just as emphatically as had the old. The oak refectory table on the dais, presented by George Lidstone in memory of William Phelps, was an exact replica of the Elizabethan-style table given by Phelps that had been destroyed. The lectern was the gift of Abraham Levine in 1945. Busts of John Finlaison and Thomas Sprague had survived the bombing and now occupied prominent positions. The anteroom adjacent to the Hall, renamed the Council Chamber, held a long-case clock and display cases. Bronze memorial tablets recalled the names of actuaries who had died in both world wars.

The 'Return to Staple Inn', as the commemorative book produced for the occasion was called, took place in May and September 1955.[22] The reopening on 31 May marked the official handing over of the completely restored building to the owners – the Prudential, represented by Sir Frank Morgan. The

The head of a mace that once belonged to the Ancients of Staple Inn when it was an Inn of Chancery. To celebrate the Institute's return to Staple Inn in 1955 it was restored by the Students' Society. Note the woolsack, a reference to the Inn's medieval connections with the wool trade and the legal profession. (See Arthur Tait, *The Story of Staple Inn on Holborn Hill*, published by the Institute in 2001.)

Institute's festivities began on 19 September with three days of open house during which more than eight hundred people passed through the refurbished premises. Thursday 22 September saw the main ceremony, at which the ancient mace of the Inn, rescued from the ruins and refurbished by the Students' Society, was carried in procession by its Honorary Secretary, Mike O'Brien, watched by a jubilant crowd of Institute and Faculty members and guests. In the evening the first dinner was held in the Hall, with many toasts, a rousing speech by Sir William Elderton and further thanks for the gifts received by the Institute since 1948 in preparation for this long-awaited day. The final event was a reception on 29 September for guests from other professions.

The Institute's homecoming was the spur to other celebratory initiatives, namely, the creation of the President's badge and Council's application to the College of Arms for armorial bearings. The designs for both were devised by Maurice Ogborn and Douglas Rich, who were keenly interested in heraldry. The badge was the joint gift of nine past Presidents and was presented by the eldest of them, Digby Besant, at the Annual General Meeting in June 1955, so that the current President, John Bunford (*), could wear it when he greeted the Institute's guests in September. It was executed in gold and enamel by the artist R. H. Hill and, like the Institute's seal, but in a different arrangement, shows the figures of Time, Plenty and Fate (the figure of Atropos, who in Greek mythology cuts the thread of life). The grant of arms was requested in March 1955 and conceded a year later by Letters Patent. The arms employ traditional heraldic

A sessional meeting at Staple Inn – this was the first one after the return in 1955.

The Institute's coat of arms was granted by Letters Patent dated 15 March 1956. It consists of a shield (in the heraldic terms used, a 'Chequy Sable and Or a Bend wavy Argent on a Chief Gold an open Book between two Hour Glasses proper'), a crest, and supporters. In the shield, the black and gold chequered ground upon which the other elements are superimposed refers to the cloth used by the medieval exchequer and thus to the actuary's concern with financial computations. The 'Bend wavy' represents the river of life and the classical 'river' separating life from death. The Chief, occupying the top third of the shield, shows the Book proper to a learned society concerned with education, flanked by Hour Glasses symbolising the periods of time which influence actuarial calculations. The crest, with the esquire's helm granted to a corporate body, is surmounted by a woolpack referring to the long association with Staple Inn. The silver lion supporters bear the Tudor rose of England on their shoulders and hold 'bezants' or gold coins. The motto *Certum ex incertis* (Certainty from uncertainty) had been chosen for the Institute's bookplate in 1901 and was thus familiar.

elements and colours to symbolise the principal concerns of the actuary and the historic associations of the Institute.[23] The end of this memorable year for the Institute marked the opening of an equally jubilant one for the Faculty. It celebrated its centenary in Edinburgh in October 1956, accompanied by the Institute's President and members of Council and numerous invited guests. In later years John Bunford would observe that the 14th International Congress, held in Madrid in June 1954, had touched off a two-year cycle of festivities for the actuarial community: besides the two British celebrations, there were important anniversaries for the Swedish, Norwegian, Danish, Dutch, Finnish, French and Swiss societies.[24]

The presidential badge was created in 1955 and presented to the then President, John Bunford, by nine former Presidents:
Arthur Digby Besant,
William Penman,
Reginald Simmonds,
Sir George Maddex,
Sir William Elderton,
Henry Melville,
Sir Andrew Rowell,
Frank Gardner and
Fred Menzler.

From the range of talent that graced the Institute during the 1950s, it seems invidious to select a few names only – except that without such a selection, the account of its life would be less colourful than was the reality. There were the Presidents, each of whom imparted his particular tone to his term of office: Fred Menzler, his mind still crackling with new ideas as it had thirty years before; Frank Gardner, self-effacing and committed to the service of the wider community; the open and genial John Bunford; Charles Wood, with his international stature and amazing memory; and, finally, Frank Redington, of all actuaries the most revered by his contemporaries as combining the highest mathematical and analytical gifts with the greatest sensitivity to their human implications. There were also those who never occupied the presidential chair, but who made monumental contributions to the profession and the Institute. Wilfred Perks, in whose forceful personality were blended 'the thorough analytical mind of the scholar with the ardour of the reformer'; the brilliant Bill Phillips, who after qualifying as an actuary went on to become a barrister; James and Francis Bacon, father and son, the driving forces in the consulting firm of Bacon & Woodrow; Rodney Barnett and Roland Clarke who largely directed the Continuous Mortality Investigation Bureau for many years; Bobbie Beard, whose breadth of interests made him the living embodiment of 'wider fields'; Frank Spratling, assistant to Menzler at London Transport and, like him, an actuary who enhanced the profession by applying its skills in new contexts.

The repercussions of inflation were not the only challenge to actuarial thinking during the 1950s. The Royal Commission on Population, appointed in 1944, had submitted its Report in June 1949 and confirmed what demographers had long been suggesting. The average size of the British family – father, mother and 2.2 children – had held steady since about 1930. Nonetheless, this figure of 2.2 fell about 6 per cent short of being able to replace the population, suggesting a likelihood of a gradual population increase until about 1977, followed by a slow but inexorable decrease thereafter. While the Report did qualify these findings, the general trend it identified (an increasing proportion of elderly people) was worrisome, and especially so in the context of the growth in pension rights and obligations under the State scheme, which was coming to be seen as a matter of increasing and grave importance by Government and the actuarial profession.

In January 1952 the Councils of the Institute and the Faculty jointly appointed a research group consisting of Francis Bacon (*), Douglas Elphinstone and Bernard Benjamin to study the growth of pension commitments in relation to the national income. The resulting study, 'The growth of pension rights and their impact on the national economy', was presented to the two bodies in April 1954 and considered the role and importance of pensions in national life. Its main purpose was to make actuarial estimates for pension provision over a thirty-year period beginning in 1951. It predicted that the proportion of elderly people in the population would rise by about 50 per cent over the following twenty-five years. The five providers of pensions – the State, the Civil Service and other public service schemes, the privately administered schemes, life office schemes and those provided by friendly societies – were examined and compared, and the conclusion drawn that the cost of pensions over the same period was likely to double, from 4 per cent to 8 per cent of national product. On the assumption that the national income remained constant, if pension rights were to grow so that in thirty years' time everyone received a retirement pension (including the State pension) of two-thirds of average earnings throughout their working lifetime, pension payments would absorb 11 per cent of national income, and under certain further conditions, as much as 14 per cent.[25] The study pointed out the importance of the growth of pension funds to the volume of savings available to finance new capital investment. Finally, the two main methods of paying for pensions were considered.

The first of these was 'funding', whereby money is set aside and a fund built up to pay for pension benefits in the future, an approach so familiar and based in common experience that its soundness seems obvious. The second was 'assessmentism', more colloquially known as 'pay as you go', in which current pensions are paid for out of current contributions and taxation. The compulsory flat-rate State scheme that had grown out of the Beveridge plan (although it began with a fund inherited from other sources) was of this type, as were most public sector schemes. Life office and privately administered schemes were voluntarily entered into by employers on behalf of their employees, and were funded by contributions from both. But while there was general agreement that funding was the necessary method for private schemes, so as to build up and safeguard the benefits, there was a marked divergence of views about the degree to which the funding principle should be applied to the compulsory State scheme. For all their obvious virtue, funded systems matured slowly; and the needs of elderly people were immediate. The money needed to pay pensions could only come from taxation and interest on investments. The payment of contributions over many years engendered the belief that a certain level of pension was receivable as of right, yet a less than rigorous assessment of likely future trends in population growth, investment and competing national priorities could result in disastrous shortfalls. The 'pay as you go' system, on the other hand, offered greater flexibility to respond to current needs, but contained a different element of insecurity. As the study pointed out,

In the case of the retirement pensions payable under the National Insurance Scheme there is one very important difference to be noted. The Government has power to raise money by taxation or by borrowing (including borrowing from the Bank of England), so that the uncertainty as to whether the money will be available to pay the benefits when they become due is limited to the question as to whether the Government will find it desirable to make it available ... the deciding factor is likely to be the prevailing trend of opinion as to the proper provision that should be made for old people.[26]

In other words, a matter that was, in the words of Frank Gardner, 'too deep for dogmatism' might be dangerously open to the vicissitudes of political expediency.[27]

The Institute and Faculty were only slightly ahead of Government in their concern for the future of pensions. In July 1953 the Chancellor of the Exchequer set up a Committee under the chairmanship of Sir Thomas Phillips with a brief very similar to that of the Joint Councils' study: to consider the economic and financial problems of provision for old age. Three actuaries – John Gunlake (*), Fred Menzler and Frederick Honey – were appointed to the Phillips Committee, and the Institute and Faculty were invited to submit a joint Memorandum of evidence. The Government Actuary, Sir George Maddex, submitted independent evidence that included statistical material prepared with the help of an Institute sub-committee.

The joint Memorandum held that the full nature of the problem of old age provision could only be considered in the context of the economic future of the nation as a whole. Its conclusions reflected the actuarial profession's concern for sound finance and social justice as well as its close acquaintance with the demographic and economic questions under investigation. While the State scheme guaranteed everyone basic subsistence in old age, those in private, or 'occupational', schemes were guaranteed a more comfortable retirement. The gradual extension of such schemes to further sections of the employed population was seen as the best means of redistributing the national income so as to provide the elderly with an adequate share. While it was recognised that full monetary funding was not really feasible for a national scheme, the contributory principle was nonetheless valuable, both as a means of providing capital for investment and an encouragement to thrift. All schemes other than the State scheme, even public sector ones, should be funded, since in this way 'pensioners become shareholders in the nation's wealth and not beneficiaries of the nation's charity'. With reference to the State scheme, one particularly idealistic recommendation sounded a prophetic note: the Joint Committee considered it 'vital that the future annual deficits that result from the absence of an actuarial fund, and the resultant burden of taxation which those deficits impose, should be continuously in the minds of all who are at any time concerned with economic policy'.[28] The flexibility of pension products, the removal of age limits and the careful setting of premium levels were all secondary to this consideration, and to the last and most fundamental conclusion, the delicate relationship between pension levels and inflation: 'If pensions grow too large, they may cause demands for increased wages and salaries from the working population who are, after all, providing the goods and services out of which the retired population has to be maintained'.[29] On the other hand, the effect of the inflation thus produced is also harmful:

the pensioner finds that the purchasing power of his pension is reduced below what he has been justly led to expect … employers commonly have to find substantial sums to meet the cost of increased pensions for existing employees. This in turn forces up production costs and price levels. A stable balance between earned incomes and pensions can only be maintained if the currency is stable.[30]

The Phillips Committee, not surprisingly, followed the actuarial lead in recommending the retention of the system of financing immediate pensions largely out of current contributions, the payment of which during working life was a condition of receiving benefit in due course. It also recommended, as one means of addressing the problem of an increasing pensioner population, the raising of the retirement age, from 65 to 68 for men and from 60 to 63 for women. But the pension question was not only of concern on account of its future implications; retirement provision had become increasingly important to Government for its fiscal implications in the present. As was mentioned in a previous chapter in connection with the formation of the Association of Consulting Actuaries, private and life office schemes were at this time proliferating at a tremendous rate as employers competed for staff at a time of full employment. Taxation concessions made setting up such schemes attractive to employers, but the tax legislation surrounding them had not kept pace with what had become a virtual 'pensions movement', and there were many anomalies. There was also the matter of the self-employed, who remained at a great disadvantage in making retirement provision for themselves.[31]

A Government Committee appointed in August 1950 had been considering these questions for several years before its vast Report was finally published in April 1954. This was the Committee on the Taxation Treatment of Provisions for Retirement chaired by Sir James Millard Tucker, of which Reginald Simmonds was a member. The Report was discussed at an Institute sessional meeting on 22 November 1954,[32] with Millard Tucker himself among the audience. While its provisions are far too voluminous even to touch upon here, those present, and actuaries generally, considered it an admirable Report, if overburdened by detail. The improvements recommended by the Millard Tucker Committee were incorporated in the Finance Act 1956: the tax regime governing the pensions field was rationalised and the way made clearer for its continuing growth. The extension of retirement provision to the self-employed in the form of deferred annuities, permitted under s.22 of the Act, led to greater things, in that they would shortly be used to offer Britain's first unit-linked contract.[33] Much remained to be done, however, to harmonise the situation of the self-employed with that of the employed.

The problem of paying for pension entitlement was by now engaging the attention of both the political parties. The pre-war, flat-rate State pension system, recast in 1948 following the Beveridge Report, was by 1956 facing a large current deficit. This was less easy to correct than might have been supposed, since merely raising the level of contributions would cause hardship to the lowest paid. The Conservative Government saw a possible solution in a move to a two-tier wage-related scheme, but had not actually divulged the details. Such a measure would bring the State into competition with the occupational pension schemes that already covered almost half of the working population, and raised the administrative nightmare of 'contracting-out' on a massive scale. Labour's suggested way forward, announced in 1957, was a scheme of 'National Superannuation' which promised employees an inflation-proof pension worth half of final salary at age 65. Both these prospects aroused actuarial unease: though different in many respects, each included a system of graduated pensions related to the total amount of graduated contributions paid before retirement, a major innovation that completely altered the future pattern of State pensions and the future pattern of costs.[34] A further Joint Committee was appointed by the Institute and Faculty Councils to study the ideas of both political parties and prepare a statement of the profession's views.

Out of the deliberations of this body during the autumn of 1957 emerged a statement entitled *National Pensions* which was issued to the press in January 1958.[35] The concerns about future costs, population changes, contracting-out and the potential conflict between the State and the occupational pension schemes were explained, but some members of the Institute, among them Frank Redington (*) – who became President in June of that year – believed that the profession's response was a matter of duty towards the future of society, and that it required greater exposure to be effective. Without a firm indication of the Government's intentions, however, a stronger statement could not be made.

It was not until 14 October, a bare two weeks before the date of Redington's Presidential Address, that the Government published its White Paper, *Provision for Old Age*, the basis of the Boyd-Carpenter scheme (named for the Minister of Pensions and National Insurance) that would become law as the National Insurance Act in 1959 and operative in 1961. Redington hastily recast his speech to make national pensions 'the major theme of his Address as indeed of his whole Presidency'.[36] The Joint Committee reconvened and rapidly prepared memoranda to Government on the financial implications of the proposals and on contracting-out. In May 1959 the redrafted *National Pensions* was published with the subtitle *An Appeal to Statesmanship*. Although it was ostensibly the work of the Joint Committee, most of the text was written by Frank Redington. Some of the phraseology is also reminiscent of Frank Gardner's Presidential Address of six years earlier. The modest-looking booklet was the subject of a press conference and several thousand copies were widely circulated – to MPs and Members of the House of Lords, to the press, to others in the pension field and in the professions. This in itself was a 'first' for the Institute and the Faculty: never before had they sought media attention, much less to assert their views in the public arena. On this occasion it was done, quite consciously, out of a sense of professional obligation to contribute their particular expertise to what was clearly going to be an ongoing debate.[37]

The 'diffident profession' momentarily – and warily – stepped into the limelight with *An Appeal to Statesmanship*, as the Institute for the first time deliberately drew public attention to an issue with grave future implications.

An Appeal to Statesmanship sets out, in less than a dozen pages, and in the usual scrupulously non-partisan language, the facts about the future costs of national pensions under the existing flat-rate State scheme and under the new schemes for graduated pensions put forward by two of the three main political parties. A brief but telling set of figures was provided by way of illustration. Although Labour's proposals were based on the partial funding characteristic of occupational pension schemes, and those of the Conservatives mainly on the 'pay as you go' principle, the chief warning regarding both was that the eventual payment of graduated pensions places additional obligations on future generations – obligations which those in the future would have no say in determining and which, in the context of the predicted shifts in population, were bound to become onerous. The present generation was mortgaging the standard of living of generations to come: 'We are promising ourselves, now, that our children will pay us larger pensions in the future than we are willing to pay now to our parents.'[38] This stark phrase was intended to resonate in the memory.

The 'Appeal' was not intended to oppose or to advocate graduated pensions, but to prompt the appreciation of the financial implications for the future that they would bring in their train. It also warned against the ease with which national pensions could 'become entangled in purely party politics'[39] – a real danger given that party spokesmen had already indicated the likelihood of changes in the State scheme following any change of government. The uncertainty in which this left employers, faced with the prospect of contracting-out of a State scheme of graduated pensions, was held to outweigh any advantage that other changes might bring. The profession's recommendation was for the creation of a 'National Pensions Council', an 'authoritative and independent body to guide the country through the financial, economic and technical aspects of this particularly difficult problem'.[40]

Regrettably, such an entity was never formed: the Boyd-Carpenter scheme that was adopted as the basis of the National Insurance Act 1959 contained an element of funding within a 'pay as you go' system which seemed sound enough, but the complexity of the new regulations was daunting, and analysis soon revealed that contracting-out benefited the better-paid and predominantly male workforce more than it did the lower paid. The suspicion grew that the Beveridge principle of a universal basic State pension as of right was being eroded in favour of the graduated scheme chiefly as a means of reducing the deficit of the existing State scheme: the extra contributions were needed to pay for present pensions, so passing on, in the way so objected to in *An Appeal to Statesmanship*, a pensions burden to a future generation.[41] The National Insurance Act of 1959 set in motion a pensions tug-of-war between the political parties that would have repercussions far into the future. Meanwhile, the Institute and the Faculty had joined forces in response to a challenge that had called forth a new spirit. Actuaries

should not be content merely to operate as backroom technicians. There is a duty to come forward and to speak out on these questions of national finance – to be prepared to contribute in a forceful if non-partisan way every time the pensions debate resurfaces.[42]

It would resurface, and this spirit itself be challenged, frequently in the years to come.

CHAPTER FOUR

On the threshold of the new age

THE impact made by *An Appeal to Statesmanship*, especially on the younger members of the Institute, tended to overshadow everything else that was happening at about the same time. By the time the dust cleared the Institute had been granted a Supplemental Royal Charter and had conducted another major educational review, but these have become hazy events, their rationale almost forgotten.

The move to obtain the Supplemental Charter came about for the most prosaic of reasons – a rent increase – and was not without its own gentle humour. Under the terms of the original Royal Charter of 1884, the Institute was authorised to pay a maximum of £3,000 a year in rent. Only in 1957, when – having rebuilt Staple Inn Hall and allowed the Institute to occupy the rest of the Inn until 1954 at the pre-war rate – the Prudential broached the subject of an increase, was it realised that new provisions would have to be gained before the Institute could comply. In its Petition to the Queen in June 1958, the opportunity was taken to request bye-laws more appropriate to the Institute's greatly expanded role since 1884 in advancing the profession. With the granting of the Supplemental Charter of 29 January 1959, the Institute gained new bye-laws and the means to amend or rescind them, the right to amend the Charters, the right to establish charitable funds, and an upper limit of £12,000 for annual rental expenditure. (The rental agreement with the Prudential, backdated to 1954, was in fact for £8,000 a year for thirty-five years, which may have seemed steep when it was agreed but which before very long had become exceptional value.[1])

Changing conditions in the world outside the Institute were by the late 1950s again exerting pressure on the established route to the Fellowship. On one hand, as the stringency of the post-war period receded and prosperity returned, there was a growing demand for actuaries. On the other, while the Lever reforms in place since 1950 had broadened the syllabus and reduced post-Part I qualification time by about a year, some examiners considered that standards in traditional areas had suffered as a result. Even with the reforms, Students were still falling by the wayside in distressingly high numbers. Of each year's intake of perhaps 140 or 150 Students, only 70 or 80 even attempted Part I, and of these only 20 or 30 ever qualified as actuaries. They did so after an average period of study of six or seven years after Part I and a period of National Service, making the age at which an actuary entered professional life undesirably late.[2]

A Committee under the chairmanship of Kenneth Usherwood (*) was appointed in 1956 to recommend ways in which the Institute's training could be improved, and the flow of actuarial Students through the process and on to the Fellowship increased. Usherwood viewed the task as one of reconsidering the Lever reforms in the light of altered conditions rather than the making of dramatic changes. These conditions, however, posed a dilemma that would resurface in the future: how to compete with other professions for the best candidates without compromising standards, and how to maintain them without creating a forbiddingly arduous route to qualification:

Since the war and with full employment and the demographic trough, the competition for technologists [sic] has become acute and industry and commerce are adopting very vigorous measures to tempt suitable boys into employment … there is a large field of physics and electricity which has a strong appeal, and much of that field is in competition with us for boys with mathematical inclinations, and offers them financially attractive posts at an early age. To graduates

The title and contents pages of the Institute Medals and Prizes Book, lettered on vellum. The names of Fellows who gain awards continue to be entered in the book, which was presented by past President John Gunlake in 1966.

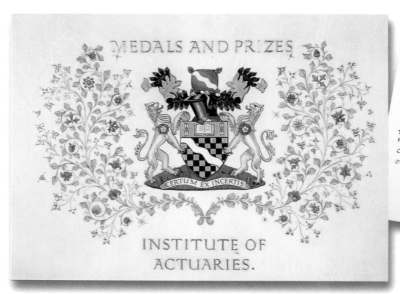

in particular it offers good employment without the need to spend the further years which the prospective actuary must devote to study. In this sort of world … we feel we shall not obtain a reasonable supply of good entrants unless we can further reduce the average period before qualification.[3]

The Usherwood Committee came to see that part of the problem lay further back, in the schools, where the fearsome reputation of the actuarial examinations sometimes dissuaded teachers from steering candidates towards an actuarial career. The Institute's recruitment team, visiting the schools each spring, naturally presented a more positive picture, but the Usherwood Committee concluded that the eighty hours of Institute examinations were a genuine deterrent. No other profession came close to imposing such a barrage, and when, moreover, 'In every section of every part of an examination, candidates are tested at near the limit of their capability', the actuarial Student's life could indeed become 'a valley of tribulation'.[4]

The Committee's recommendations centred on three main areas: attracting good candidates and getting them rapidly through Entrance and Part I, weeding out the unsuitable, and reducing post-Part I qualification time. Eliminating the entrance examination in English was a bold step, but one which was justified, even for overseas candidates, on the grounds that later training would test the same abilities. Time limits were set for taking the Part I examinations, where core subjects such as probability were studied, with the intention of speeding the progress of the good Student and shaking out the less able before they expended too much of their own and tutors' time. Finally, the fifty-four hours of examinations attendant on Parts I to III were cut to thirty-five hours through a drastic reduction in the amount of 'problem-solving' in each exam, the greatest saving being in the bedrock subjects such as compound interest and life contingencies where course-work at a later stage of training would provide reinforcement. In general, the Lever canons of parallel training, progressive approach and specialised emphasis were allowed to stand. The regrouping of closely associated subjects, the freeing up of the order in which the examinations in them were taken, and the banishment of the exam in reversions were among the modifications that together added up to a major saving of time. The underlying emphasis was 'on making the examination tests less exhaustive and less penetrating than they are at present' and thus to help the able Student, 'provided he works with assiduity', to qualify in four years, and the less-gifted or less-industrious candidate in six. A review of education at five-yearly intervals was advised, the need to keep abreast of change being seen as a very real obligation.

The Usherwood Committee's Report appeared in April 1958, with its recommendations coming into effect in 1960. One idea it had suggested, given the predominantly London-based Student body, was oral tuition directed towards the examinations, to supplement the correspondence courses and the discussion classes already held. Faith was expressed that somehow the necessary manpower could be found to undertake this. Existing tutors already carried a heavy load, and this proposal could be implemented only partially, by drawing upon the ranks of the newly qualified. In this period, as before the war, the young actuary became 'a debtor to his profession' as soon as he qualified, and his energies – such as they were after his long ordeal – were quickly harnessed.

The consideration of just how reliant upon volunteer effort the Institute was suggests not only a professional body compelled to live within the means generated by its members' subscriptions,[5] but one whose members were deeply committed to it. One of the few paid staff was Allan Dale, who in 1939 succeeded the venerable Jarvis as Assistant Secretary. His title was upgraded to Secretary in 1952, after he had seen the Institute through the war and its aftermath. Dale handled all the administrative and Council affairs with the help of four salaried clerks, and his discretion and capacity for work are still recalled. The Actuarial Tuition Service (ATS) tutors were modestly remunerated for the mountain of assignments they marked, but the Institute *Journal* was edited, the Library managed, the *Year Book* produced, the Appointments Board organised and the Mortality Investigations carried on by a succession of Fellows whose only recompense was the satisfaction of serving the profession. The Institute's governing body, the thirty-strong Council, provides a further illustration of the same point. Those nominated for election were usually already known for having put back into Institute life something of what they had gained from it.[6] The matters dealt with by Council at its ten meetings each year increased greatly from about 1950. Sub-committees composed of both Council and non-Council members were deputed to report on everything from the need for new textbooks to impending legislation.

By 1963 there were twenty such sub-committees, most of them meeting at least as frequently as Council itself.[7] A quick analysis reveals that four men – Arthur Steeds, Leonard Hall, Herbert Tetley and Francis Bacon – each served on six of them; and three others – Norman Benz, Bernard Benjamin and Bert Haycocks – on five. Steeds and Haycocks were at the same time Chairman and Secretary respectively of the ATS, while Bobbie Beard and Frank Redington sat on four sub-committees each and in addition ran the Continuous Mortality Investigation (CMI) Bureau. Jo Hamilton-Jones, whose work with the Mercantile & General frequently took him abroad, furthered the Institute's contacts wherever he went and still managed to help with the Library, the CMI and several committees. Quite what such generosity on the part of these and other Fellows of the Institute amounted to in man-hours is impossible to gauge.

The Institute's Gold Medal was instituted in 1920 but it was not until 1927 that the first was awarded, to George King. Subsequent medallists were George James Lidstone (1929) and Sir William Palin Elderton (1937).

There were also the personal projects, such as the history of Staple Inn written by Maurice Ogborn[8] and Fred Menzler's history of the Students' Society[9] (on which Dennis Gilley also worked behind the scenes and which was later updated by Colin Stewart), both of which similarly represented the gift to the Institute of much time and dedication. The individual research that resulted in papers for sessional meetings and *Journal* articles was a further means of honouring the Institute's motto, 'I hold every man a debtor to his profession'. taken from the preface to Sir Francis Bacon's *The Elements of the Common Law of England.* In a very few cases the body of work built up over a period of years, which might include the discussion of sessional papers as well as the papers themselves, represented a contribution and stimulus to actuarial thought that justified the award of the Institute's Gold Medal. The first two recipients after the war were Wilfred Perks (*) and Bill Phillips in November 1964, enlarging the select band so honoured to five (the first three being King, Lidstone and Elderton).

Presentation of Gold Medals by Herbert (later Sir Herbert) Tetley to Wilfred Perks and Bill Phillips OBE, on 23 November 1964.

The Institute's Charter prescribed that its office-holders were to be elected from among the Fellows, but in practice, this had come to mean 'from among the members of Council'. The President's duties were narrower in scope than they have become since, frequent trips abroad not yet having become an essential component of the position. It was customary for a President to have served previously as one of the four Vice-Presidents or as Treasurer, and possibly as one of the two Honorary Secretaries as well.[10] Such a well-defined progression reinforced the sense that within the Institute everything was well regulated and unlikely to produce many surprises, pleasant or otherwise. To the outsider – if not to the hypothetical 'man in the street' (who would probably have disclaimed all knowledge of actuaries) – the Institute, secluded from the bustle of High Holborn, remained the semi-collegiate enclave it had been before the war. This image of being at one remove from the fray was more and more at variance with the intensity with which actuarial concerns touching on the future of the nation were debated within the venerable walls of Staple Inn. This contradiction between image and reality would accompany the Institute for several generations yet, and was one to which it would have to devote considerable effort to dispel.

Basic to the projection of the actuarial *persona* in the years ahead was the ideal of professional independence and integrity, the restatement of which, by the late 1950s, was claiming an increasing amount of committee time and deliberation. The collective slogan of 'freedom with publicity' which Institute spokesmen had so often cited before the war was no longer suitable in the altered social climate of post-war Britain. The professions – actuaries included

– were now under pressure to justify the privileges they were widely held to enjoy, while the sense of service traditionally ascribed to them seemed less credible in an increasingly sceptical and materialist age. The actuary obviously had to understand and comply with the legislation governing his activities, but Council had never sought to incorporate in the Charter or Bye-laws a comprehensive code to govern members' professional conduct. The *Year Book* included some notes on the subject, but as the introduction to them made clear, the Institute relied upon the conscience of each individual member and the collective conscience of the profession.

The issue that led to the first departure from the principle of 'freedom with publicity' outlined above was that of the professional independence of the actuary and the advice he gave in changing economic conditions and new contexts. Concern with this would extend far into the future, as more diverse employment opportunities became available. Since most actuaries were employed by life companies, a great many of which were building up substantial group and occupational pensions business in the twenty years after the war, the question of the life office actuary's relationship to the clients of his employer was basic. The 1950s saw an increase in the number of firms of insurance brokers, some of which publicised themselves as 'consultants in actuarial finance' in direct competition with both the life offices and the consulting actuaries. Such firms offered a new employment avenue for actuaries, but the need for clear lines of demarcation between what was done as an independent professional and what was done as an employee became acute. Were an actuary in such a firm to be asked to value a pension fund, for instance, the Institute's view was that he might do so only in a direct capacity, setting and receiving a proper fee; for otherwise, he was not 'independent' in any meaningful sense, nor 'professional', in that his employer sought and gained business by commercial means. Not surprisingly, resentment arose between the actuaries in these firms, who found the Institute's standards restrictive, and the consulting actuaries who viewed them as an essential safeguard against what they saw as a *parvenu* commercialism.

With members of the Institute on both sides, this question, together with transgressions of the rule that forbade FIAs to advertise, probably occupied the Professional Conduct Committee more than any other. But there were also the anomalies (such as the actuary resident abroad, yet acting for clients in Britain; or the actuary acting in a professional capacity in partnership with non-actuaries) for which guidelines had to be created, as well as the occasional moral dilemma that required a clear lead from the Institute. Once the Professional Conduct Committee had pronounced upon the matters drawn to its attention, the problems were usually resolved by a directive, but there was no doubt that issues of professional conduct were by now arising more frequently. In September 1959 the Institute set up a Professional Guidance Committee to replace the former one advising on professional conduct. It had met thirty

BILL'S MEDAL

You've 'eard of William Phillips, per'aps?
    A lad of bull-dog breed,
'Oo wrote some actuarial stuff,
    (A most *unusual* deed).

In bygone years he wrote and wrote
    And when the work was done,
Our Herbert had a medal struck,
    A most attractive one.

So Bill came up t' Institute,
    In famous London Town;
A porter in a fine top hat
    Was walkin' up and down.

The Porter stopped and looked at Bill,
    "Excuse me, mate," said he.
"Might you be Actuary William Phillips?"
    And Bill said "Ay, that's me".

"Well, go on in," said Porter chap
    In language loud and chill,
"Bert's got a medal there for thee!"
    "I know 'e 'as," said Bill.

Well, Bill pushed open door of Inn,
    And stood in 'oly 'ush;
He found himself inside a room;
    All marble busts and plush.

A boy called Page in red cocked 'at
    And breeches white and blue,
Said "Is your name Bill Phillips, lad?"
    "It is," said Bill, "'Ow do."

"Don't loiter then", said Page-boy sharp,
    "Like schoolboy feeling ill,
"Our Bert's got medal there for thee."
    "I know 'e 'as!" said Bill.

Upstairs Bill met Fred Menzler,
    A top-'at on 'is 'ead.
'Is trousers they were velveteen;
    One leg was blue – one red.

'E glanced at Bill all 'aughty-like
    And asked 'im "Might you be
William Phillips – Actuary?"
    And Bill said "Ay, that's me."

"Well, don't keep Bert all night," 'e said,
    "Surprised at thee, I be.
'E's got thy medal there, 'as Bert".
    "I KNOW 'e 'as," said P.

But when Bill came on Council chaps,
    His awe he couldn't smother;
For there sat Bert – one hand held quill
    And gavel was in t'other.

Bill grasped the situation like
    In less than half a jiff,
He gave a very smart salute
    And knocked 'is 'at skew whiff.

"This must be William P." said Bert.
    "That's reet," said Bill, "I be."
"Well, I've got medal 'ere for thee."
    "I KNOW thou 'ast," said P.

"Don't be impatient Bill," says Bert.
    "Before 'tis 'anded you,
There's certain grave formalities
    Which must be gotten through."

"'The medal's granted William P.'"
    (Our Bert began to read,)
"'For writing actuarial stuff;
    (A most unusual deed).'"

"'All kinds of things 'e wrote about,
    From serving at the Pru'
Now tell me Bill, 'ow come you do
    This deed so brave and true?'"

"Well now," said Bill, "'twas like this 'ere –
    Joe Burn was very tough
And told us boys to start at once
    On actuarial stuff."

"It's very good of you", said Bert,
    "To write this stuff so well,
I'm sure you'd write us volumes more"
    "I would!" said Bill, "Like 'ell!"

"Did you 'ear that!" said Bert to Ken,
    "of all the flipping jerks!"
"We won't give 'im the ruddy thing"
"We'll give them both to Perks".

'Bill's Medal' (poem). Bill Phillips was noted for his sense of humour, celebrated here along with the award of the medal in question. 'Bert' refers to Herbert (later Sir Herbert) Tetley and 'Ken' to Kenneth Usherwood. The poem was written by Charles Wood, President 1956–58, in October 1964.

times by January 1962, and in March of that year approved a set of 'Basic Principles' covering the four areas of impartiality and independence, relationship with the client, advertising and publicity, and fees, with some general points and a summary of Council's views over time on specific problems.

A major influence was the determination of fee-charging consulting actuaries practising in partnerships to be clearly distinguished from those employed by the insurance-broking firms, which were paid by commission and operated under limited liability. The fierce competition between the two groups for self-administered pension fund business highlighted the whole question of the actuary's professional independence; and thus the 'Basic Principles' distinguished strongly between direct professional advice and the 'indirect' advice given by the actuarial staff of a company, which was then passed on to its clients. An amended version of the basic principles, drafted mainly by Frank Spratling (*), became the 'Memorandum on Professional Conduct and Practice' (MPC), dated 1 May 1965. This set out the general course to be adopted in particular circumstances, but could not, of course, cover all contingencies.[11] It was emphasised that the Institute would supply guidance for specific instances not covered, and that it was each member's duty to ask for such guidance, if in doubt as to a course of action. In 1971, on the advice of the Monopolies Commission which was at that time examining the professions, the MPC was reworded by the Professional Guidance Committee chaired by Harold Purchase to allow employed actuaries to operate on much the same basis as consulting actuaries. To some this remained a regrettable blurring of distinctions and was seen as the thin end of a wedge; others saw it as an accommodation to realities that, if viewed positively, could result in the widening of the scope of the profession. (The tension between these points of view remained a feature of Institute debate until 1984. In that year the revision of the MPC by Brian (later Sir Brian) Corby (*), by then Chairman of the Professional Guidance Committee, eliminated the distinction between direct and indirect advice and established a clear set of principles for all, whether employees, partners or directors. In the light of this, the Association of Consulting Actuaries amended its constitution in 1988 to enable any actuary engaged in consulting to belong, regardless of the corporate structure of their employers.)

Up to now, the disciplinary measures available to Council in the event of 'unprofessional conduct' or 'bringing the Institute into disrepute' were in theory administered by a standing Investigating Committee reporting to a Special Meeting of Council, and appeal was to a Special General Meeting of the membership. (All of this was enshrined in the lengthy bye-law 62 of the Bye-laws ordained by the Supplemental Royal Charter of 1959.) In practice, disciplinary procedures had never been resorted to, although there had been a few instances in the previous hundred years where members had resigned on having a complaint made against them. This situation would alter within a few years, and more will be said about it in due course.

Issues arising from concepts of professionalism were only one element in a panorama which, as actuaries who were active in the Institute during the late 1950s and early 1960s recall, was undergoing a great deal of change in a comparatively short time. Much of this impression derived from technological advances. One that had been appreciated early on and was now being increasingly adopted in the environments where actuaries worked was electronic data processing, the commercial aspect of the immense field of electronic computing. At its origin twenty years before, the electronic processing of data had been purely experimental. In 1936 when he presented his famous paper, 'Binary Calculation' to an Institute sessional meeting, Bill Phillips (*) had described the characteristics of a high-speed calculating device that would use electronic components and the binary system, prefiguring the later development of computing. He was also visionary in predicting the importance such devices would have in insurance and allied fields.

The first applications of electronic data processing had nothing to do with insurance, however, but with statistical and probability analysis. From 1937 onwards, as war with Germany appeared ever more probable, the experimental approach gave way to practical uses under the aegis of British and American military operational research groups. In Britain teams of scientists were formed to study the strategic and tactical problems involved in military operations. These kinds of problems required the analysis of large amounts of data and systematic testing using multiple variables, in a way that was second nature to actuaries, although theirs was only one of the many scientifically trained professions that supplied the relevant personnel. It was with activities such as gauging the effectiveness of anti-submarine measures, the uses of radar, and reducing aircraft loss that Fellows of the Institute were involved during the war as part of the larger overall field of what became known as 'OR' or 'oper-

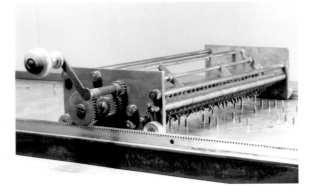

The binary calculator devised by Bill Phillips in 1936 to illustrate binary theory, which was basic to the development of computers and computer programming.

ational research'. 'OR' meant simply the use of scientific methods to provide a quantitative basis for decision-making. National security was the force driving the development of machines that could produce rapid calculations from vast arrays of data and multiple variables. (Code-breaking soon became a priority, and thus were conceived the earliest computers – Colossus by the British team at Bletchley Park and the University of Pennsylvania's ENIAC.)

After the war, it was predictable that actuaries who had been employed in OR should see the implications of electronic data processing for their own work, especially in life and pensions, so much of which involved countless small calculations and the analysis of probabilities. Existing means for calculation had served generations well, but were, by comparison with what came after them, both time consuming and labour intensive. The most basic of these, used for fairly straightforward calculations, were the Cotsworth tables and the Fuller's cylindrical slide-rules, which were common in the late 1940s (the latter, colloquially known as 'guns', still had their devotees in the 1970s). Then there was the arithmometer, a wholly mechanical machine whose speed depended entirely on the dexterity and stamina of the operator. A nineteenth-century invention, it would be succeeded by machines that remained a common fixture in life offices well into the 1960s. They were used for premium calculations, which had to be checked and cross-checked by other operators. The Rolls-Royce of hand calculating machines was the Brunswiga. Many offices were equipped with these, as were the Government Actuary's Department and the consulting firms. Peter Cox (who served under six Government Actuaries and himself became a Deputy GA) recalls that they 'weighed about ten pounds and made a grinding noise. One rotated a handle on the right-hand side, having first arranged for the number to be operated on by pulling down levers, one for the units, another for the tens and so on.' Others recall that these machines were prone to jam from time to time.[12] By the 1950s they had become old-fashioned and many actuaries preferred the new lightweight electrically powered calculators, many made by Monroe, but in some very traditional offices sets of tables or 'ready-reckoners' continued to be preferred to any kind of calculating machine.

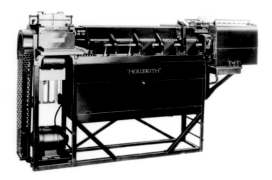

For the handling of the large volumes of data involved in valuations there were the two mechanical punched-card systems manufactured by the rival firms of Hollerith and Powers-Samas. Both systems dated from early in the century, and by the 1920s almost all life offices had installed one or the other. By the 1950s, however, the demands being made upon them meant that they were ripe for replacement, even if they were not strictly speaking obsolete. The electronic computers produced by Ferranti, IBM and others, on the other hand, required specialist knowledge to program and operate them, and a considerable financial outlay – the price of greater speed and capacity, and the promise of a reduction in manpower costs.

Tabulating and sorting machines (1924) developed by the Hollerith company – founded in 1896 and the forerunner of International Business Machines (IBM) – which used punched coded cards derived from the model of the Jacquard loom to register, sort and analyse large quantities of data.

Actuaries had a natural advantage in understanding the mode of operation and the capabilities of electronic devices, and the Institute was uncharacteristically prompt in endorsing interest in them. In February 1953 Dr B. V. (later Lord) Bowden was invited to speak to the Students' Society on 'Electronic digital computers', and in April Ronald Michaelson presented a sessional paper dedicated to 'Large scale digital computing machines'.[13] This set out the advantage of the thermionic valve over the mechanical relay in communicating, at some million times a second, the binary 'pulses' that represented numerical values. At the stage of development at which computers then were, however, the programming, printing and checking of results for accuracy dominated computing time. The computer was only economic if the program could be created in less time than was required to carry out the task by other means, and if the results represented an improvement in rapidity and accuracy compared with mechanical methods. Once these standards were guaranteed, the life office computer could undertake all the work of the punched-card systems, as well as other fairly straightforward tasks involved in producing renewal notices, receipts, commission statements, bonus notices and the printing of policies. Routine sequences of calculations, which habitually required hours, days or even weeks of clerks' time, could be done in a fraction of that time, without any real change in an office's basic methodology.

The German made 'Tim' ('Time is Money') calculating machine, introduced in 1907, was the first 'four-function' type, and could perform addition, subtraction, multiplication and division. This electrical Monroe model was the first to offer fully automatic multiplication and division. The Munroe range was the work of J. R. Munroe and F. S. Baldwin, the inventor of the barrel calculating machine. These were smaller, lighter and easier to use than arithmometers. The early Brunsviga shown (below) was such a machine. All of these machines underwent progressive refinement and their later versions were the mainstays of insurance offices until the 1960s.

More complicated tasks that demanded a higher degree of understanding on the part of the operator, such as valuations, or the calculation of surrender values or of the amount of surplus to be distributed, were where the actuary could make his contribution.

It was natural that in the early stages computers in insurance offices were perceived mainly as a means of speeding up tedious work and reducing costs, but as they were further developed, their more radical advantage of being able to perform more complex calculations succeeded straightforward data processing as the prime focus of actuarial interest. At the Institute, interest had been aroused, not only by Michaelson's paper, but by the Reports produced during the previous five years by the Society of Actuaries in the United States. In July 1953 the Institute set up an Electronic Computers Committee chaired by Kenneth Usherwood, who was intrigued by the potentially revolutionary significance of computers for life office work. Besides acquainting themselves with the capabilities of the various kinds of machines, the Committee sought to make the manufacturers aware of the needs of the actuarial profession with a view to influencing design. For a time the emphasis was on finding the way around the new field, but it was soon realised that the potential applications were so wide that study groups to concentrate on specific areas were necessary. In April 1955 seven such groups came into being, led by men such as Herbert Tetley (*), soon to be appointed GA, Bobbie Beard and Bill Phillips. The groups focused on how computers could revolutionise the work of such fields as pensions, large-scale group pensions, and ordinary and industrial branch work. One group monitored the material being produced abroad, while another maintained links with the British computer manufacturers.[14]

The influence which individual actuaries' exposure to the new areas of computing and programming had in their respective offices probably depended on the individual's position and role in decision-making, and also on the degree to which management was prepared to embark on the process of change. Some offices were quick to computerise, while others were slow, but by the mid-1960s most were in the course of modernising. The consulting firms also began to buy mainframe computers, with R. Watson & Sons being the first (and reputedly the smallest firm in the country) to do so with the purchase of an IBM 1100 in November 1966. One problem was the standardisation of data into a form that could be read by a computer,[15] but once this was accomplished the computer could take over a great deal of mechanised work and produce better results in less time, with a significant reduction in staff. Since computers function in a strictly logical fashion on the basis of the information put into them, it is perhaps fanciful to speak of their 'creative' potential, but they do seem to have stirred the creativity of actuaries in a way that was felt at the time to be exciting and liberating. An existing technique such as the 'matching' of investments could be intensified and refined, and new life and pensions products conceived, tested and perfected, with a comparative ease undreamed of even a few years previously. A landmark was reached with the launch of unit-linked policies by a number of life offices from 1959 onwards. These were policies in which a portion of each premium buys life assurance, while the rest buys units of a portfolio of equities, on the performance of which the benefits depend. In the prevailing climate, with no end in sight to the 'cult of the equity', such contracts were soon producing a better return for investors than the bonuses attendant on the mixed funds of with-profit contracts. The unitised concept soon spawned an array of unit-linked savings vehicles with which many actuaries became involved. Within the Institute, computerisation, unit-linking and investment techniques provided the subjects for various sessional papers. The use of computers enabled actuaries to take account of a wider range of statistical data than had previously been possible. One who applied the new tools to update established methods was Gordon Pepper (*), who in October 1963 presented a paper on the role of gilt-edged securities in a modern portfolio, and described how an electronic computer could be used to assess the relative merits of any two British government stocks. The greatest interest in computing and its applications came, predictably enough, from the Students' Society. Its computer programming courses and Computer Study Group were led by Sidney Benjamin (*) (no relation to his equally eminent but slightly older contemporary, Bernard Benjamin). He started his career in 1952 at the Prudential

viii   THE TIMES SUPPLEMENT ON THE ACTUARY'S PROFESSION MONDAY MAY 25 1964

Toys for magnates

IN 1961, AT VERY short notice, the Students' Society of the Institute of Actuaries invited its members to apply for a computer course which it intended running at the institute. There were to be 12 fortnightly lectures each of two hours, with several hours of homework between lectures, and a final practical of two sessions on a machine. The notice advised that students who were still studying for the examinations (as opposed to "students" who had already qualified as fellows) should not apply.

The committee hoped to fill perhaps 25 to 30 places. Over 70 applications were received and a second course had to be arranged for the following year. It now seems likely that a high proportion of fellows newly qualifying each year will apply for the computer course as a post-graduate exercise. What started as an activity for the society's 1961-62 session is taking on the appearance of an optional part of formal actuarial training.

As more companies acquire computers many actuaries are learning programming in their own offices, and it

By SIDNEY BENJAMIN

pany is financially sound. At the same time he carries out several other investigations, especially valuations on different assumptions, in order to obtain a broad picture of the office's financial position.

With the computing power of future machines it will be possible to project the future course of events on thousands of different bases. Even with the speeds of present printing devices, say 50 lines a second, it would be possible to print out all the results in a few hours. This is the second stage of familiarity because two roomsful of

Actuarial students receiving instruction in computer programming, 1964. The first formal course in 1961 was intended for twenty-four Students, but such was the interest that there were more than seventy applications.

under Frank Redington and Kenneth Usherwood, and was sent back to Cambridge by the latter to learn computer programming. His papers – 'Computers and actuarial science', 'Putting computers onto actuarial work' and others – generated much excitement and discussion.[16]

At Staple Inn the impact of computerisation was felt in two additional areas. The first was upon the Actuaries' Investment Index, the index of prices and average yields of securities which had been produced since 1930 and which was available monthly by subscription. The index had grown out of a joint investigation of investment research by the Institute and Faculty, and had been periodically reviewed and amended to take account of changing conditions. In 1953 a completely new series was started, dating back to 1946. A wider selection of ordinary shares involving twenty-seven industrial groups was made, showing the experience in groups according to the nominal rate of dividend of each security; indices of debenture stocks and of gilt-edged securities were also included.[17]

By 1960 the index was encountering competition from newer, computer-designed rivals, and the Institute's Council feared that its shortcomings made it a poor advertisement for the profession. Partly to offset the financial burden of bringing it up to date and partly in search of a 'partner' that could ensure a new index a wide circulation, the Institute approached the *Financial Times* in March 1960. A scheme for a daily index and analysis of a number of fixed-interest

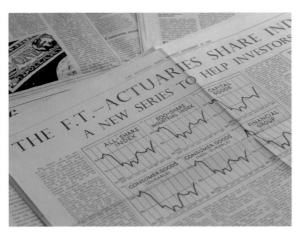

stocks and the shares of some five hundred companies quoted on the London Stock Exchange had been prepared by Bert Haycocks and Jack Plymen (*) using the latest computer applications. The shares were divided into thirty-one sub-groups and a system was devised whereby the index could be kept up to date and continuity maintained in a way that had never before been possible. The 'FT–Actuaries' Share Index' began publication on 26 November 1962, with a base date of 10 April 1962, the data on the constituents being collected by the staff of the *Financial Times*. Publication of the old index ceased on 31 December 1962. Haycocks and Plymen presented an account of their work to an enthralled ses-

A revised Financial Times–Actuaries' Share Index, incorporating the work of Bert Haycocks and Jack Plymen, was inaugurated in 1962.

sional meeting in March 1964, explaining that the 500-share Index reproduced the performance of a standard portfolio of equities in which each holding was maintained in proportion to the market valuation of the whole equity capital of the constituent concerned. The use of the computer made it possible to analyse daily an impressive volume of investment data to provide, not just the price–earnings–dividend profiles of earlier indices, but an aid to investment policy, a benchmark against which to check the performance of a managed investment portfolio, and a historical record of equity progress.[18]

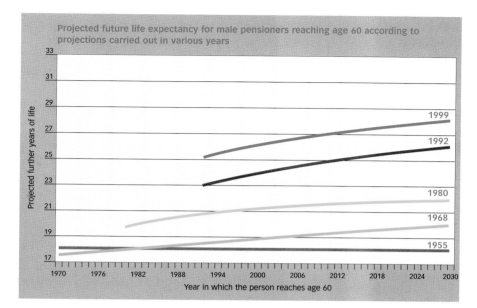

Projected future life expectancy for male pensioners reaching age 60 according to projections carried out in various years

The Continuous Mortality Investigation Bureau collects and analyses data on policyholder statistics volunteered by participating life offices to produce mortality tables and project mortality trends. This chart shows how projected life expectancies for people aged 60 have changed as experience has unfolded over the second half of the twentieth century.

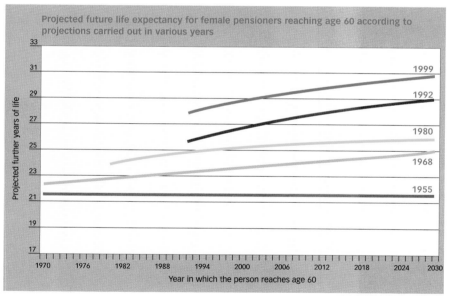

Projected future life expectancy for female pensioners reaching age 60 according to projections carried out in various years

The second area where computer technology had great effect, although not until somewhat later, in the 1970s, was in the work of the CMI Bureau. This worthy but largely unsung entity had been collecting and analysing the mortality and morbidity experience of UK policyholders, in the form of data from sixty British offices, since 1924, supervised by a Joint Committee of the Institute and Faculty. In this it followed the precedent of pooling data set by the original 'Seventeen Offices Experience' of the 1840s. Its purpose was (and still is today) to produce standard mortality tables according to the needs of the profession which – via the Committee – determined the basic data and method of graduation to be used. There were various investigations – assured lives, annuitants, children's deferred assurances and so on – for each of which male and female data was returned, and, beginning in 1964, a study of male assured lives analysed by cause of death. Computerisation transformed the work of the CMI Bureau, and its essential task of collecting and analysing data became almost routine. The question of how best to use the new technology then became pressing – as a later Report put it, there was 'a great temptation to use the sophistication of the systems to produce a vast array of results on every conceivable basis'.[19] This temptation was resisted, and instead, the CMI sought new ways in which to analyse its data, and proceeded to comparisons which would not have been possible previously. The results obtained were of fundamental importance to the life assurance industry and, as the same Report emphasised, to the actuarial profession as a whole:

The contributing offices have, annually, a detailed analysis of their own experience together with the combined experience of all offices transacting similar forms of business. In the periodical publications of the Committee, 'Continuous Mortality Investigation Reports', the profession has a series of reference points by means of which trends can be studied and the suitability for use of the various standard tables currently available can be judged. The CMI Bureau's computer systems have provided the Committee with tools that enable it to explore all its data. This will lead, gradually, to the actuarial profession increasing its understanding of both mortality and morbidity. Here computing is serving our profession.[20]

The computer has, of course, become the instrument of global change since those words were written about one basic field of actuarial study, but it is satisfying to recall that actuaries were among the first to see the potential of computers to extend the dimensions of their own area of expertise. That expertise was becoming ever more essential to developing economic and social systems, the irony being that outside the Institute and the financial institutions where actuaries were found, it still was seldom understood to be so.

CHAPTER FIVE

Greater recognition

PEOPLE who bought *The Times* of Monday 25 May 1964 received an unexpected 'bonus' in the form of a *Supplement on the Actuary's Profession*, published to mark the 17th International Congress of Actuaries set to open the following day. Those who had time to digest the articles gathered together in the *Supplement* would have learned quite a lot about the profession, its history and its multiple roles in finance and the national economy. Even as they read, some eight hundred members of that profession, representing the actuarial associations of twenty-two countries, were converging on London to join several hundred Institute and Faculty colleagues.

Preparations for the Congress had gone on almost since the closing four years earlier of the previous one in Brussels. The 17th Congress was the most ambitious gathering yet; it had three official languages and its proceedings would eventually run to four volumes. The papers to be given represented the latest work in actuarial science, in the life and pensions fields, and in newer ones such as computing, game theory, risk theory and forecasting. (Readers of the *Supplement* might have been surprised to learn that actuaries had anything to do with these newer areas.) It was ambitious, too, in that it was held in two centres, beginning in London on 26 May, and finishing in Edinburgh on 3 June, hosted by the Institute and the Faculty. It proved an exhilarating, if exhausting, week, for once the meetings and lectures at Church House, Westminster, were over, the social events and ceremonies began. Guildhall and Burlington House in London and the George Street Assembly Rooms in Edinburgh were among the venues (the latter city was distinctly chillier than London, and some wags claimed that the Edinburgh Woollen Mills did a brisk trade during the Congress). The heaviest speech-making duties fell naturally upon the President of the Institute, Kenneth Usherwood, and the President of

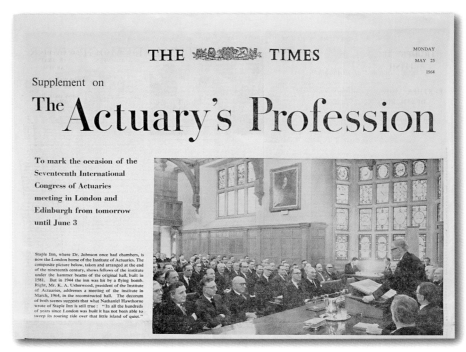

The 17th International Congress prompted a special Supplement on the profession in *The Times*. Kenneth Usherwood, President 1962–64, was shown addressing the delegates in the Hall.

the Faculty, Trevor Haynes, but many others acted as organisers, interpreters, guides and hosts. The Institute had not hosted a Congress since 1928, although the centenary celebrations in 1948 and the return to Staple Inn in 1955 had each brought the actuarial community to London. Since most senior British actuaries made a point of attending the now quadrennial (formerly triennial) congresses wherever in the world they were held, the 17th Congress was a further occasion for the renewal of long-standing friendships.

It was noticeable that at this Congress, non-life subjects enjoyed more official attention than at similar gatherings in the past. Until fairly recently the Institute had taken little notice of non-life, or 'general', insurance, reflecting the comparative scarcity of actuaries directly involved in it. The conclusion that this area went unexplored by British actuaries would nonetheless be unfair to its champions, whose small number was offset by a more than ordinary degree of determination to bring general insurance into the profession's sphere of influence. If at the 1964 Congress this determination was shown to have succeeded, it had not done so without a struggle.

Even in the nineteenth century, papers on general insurance topics – fire and property, marine, employer's liability, personal accident insurance and reinsurance – were published in the *Journal* from time to time. Later, motor and aviation insurance made their appearance, but in general the focus in the United Kingdom had remained life insurance, with its closely associated fields of long-term sickness insurance and pensions. This was in contrast to the situation in the United States, where the need for a statistical basis for workers' compensation insurance was recognised early on.[1] In continental Europe, actuaries and academic statisticians took an interest in the mathematical basis of non-life insurance somewhat in advance of their opposite numbers in Britain, but by 1950 Bobbie Beard (*) was in touch with several actuaries working in reinsurance and at the Scheveningen Congress of 1951 there were four papers on non-life subjects. In the run-up to the next Congress in Madrid in 1954, a circular letter from a small group of continental actuaries brought the request for a new association dedicated to the study of non-life insurance to the attention of the Congress Permanent Committee. Despite assurances to the contrary, the proposal was seen as potentially divisive, partly because the congresses' increasing size and level of social activity were considered by some to be diminishing the time available for non-life and newer subjects,[2] and the idea of smaller gatherings devoted to single areas was gaining support.

If ASTIN – the proposed Association for the Actuarial Study of Non-Life Insurance – was regarded with suspicion at international level, it had to struggle against resistance to change on the part of the Institute as well, rather as the Association of Consulting Actuaries had done a few years earlier. The Institute, which set up an ASTIN Committee at Beard's behest in November 1954, recognised that non-life subjects came within its own remit, but was unwilling to go further than approving a gradual approach in collaboration with the Chartered Insurance Institute. Even this fell through six months later, when the conclusion was reached that 'whilst there may be matters in non-life business which are worthy of theoretical investigation, there is no general awareness of any outstanding problems of such a character as to create a demand for statistical investigation'. ASTIN's promoters were held to be riding a hobby-horse of their own construction: the companies transacting non-life business were unlikely to take a lead in collecting data, or to supply it where it existed, and the ASTIN Committee thus recommended that the Institute take no further action in assisting the formation of a non-life study group in the United Kingdom.[3]

Following his retirement, Bobbie Beard was appointed Visiting Professor in Mathematics, first at the University of Essex, then at Nottingham. His work as an insurance adviser to the DTI brought him an OBE in 1967. He was awarded the Institute's Silver Medal in 1972.

ASTIN finally came into being, thanks to the persistence of Beard, Sir George Maddex, and others from continental Europe and the USA, at the 15th Congress in New York in 1957, when the Permanent Committee amended its regulations to permit the formation of a 'Section' for the study of a special subject. ASTIN quickly began producing a Bulletin and soon organised a colloquium at La Baule, France, in June 1959 and a second at Rättvik, Sweden, in

1961. These colloquia were increasingly well attended, and by the time of the sixth one, in Arnhem in 1966, one-quarter of the total membership of the Permanent Committee belonged to ASTIN. Bobbie Beard continued to play a prominent part in it with particular reference to the motor industry, for which he made the first systematic collections of statistical data from a number of European and British companies. His findings represented a practical step towards international agreement on methods of assessing reserves in non-life business.[4] The eighth colloquium – held in Sopot, Poland, in 1969 – was the first international actuarial gathering held behind the Iron Curtain, and was attended by actuaries from thirteen countries. The ASTIN meetings provided a forum for the airing of new and complex problems in aviation and marine insurance, and in the theory of risk. Very large risks – natural catastrophes such as earthquakes and floods, as well as man-made ones such as the thalidomide tragedy and oil spills – were recognised as being unquantifiable by actuarial methods, but their classification and statistical analysis was still considered to be of value, even if only to highlight areas of inconsistency.[5]

In retrospect it seems strange that in the UK so few actuaries were employed in non-life areas, even in composite companies that employed them on the life side of the business,[6] and that for so long general insurance remained the preserve of the few. Wider actuarial interest in it was stirred during the 1960s, however, by the rapid development of the motor industry. Since the war the number of vehicles had increased to the point where the UK had the highest ratio in the world (with the exception of The Netherlands) of cars per kilometre of road, offering an obvious opportunity for motor insurance. While a number of long-established companies were engaged in this field, even

The ASTIN colloquia allow for relaxation as well as serious presentations: here (above), Sidney Benjamin finds time to sketch the harbour at Puertimão, Portugal, where the thirteenth colloquium was held in October 1975, and (right) Frank Guaschi addresses the fourteenth colloquium in Taormina, Sicily, in October 1978.

these, in the days before widespread electronic data processing, sometimes lacked a firm statistical basis for their ratings, making the calculation of reserves to cover known and unknown liabilities a matter of guesswork. By 1967, however, the motor statistics bureau of the British Insurance Association (BIA) was receiving data from many companies, as data storage on magnetic tape became more widely used. Given a growing vehicle market it was not surprising that new companies specialising in motor insurance began to proliferate, resulting in fierce competition to undercut the 'tariff' agreements that existed among the older companies by offering lower premiums and higher no-claims discounts. Compared to life insurance, general insurance was undersupervised, making fraud in that sector easier to perpetrate and harder to detect. Judged on premium income and known claims, a company could appear profitable, but the revelation of its full claims history sometimes told another story. Membership of the BIA could give a misleading impression of respectability. The Fire, Auto & Marine was one such company, founded in 1960 and admitted to the BIA despite protests from other members.[7] Its spectacular demise in 1966 was a wake-up call to the Board of Trade, which wisely consulted ASTIN and in particular Bobbie Beard about how to improve the information available to the supervising authority about non-life insurers. Colin Stewart (*), then Principal Actuary in charge of the insurance division at the Government Actuary's Department (GAD), was also consulted, although the GAD at that point played only a limited part in the routine supervision of non-life insurance companies.[8]

Competition for motor insurance business intensified still further with the abandonment of agreed premium rates by the tariff offices in 1968. Both the Insurance Companies Act of 1967 and the Insurance Companies (Accounts and Forms) Regulations of 1968 tightened up the information requirements, so that general insurance companies had to report on the year-by-year settlement of claims and the amounts estimated to be outstanding. Within a few years the GAD would be able to analyse these returns and advise the Board of Trade (from 1970 the Department of Trade and Industry, or DTI) on the apparent adequacy of the reserves for outstanding claims. Unfortunately the returns were still too few for the analysis that might have averted the mightiest collapse of all, that of the Vehicle & General, in March 1971, leaving one million motorists without insurance cover.

The 'V&G' was not an overnight sensation like the Fire, Auto & Marine (whose proprietor went to gaol). It was one of the older companies selling motor insurance, dating from 1926, but in recent years had grown extremely rapidly. It too was a member of the BIA. A Government-appointed tribunal spent nine months investigating the role of the various parties to the debacle, including the DTI. Its Report eventually revealed the continuing inadequacy of the information required of non-life companies, as well as the limited powers of the Board of Trade to intervene in their affairs. Perhaps the most glaring

The motor insurance industry in the UK has seldom had to contend with claims resulting from tornadoes, but bizarre weather – as in the 'Great Gale' of October 1987 – can nonetheless bring about sizeable losses.

revelation was the lack of formal actuarial involvement in general insurance. Of this, the Institute (which had hastily set up its own enquiry in advance of the Government's) was of course well aware.[9] What it had not expected was the tribunal's seeming hostility to the use of actuarial methods to evaluate a company's reserves. As a review in the *JIA* commented, 'it was not clear from the Report that the Tribunal actually understood the so-called "actuarial method", which is purely the application of valid statistical techniques to an insurance company's operation'. Surprisingly, the tribunal had observed that motor insurers' liabilities could be spread over several years and that there could be wide variations between companies as to the risks they held, but it did not see (as the *JIA* piece put it) that such conditions made 'the adoption of actuarial techniques, rather than ratio comparisons, highly desirable as the means for assessing the reserves required to meet outstanding claims'.[10]

Such adoption was a distant prospect in 1972 (it would not occur until nearly the end of the century) but the question of how to assess and ensure solvency, which emerged as a primary concern on the part of the tribunal, was of particular interest to actuaries, given that insurance company failures reflected upon the whole insurance industry, with which the name of the profession was so inextricably associated. Here was an area upon which the profession was well qualified to advise, but it could contribute only to the degree that its methods were accepted and their purpose understood. The DTI took a more enlightened view than the tribunal had done and employed Bobbie Beard, following his retirement from the Pearl, as a part-time adviser on the supervisory aspects of non-life insurance.[11] The Institute, through its own committees and through its discussions with the DTI (to which Sidney Benjamin contributed a great deal), sought the gradual recognition of the need for soundly based calculations and of criteria for the adequacy of reserves, but most of all, for some form of actuarial certification of the valuation of liabilities. Continuing resistance to these ideas eventually forced the Institute to accept that in non-life insurance the profession enjoyed little of the standing it had acquired in life and pensions.[12] This was due in part to the reluctance of the managers of non-life companies to admit any formal actuarial involvement in their business.

There was much groundwork to be done – and so, in October 1974, twenty years after the idea had first been suggested, a General Insurance Study Group (GISG) on almost exactly the same lines as the original proposal emerged from an initial seminar organised by Hugh Scurfield in Norwich. A quarterly bulletin known as *GIRO* (for General Insurance Research Organisation), edited by Brian Hey (*), was quickly launched to keep the sixty-strong membership in touch with the Group's research in four key areas: catastrophe risks, motor insurance statistics, reserves and market statistics. As the first number of the *GIRO Bulletin* stated, the aim was to provide practical solutions, for 'whilst mathematics and model building remain basic tools of the statistician, they are relatively trivial, at present, compared with the problems of data collection and analysis'.[13] These problems were easier to resolve now than they had been earlier, thanks to electronic data processing. Another of GISG's objectives, carried out through the *GIRO Bulletins*, was the development of educational materials. The work of Sidney Benjamin was instrumental in enhancing interest in the ways that actuarial methods could be applied to general insurance, and in getting the subject included in the Institute syllabus. General insurance finally came of age in Institute terms with the publication of Bernard Benjamin's *General Insurance*, a textbook based on the papers produced for Group meetings, in 1977. This established the basic syllabus for the study of general insurance as a compulsory subject and from 1978 qualification was made dependent upon passing an examination in it at Fellowship level.

Problems in the conduct of motor insurance business led to tighter regulation of that area, but it was not long before the life insurance sector similarly came under scrutiny, with important results for actuaries. The corollary to 'freedom with publicity' was actuarial reporting on the financial condition of life assurance companies, performed and publicised on a regular basis. For almost a hundred years after the Life Assurance Act of 1870 there was 'surprisingly little change in regulation, and a very modest level of active supervision by the Board of Trade', and even in the late 1960s the GAD had only one full-time actuary advising the Board of Trade on the financial strength of life offices.[14] The intervals at which companies were required to file a report could be as long as five years until 1968, when it became three years. This still left what might prove to be dangerously long periods between valuations. The Insurance Companies' (Accounts) Regulations 1968 altered the format of returns to the Board of Trade and stipulated that life office actuaries were to value companies' liabilities having regard to the nature and term of the assets, but this fell far short of what the Institute and Faculty on one hand, and the GAD on the other, had come to see as desirable by the early 1970s. Quite apart from the V&G affair – a non-life embarrassment – the rapid increase in the number of small proprietary life companies was giving cause for concern. The discussions of insurance matters that were simultaneously taking place among actuaries of the European Community, aimed at paving the way for a free market in insurance within the EEC, pointed towards the need to reinforce the actuary's role in the supervision of long-term insurance in the United Kingdom.[15]

Bernard Benjamin, President 1966–68, accepting his Institute Gold Medal on 27 October 1975. Looking on are, (left), Gordon Bayley, President 1974–76, and (right), Peter Moore, who would become President 1984–86.

The Insurance Companies (Amendment) Act 1973 introduced the concept of the 'appointed actuary', though not the actual phrase; what it said was that every insurance company transacting long-term insurance business should 'appoint an Actuary' who must be over 30 and be a Fellow of the Institute or of the Faculty. The title, which was consolidated into s.15 of the Insurance Companies Act 1974, passed quickly into the terminology of the profession. The provisions of this legislation upgraded the actuary nominated by the company to an identifiable professional figure whose monitoring responsibilities were from here on to be permanent, and much greater. The valuation of liabilities and the determination of surplus were now an annual requirement, as was a certificate detailing the amount of the required minimum solvency margin and the adequacy of the reserves provided in respect of the liabilities of the long-term business. The appointed actuary also had to certify that the data used for the valuation would indeed support it, and that the premiums charged were sufficient to cover the corresponding liabilities, in the context of the company's overall financial position.[16]

By 1974, however, inflation was rampant and the equity and property markets were flagging, and some of the smaller companies that had sprung up to take advantage of the boom conditions of the 1960s were coming under pressure. Over-extended in the amount of business they had written, undermined by guarantees that had begun to bite, and under-supplied with reserves, a number of them proved unable to ride out a prolonged depression of market fortunes. The London Indemnity & General Insurance was one of several that were rescued after becoming insolvent, but the Nation Life was not so fortunate and was wound up.[17] The appointed actuary system was barely established before the need to underpin it with more detailed guidance from the profession became essential. Led by Gordon Bayley (*), President of the Institute from 1974 to 1976, the Institute and Faculty set up a Joint Committee on Financial Standards, chaired by Mike O'Brien (*), which produced the first draft of 'Actuaries and Long-term Business', issued in May 1975 as a guide. Setting out in greater detail the responsibilities of the appointed actuary, 'GN1' (for 'Guidance Note'), as it soon came to be called, was the first major step in constraining actuaries' freedom in giving advice. 'Freedom with publicity' would remain a cherished ideal, but it was necessarily being supplanted by a more pragmatic approach that brought the expertise of the profession to bear on recognised deficiencies in the functioning of the insurance sector rather than letting that initiative pass out of the hands of the profession. In so doing, collaboration between the Institute and the GAD, where Edward (later Sir Edward) Johnston (*) had recently taken over as Government Actuary (GA), was much enhanced. The GAD came to see active supervision as essential, with consequent expansion of the team involved in overseeing the life insurance area.[18]

As a later GA – Chris Daykin – has pointed out, a singular feature of the UK appointed actuary system is the extent to which it is governed by professional guidance, rather than by legislation or the direct requirements of the insurance supervisory authority.[19] Perhaps the most fundamental change effected in 1973 was the transfer to the appointed actuary of much of the responsibility for monitoring the financial strength of a company. This in a sense made him the guardian of policyholders' interests, and though he was constrained by explicit ethical considerations, he continued to have to exercise a considerable degree of professional judgement. GN1 stipulated that the appointed actuary must be satisfied that his company was 'at all times solvent' during the year (which seemed to imply the need for constant valuations, but which Mike O'Brien recalls his committee interpreting, in the light of common sense, as applying only 'where an end of year picture was near the edge').[20] Such a degree of confidence was only possible if the appointed actuary had access to, and was kept informed of, all the aspects of the company's activity that had a bearing on its financial position (such as premium rates, investment policy, reinsurance arrangements and distributions of profit to policyholders and shareholders) and could estimate the effects of these various factors between valuations. He was to have the right of direct access to the Board and the right to be present at discussions likely to affect the company's financial future. In the event that a Board persisted in a course likely, in his view, to damage the company financially, he was required to alert the DTI. This 'whistle-blowing' function was not designed to ensure that he had an easy life (on the contrary, it could make him an object of suspicion), but it put teeth into the day-to-day monitoring that was being substituted for sporadic external supervision, and kept the appointed actuary's sense of professional duty on its mettle. He was also obliged to certify each year that he had complied with the mandatory actuarial standards of practice. (This was an aspect of his position that in years to come would be reinforced by the Institute and Faculty through ongoing professional development and annual practising certificates.[21])

The introduction of more detailed guidance resulted, fairly predictably, in the first allegations of non-compliance. Whether inadvertent or deliberate, these had to be investigated, and for the first time in living memory, the Professional Conduct Investigation Committee (PCIC) met early in 1975 to consider a formal complaint against a member of the Institute. It was only when the existing disciplinary arrangements were put into practice that it was realised how time consuming and cumbersome they were. Under bye-law 66 (bye-law 62 until some amendments brought about a renumbering of the Bye-laws) a complaint dealt with by the PCIC could be dismissed, the conduct in question deprecated, or the matter passed to Council for further action. In the latter case, the member had the chance to defend himself at a Special Meeting of Council requiring the attendance of all of its thirty members. Council then had to decide whether the complaint was well founded, and if so, whether to admonish or suspend the member, call upon him to resign, or expel him. The latter two courses left the accused the avenue of an appeal to the Institute membership (three-fourths of which had to confirm or vary the penalty), but this, bearing in mind its 1,800-strong international roll-call, was no longer the feasible next step it had once been, even had all those entitled to attend been able to squeeze themselves into Staple Inn Hall.

Other, more complex issues, coupled with a second complaint following closely on the first, led the PCIC to conclude that the disciplinary provisions had to be amended. While the current three-stage process – investigation, adjudication and appeal – was to be retained, Institute members were informed by circular of proposed changes to bye-law 66 that would enable Council to act as the final arbiter in the event of an appeal and lower the 'threshold of complaint' to provide a mechanism for the airing of 'grievous misgivings' about a member's conduct, even where the firm conviction of wrongdoing was absent.[22] The Special General Meeting of 26 April 1976 (reconvened on 17 May) was expected to generate intense debate, but the eloquence with which matters of principle were raised, in particular by Dennis Gilley (*), impressed the occasion indelibly upon the Institute's collective memory. (Rather like having witnessed 'the trial of Hilary Seal', having been present at these SGMs confers venerable status on the Fellow who recounts his version over coffee at a dining club dinner.)

The resolution failed to receive the requisite two-thirds of votes in favour, either at the May SGM or in a subsequent poll, and Council was forced to seek a new way forward. An *ad-hoc* committee was set up, which during 1977 prepared and sent out a consultative document and questionnaire to the entire membership. The points at issue were too detailed to summarise here, but chiefly concerned Council's role as either adjudicator or as appeal body, the rights of overseas members, and problems surrounding the proposed 'threshold of complaint'.[23] The process of collecting and sifting the replies went on for over a year, since although 'some 95% of those who replied wanted change, there was no such unanimity as to what the change should be'.[24] It was not until 26 June 1978 that an SGM was held to approve the substitution of a new bye-law 66 for the former one. Under the proposed new bye-law, the adjudicating body was an annually constituted tribunal of twelve Fellows not already on Council, half to be elected and half to be Council nominees. Council remained the appeal body, but required the attendance of only twelve of its thirty members to sit as such. This time, again after lengthy debate, the resolution was passed unanimously.

While the details of bye-law 66 were particular to the Institute, the kind of searching examination of procedures that it had carried out was not. Other professional bodies (such as the Institute of Chartered Accountants, which had already issued an 'Ethical Guide') were similarly concerned with the nature of behaviour which justified disciplinary action, and with 'the maintenance of public confidence in the standards to be expected from a professional man'. The central problem that had occupied the Institute of Actuaries was

one of achieving a balance between two aspects, neither of which is capable of precise definition. On the one hand we must not be in a position where a Member could be deprived of his livelihood unjustly, unreasonably or capriciously. On the other hand, in terms of maintaining public confidence in the profession … it is equally important that a Member who can reasonably be regarded as seriously at fault should not be immune from disciplinary action.[25]

The Institute's resolve to put the actuarial house in order, as evidenced by the reform of its internal disciplinary code and the issue of what became a series of Guidance Notes or 'GNs', reflected – but also sought to pre-empt – a similar tendency towards increased regulation and consumer protection in the public sphere. The life insurance and pensions industry had experienced great changes and reversals in the previous decade. Inflation, which as long as markets were buoyant had formed part of the equation of prosperity, wrought havoc under less favourable conditions. One consequence of the dramatic fall in stock market prices and the collapse of the property market late in 1974 was the rash of company failures mentioned above. Across the industry, the value of the investments to which benefits payable under many insurance policies were linked had experienced a substantial fall. The Institute and Faculty were invited to advise on legislation arising from these adverse circumstances. Meanwhile, measures such as the Policyholders Protection Act 1975 and the Social Security Pensions Act 1975, together with increasingly complex tax requirements and the rules laid down by new supervisory authorities such as the Occupational Pensions Board, placed further demands upon the judgement of appointed and pension scheme actuaries and added to the regulations with which they had to comply. Overall, their risk of becoming liable to prosecution in the event of error increased dramatically. The inclusion of a note on 'Legal liability' in the *Year Book* for 1975–76, immediately following the 'Memorandum on professional conduct', illustrated Council's concern that members of the profession be cognisant of shifting perspectives.[26] In little more than a decade after the first 'MPC' in 1965, the environment in which the actuary carried out his work went from one of relative freedom to one governed by greater regulation and supervision.

A major area with which the Institute had remained concerned and as closely involved as it could be was pensions, although it often seemed that successive governments paid only polite attention to its views. The profession's plea for 'an authoritative and independent body' on pensions issues, first made in *National Pensions* in 1959, was reiterated in 1962 in a letter to the Chancellor of the Exchequer (Reginald Maudling, the son of the former senior partner of R. Watson & Sons and Institute Vice-President) and the National Economic Development Council, in the context of concern at the increasing share of national resources likely to be needed to meet developing pension costs. Institute Working Parties were formed in the same year to consider both national pensions and the scope and adequacy of private pension provision, the latter undertaking an annual statistical report on both insured and self-administered schemes. The Life Offices Association Joint Committee on National Pensions, which was chaired by Frank Redington and included a number of Institute members, monitored the plans put forward by the political parties on a regular basis, while at the Institute, sessional meetings were frequently devoted to pensions topics. The importance of occupational pension schemes in overall national pension provision was repeatedly emphasised. By 1963, as the Institute's statistical reports revealed, such schemes covered some eleven million active members, or more than half the male working population, and were increasing by some 3 per cent a year. Total funds amounted to more than £5,800 million,[27] and their net increase accounted for more than one-third of total net personal savings.[28] Such savings helped to finance the creation of real assets that would provide the pensions when they fell due. The State system, on the other hand, continued to operate at an ever-increasing deficit. As Bill Phillips told the International Congress in 1964, 'no secret has been made of the fact that part of the new graduated contributions is budgeted to meet the deficiency caused by increases in the basic flat-rate pension'.[29] The concerns expressed in *National Pensions* were, if anything, more acute than in 1959. There were also fears, once Labour returned to power in 1964, that the rumoured new State pension plan would include a system of graduated State pensions linked to an index of wages or prices. Plans announced at the Labour Party Conference in 1967 increased these misgivings, with at least one prominent actuary foreseeing the creation of an overlap with the benefits of occupational schemes, the appreciable reduction of the latter and the transfer of contributions and funding from occupational schemes to the State – an alarming prospect that was felt to be contrary to the national interest.[30]

It was not until the release of a White Paper entitled *National Superannuation and Social Insurance* (Cmnd 3883) early in 1969 that a clear indication was given to which the profession could respond. The 'Crossman scheme' (named after the Secretary of State for Social Services) was a fully graduated scheme on a pay-as-you-go basis, and kept faith with the contributory principle and compassionate aims established by the Beveridge plan. Its anticipated repercussions upon occupational schemes were not yet altogether clear: the means of contracting-out that it proposed were extremely detailed, and the uncertainties they raised, together with questions relating to the proposed preservation of pension rights for employees who left their employers' service before pensionable age, ensured the White Paper a lengthy discussion at an Institute sessional meeting on 24 March 1969.[31] The great breadth of opinion that emerged was proof, as President Jim Pegler emphasised, that

the Institute was not expressing an official view of national pension schemes. The opinions expressed were those of members as individuals … What was common to them all as actuaries was the determination to show, as clearly as possible, the financial implications for the future of decisions taken in the present.[32]

A meeting of Council in April 1969 during the presidency of Jim Pegler 1968–70.

At the far end of the Council Chamber, from left to right (far top table): Norman Page (Secretary), Dennis Gilley (Senior Honorary Secretary), Jim Pegler (President), Peter Cox (Vice-President), Walter Bailey (Treasurer); (far left-side table at vertical): Mike O'Brien, John Waugh (Assistant Secretary), John Wykes (Assistant Secretary), Arthur Elliott (Deputy Secretary); (middle table at vertical) Jo Hamilton-Jones, Peter Moody, (faced by) Peter Francis, Arthur Steeds and Deryck Spackman; (far right table) Colin Cornwall, Colin Stewart, Bernard Benjamin; (third nearest row) Tony Lamb, Gilfrid Day, Marshall Field, Monica Allanach; (second row) George Ross Goobey, Charles Clarke, Sidney Benjamin, Alfred Edward; (first near row) Ronald Skerman, Peter Moore, Harold Purchase.

But despite some generous praise for the scheme, those financial implications left many members of the Institute perturbed. In a letter to the editor of *The Times* dated 3 April 1969, and signed on behalf of the Institute and the Faculty by their respective Presidents, Jim Pegler and Ernest Bromfield, the doubts shared by the two professional bodies were made public. They centred, once again, on the ramifications for future generations, but also on rumours that the demand for occupational schemes might be artificially constrained:

The White Paper emphasises the importance of sharing pension liability between the state and the private sector. This is important because the state scheme is on a pay-as-you-go basis, which throws a heavy and increasing burden on the future, whereas private schemes are funded in advance and thus reduce the strain on the future. They also provide a substantial part of the country's current savings which are vital to the national economy.

We have read with some misgivings the reports of recent speeches which seem to indicate the Government's view that it may be necessary to restrict the volume of contracting out. This may restrict the immediate cost of the state pension provisions, but only at the expense of throwing a heavier burden on our successors and of reducing the volume of current national savings. Under the proposed scheme the present generation of workers promises itself a higher scale of state pensions than it pays to present pensioners. It is dangerous, at the same time, to arrange the finances so that a greater proportion of the cost of these higher pensions is passed on to the next generation.[33]

The details of the scheme were not yet finalised, and the Institute was among the organisations asked by the Department of Health and Social Security to comment upon the Consultative Documents dealing with the contracting-out arrangements and with the preservation of pension rights. This included the vexed question of transfer values,[34] which with the growing mobility of the workforce in recent years was now an area needing reform. The Council of the Institute also considered that there could be great benefit in taking direct action to educate employers and the public generally in the principles and terminology involved in pension schemes and their funding. The result was *Funding Occupational Pensions*, issued jointly by the Institute and the Faculty in November 1969 and sent, like *National Pensions* ten years earlier, to all MPs and members of the Confederation of British Industry, and circulated widely through other organisations in the pensions field.[35] On 19 November 1969, Richard Crossman was the principal guest at the Institute's Biennial Dinner, and spoke forcefully about the desirable balance between the State and occupational schemes, and especially about the problem of labour mobility and non-transferability of pension rights. This was a question on which actuaries were not so much divided as capable of seeing both sides of a true dilemma: the burden that enforcement under the new scheme would impose upon employers, versus the existing unfairness to employees who changed jobs in mid-career. Even Crossman was prepared to admit that conceding preservation would increase the cost of occupational pensions by as much as £20 million to £25 million a year, but he considered it a cheap price to pay for the benefit to millions of employees that would result.[36]

The Crossman scheme was scheduled to come into effect in April 1972, but events took an unexpected turn when Labour lost the 1970 General Election, and all the preparation for the scheme's introduction was suddenly rendered superfluous. In 1966, however, some members of the Institute had been approached by the Conservative Party to comment on its proposal for a funded national scheme. The plan devised by Keith Joseph, enacted once the Conservatives were in power as the Social Security Act 1973, would have required all employees to be covered by earnings-related pension arrangements supplemental to the basic flat-rate State pension, whether occupational schemes or a new 'Reserve Pension Scheme' offering roughly equivalent benefits to employees who chose not to enrol in an employer's scheme. It was thus intended to encourage the development of occupational pension schemes. In theory, as Frank Redington explained in his 'Reminiscences about National Pensions' – perhaps the best brief account of the development of actuarial thought about State scheme funding[37] – he and his actuarial colleagues should have been pleased ('on the grounds of self-interest', since the profession was so intimately connected to the occupational pensions field) but had come to have misgivings about the slowness to mature of a funded State scheme. That these objections were held on economic as well as social grounds had been made clear to the Conservatives. In the event, the Joseph scheme never came into operation. The oil crisis and the industrial unrest of 1973–74 brought another General Election and a Labour victory in its wake. A new scheme was developed by Minister of State Brian O'Malley, under Secretary of State Barbara Castle, heavily based on advice from George Newton at the GAD. This emerged in 1974 as a White Paper entitled 'Better Pensions'. A Bill was hurried through the parliamentary process with a fair measure of cross-party agreement and enacted in September 1975, to become operative in 1978 as the State Earnings-Related Pension Scheme (SERPS), about which more is said in the next chapter.

Opening the Institute's discussion of the paper on 25 November 1974, the basic problem underlying the recent attempts at pension reform was summarised as 'how to reduce reliance by the elderly and the sick on a supplementary means-tested benefit which, though intended as a safety net for exceptional cases, had become a vast platform supporting two million people'.[38] The situation was made more difficult by the ravages of inflation. The White Paper sought to address several anomalies, such as the preservation of pension rights, and the position of widows, the sick and the elderly. The succession of schemes in the comparatively short period since the war had created a burden of detail that had to be honoured, altered or added to, with the result that 'Better Pensions' seemed vastly complicated. The right of early leavers with five or more years' pensionable service to the preservation of their accrued retirement benefits was a survival from the 1973 Act. New elements in the mix were the inflation-proofing of State pensions (and of guaranteed minimum pensions for occupational schemes), and equality of treatment for women, despite the continuing disparity in retirement ages: women at 60, men at 65. The discussion touched upon all of these, and while contributors saw the complexity and practical difficulties of implementation, they seem also to have been heartened by the accommodating approach taken by a Government attempting to reach consensus among competing interests. It gave hope that 'Better Pensions', once put into effect, would not be automatically jettisoned should another change of government take place, and hence that if the difficulties could be overcome, stability could at last be achieved.

CHAPTER SIX

A broadening panorama

B Y the mid-1970s the life offices were still employing the majority of actuaries, but the proportion of Fellows and Associates thus employed, relative to the Institute's overall UK active membership, had undergone a significant reduction in the previous decade. In 1966, for example, of the 700 active Fellows of the Institute in the United Kingdom, 515, or 73 per cent, worked in the life offices. By 1978 the comparable figures were 1,255 and 789, or 62 per cent.[1] The buoyant economic climate that lasted until the slump of 1974 encouraged the rise of the consulting actuarial partnerships and the firms of pensions insurance brokers handling pensions, while increased product choice, together with new legislation, had increased the need for the advice they gave. Consulting practice, the Stock Exchange and industry offered the largest sources of alternative actuarial employment to the life offices, although the actual numbers were as yet very modest. For all their importance within the profession, there were only 150 consulting actuaries in the UK in 1974 and 273 in 1985. (The comparable figures for actuaries in pensions insurance broking firms were 44 in 1974 and 130 in 1985.) Until 1972, when Geoffrey Heywood (*) of Duncan C. Fraser became President of the Institute, there had only ever been one consulting actuary President: John Gunlake of R. Watson & Sons, from 1960 to 1962.

Consultancy and the needs of the pensions insurance broking firms (more often known as pensions consultants) engaged in pension fund work would continue to attract newly qualified actuaries in increasing numbers through the 1980s and beyond. Rising prosperity and changing work patterns and job expectations made the relative independence and increasing variety of the work in these areas highly appealing. The consulting practices were involved in the setting-up of the new unit-linked life assurance companies during the 1960s, going on to advise major insurers on new products, mergers and acquisitions, as well as acting as appointed actuaries to the smaller UK and overseas insurance companies. Consulting actuaries often mention independence and variety, along with the enlivening experience of dealing with clients and the stimulus of working in partnership, as outstanding features of their work. The impression that emerges from their recollections is that the value of independence lay less in the possibility of organising their own time (although that was part of it) than in that of exercising their own judgement on clients' behalf. The responsibility was sobering, but also exhilarating: 'one had the sense of doing something worthwhile, and of how one's technical expertise had to be grounded in one's integrity' was how one retired consulting actuary recalled his work with pension fund clients.[2]

An additional ingredient in the rise of the consulting practices was the advent of the smaller computer. The range of actuarial calculations made possible by these machines created new positions for actuaries, contrary to earlier fears that they would have the opposite effect. This at least was the experience of R. Watson & Sons, which found itself engaging more staff to carry out the tasks which its IBM 1100 computer enabled the partnership to perform. By the 1970s some consulting practices, Watson's among them, had developed investment performance measurement services for their pension fund clients, out of which later grew other kinds of investment consultancy, such as asset liability modelling, investment manager selection and the design of investment management structures.[3]

John Gunlake, President 1960–62 and the first consulting actuary to hold the office. The comments on professional ethics in his Presidential Address influenced the Memorandum of Professional Conduct and Practice produced in 1965.

Another factor for change became apparent when, in 1975, the total number of women members of the Institute (287 Fellows, Associates and Students) for the first time comprised more than 5 per cent of its total membership of 5,376.[4] The number of women Fellows had always been very small: since 1920, when (following Geoffrey Marks's suggestion) the legal barrier to admitting women to the Institute was removed, only nine had gained the Fellowship by 1955 and twelve by 1965. Then came the widening of higher education and a sudden influx of women students. Eleven women – the largest number in any single year thus far – qualified together in 1975, bringing the number of women Fellows, past and present, up to thirty-five. From then on, the number of women taking up actuarial studies increased dramatically and with each passing year the number of them qualifying rose. While the Institute and the profession remained predominantly male, women became a more visible, vocal and participating minority. At the time of writing women constitute some 20 per cent of total Institute membership.

It would be interesting to consider[5] whether the actuarial profession was singular in its lack of appeal to women, or whether their numbers merely reflected the profession's smallness compared to others, such as medicine, dentistry, law and architecture. Such a study would require broader analysis and comparisons than are possible here, but it is probably fair to say that women training for any profession found the going hard until the sea-change in education and social *mores* of the 1960s and 1970s, especially if they had family responsibilities. Andrew Davidson (President of the Faculty from 1948 to 1950) observed that 'actuarial life … leaves little room for those flashes of intuition with which the fair sex are generally supposed to cope with life's little difficulties', but the difficulties, for would-be actuaries who happened to be female, were neither little nor resolvable solely by 'flashes of intuition'.[6] Early on, the rule in most life offices that women forfeit their jobs on marriage had meant that the kind of in-post actuarial training available to men was not really available to women unless they remained single until they qualified.[7] There were thus few senior women in the financial and insurance fields as role-models for younger career women after the war, themselves still few in number. There is little doubt that – before or after the war – the long and daunting road to the Fellowship was incompatible with home-making and child-raising unless a woman had an exceptionally supportive husband.

For a single woman, on the other hand, the obstacles to achieving the Fellowship were in theory no greater than for a single man, and to be surmounted by exactly the same means as were demanded of any Student. The deciding factors, as in any other professional field, were innate ability, hard work and a blend of fascination with the subject matter and a passionate sense of purpose. This is certainly the view of Monica Allanach, who was the first woman member of management of the Prudential Assurance Company and in 1968 became the first woman elected to the Institute's Council. Both she and Pat Merriman of Bacon & Woodrow, the first woman partner in a firm of consulting actuaries, qualified in 1951, and affirm that they were accepted on their merits by their male actuarial colleagues and within the Institute, whatever the inequalities of pay and conditions prevailing at the time. As an active participant in the Students' Society, Monica Allanach appreciated that female actuarial Students might still experience a sense of isolation. She and Pat Merriman sought, by creating regular informal opportunities for the handful of women in the profession to meet, to foster the exchange of views across the generations and provide encouragement through the examinations.[8] These gatherings began in 1954 and usually consisted of a meeting with an invited speaker (frequently a woman member of another profession), who was the guest of the group at dinner afterwards. They continued, the average attendance rising to sixty-five by the 1980s, until they were superseded by the Lady Actuaries' Dining Society in 1985. At the time of writing this dining club still meets regularly.

At the 125th anniversary celebrations in 1973, Monica Allanach presents the Loyal Address, sharing the dais with Geoffrey Heywood, President 1972–74, and Dennis Gilley, Vice-President.

There was no bar to women FIAs becoming members of the existing dining clubs – and some did, there being a wide variety to choose from and no lack of willing nominators. The dining clubs had proliferated over the years and each had its own *raison d'être* and rules; most of the more active Institute members living with reasonable access to London belonged to one or more. After the granting of the Royal Charter in 1884 and the healing of the breach between the secessionist Actuaries Club and the Institute, the Actuaries Club remained the dining club of the older, most eminent members of the profession. As it always included a number of Council members, it met after Council meetings. The Gallio Club, founded by five young actuaries in 1903 as a forum for discussion, had soon evolved into an alternative dining club that entertained the authors of the papers presented at sessional meetings and any other Institute guests. These were the two longest-established clubs, but to neither of them could a member invite a private guest. The Fellowship Club came into being in 1910 to fill this particular need; its major distinction was that it entertained a guest speaker. While by the 1970s the Woolgatherers' Club (whose conversation ranged over every subject except matters actuarial) had ceased to exist, the Phiatus Club, founded in 1948 by actuaries whose training had been interrupted by the war, was still going strong. There were also newer foundations such as the 59 Club (dating from that year, whose members went in for organised walks and opera outings), the Debtors Club (founded in 1960 for actuaries under 40, who were still 'debtors to their profession') and the Ornaments Club (formed in 1970 for the 40-year-olds ejected from the Debtors). Some clubs were linked to particular kinds of work: the Denarius Club (1923) was founded for actuaries working in industrial assurance and the collecting societies, and enacted the ritual of passing a real Roman denarius around the dining table in homage to the 'penny-a-week' insurance tradition. The Argonauts Club (1954) (from the idea of navigating unknown waters) catered for actuaries employed in 'non-traditional areas'. The Various Actuaries Club drew its members from across the whole profession and, like the Ultimate Club (which absorbed an earlier one called the Rejects consisting of those failing to be elected to Council), was formed in 1975.

The clubs have always been (and at the time of writing, remain) an essential part of Institute life, supplying the setting for the development of friendships that complemented the ways of contributing to the profession provided by the Institute proper. The dining clubs could seem staid, however hard they tried to attract younger members. The Students' Society, on the other hand, offered an array of social activities as well as 'General Meetings' at which the fruits of original research were presented. It also ran study groups and courses on subjects of current actuarial interest. Over the years the purpose of the Society had shifted away from the original one of assisting Students to prepare for the examinations. In parallel with the growing tendency towards graduate entrants and partial exemptions from the examinations, it had become an essentially post-qualification association. In 1966 its rules were altered to allow actuarial students from the London School of Economics and other institutions to participate in its activities. Emphasis now was on keeping actuarial students abreast of knowledge in a multitude of newer areas, and the Society's *Journal*, which published the papers given at general meetings, supported this aim. The Society has made a particularly valuable contribution through its support of the Institute Library. Until the 1970s the Library consisted largely of texts contributed by their authors and bequests from senior actuaries, but there were many gaps and little of historic value. Then, with funds from the Students' Society, a systematic policy of building up the collection was set in motion under the guidance of Chris Lewin and Trevor Sibbett. The acquisition of many early mathematical and scientific works has made the Institute Library a significant resource for actuarial history. Some of these treasures were included in the exhibition on the history of actuarial science in the United Kingdom that formed part of the Assembly held in 1973 to mark the Institute's 125th anniversary.

Membership of the Students' Society Committee, especially serving as Honorary Secretary, was often a stepping stone to being elected to Council. Not all of the Society's activities were serious. The 'entertainments' that rounded off its biennial dinners were written and produced by Bernard Fison and Jim Lagden over a twenty-year period, and revealed the irreverent and witty side of the actuarial *persona*. These musical offerings ranged from *Unprofessional Conduct* in 1960, through *The Godfather* (centring on a powerful President from Liverpool), *Cinderfella, or Get Your Kicks Under Bye-law 66* in 1976

The Denarius Club, one of the older actuarial dining clubs, dates from 1923. Members pass a Roman denarius around their dining table in homage to industrial insurance, which was widely sold door-to-door by the agents of the large insurance companies and collecting friendly societies.

to *Butch and the Kid – The Later Years* in 1979, featuring 'Gilley the Kid'. As their titles suggest, these revues were highly inventive, full of merciless take-offs and actuarial in-jokes. Those who were the objects of the fun were sometimes caught unawares, but took it in good part.

The Students' Society was able to involve many members in its activities until about 1970; then, in common with many similar organisations, it began to feel the effects of the migration of employment from central London to the suburbs and the provinces. A new, informal actuarial magazine, the lighter-hearted *Fiasco,* was launched in February 1978 to keep a by then more scattered membership in closer touch with current actuarial concerns. In 1978

The Institute Library possesses a notable collection of works connected with the early history of actuarial science. They are regularly consulted by scholars, and are occasionally exhibited, either on loan or as in the Institute's 100th and 125th anniversary celebrations in 1948 and 1973, and the 75th anniversary of SIAS in 1985.

(like the Institute, which had done the same a year earlier), the Society adopted postal voting, acknowledging the reality of a geographically dispersed membership and the right of members at a distance to take part in elections and Special General Meetings. A long debate about changing the Society's name carried on through the 1970s, finally coming to fruition in 1985 shortly after its 75th anniversary. Since then it has been known as the Staple Inn Actuarial Society, which better reflects its role in stimulating an ongoing interest in actuarial questions, regardless of members' status or age.[9] A similar function was performed by the regional actuarial associations that existed in some of the major cities. Several of these were quite venerable ones, the oldest being the Birmingham Actuarial Society, dating from 1924.

With the advent of the 'Appointed Actuary' came the recognition that the training given by the Institute would again have to be updated. The recommendations of an education review chaired by Ronald Skerman (*) in 1967 came into effect in 1970–71, and had barely settled down before a further review was set in motion. The Skerman review was the third since the war, and revealed the education of actuaries to be beset by some intractable problems. Qualifying time was still on average six years or more, pass rates relative to examinations taken were dismally low at around 30 per cent, and the Actuarial Tuition Service (ATS) was woefully undermanned. The problems were rendered more acute by the need for candidates to assimilate new knowledge when it had not yet become clear what elements of the existing syllabus could be trimmed to compensate. The Skerman review brought about a number of small reforms intended to result in a saving of time overall. An aid to this was a shift away from tests of memory in favour of 'practical applications' that would 'test an understanding of fundamentals'. Computing was to be introduced earlier, in the light of the influence it was having on basic subjects such as compound interest and life contingencies, and greater exposure to operational research and numerical analysis was to be given. Most importantly, the seeds of closer future collaboration in education between the Institute and Faculty, already well rooted in the very nature of the two professional bodies, were encouraged to grow by having some searching light shone upon them. The differences were acknowledged (the Faculty was carrying out a similar study): where the Institute emphasised probability, the Faculty stressed life contingencies; the Faculty syllabus included and examined demography as a separate subject, while the Institute was about to scale down even the amount of general demography's study required up to then; the Institute's training included computer programming and investment, while the Faculty's did not. The two bodies' approaches to the same subject had on occasion required the ATS to produce two different tuition courses, with obvious repercussions for the authors of textbooks.

All of this was the prelude to the more radical overhaul of actuarial education by a Committee chaired by Colin Cornwall and appointed by Council in September 1973. Its instructions were to review the tuition and examination system in the light of developments – the insurance company failures, investigations and legislation – in the fairly dramatic period since the Skerman review. The first of its two Reports dealt with the general framework of the examinations and related matters and was accepted by Council in February 1975. A number of important changes arose from it. Taking into account the number of actuaries already working in that field, and to encourage others, the Committee made general insurance a compulsory subject. In an apparent *volte-face*, the subjects on which more emphasis had been placed only a few years earlier – such as computer programming, numerical analysis, OR and advanced statistics – were scaled down again. This was interesting: at the Institute's Biennial Dinner in 1967, the then President, Bernard Benjamin (*), had called actuaries 'the most computerised of all the professions', and had alerted them to a modern ailment called 'computer hypnosis', the symptoms of which were 'technological euphoria' and 'electronic idolatry'. (While the computer 'could immensely extend the impact of cerebral activity … it could not be a substitute for it'.) The Cornwall Committee put the actuarial love affair with the computer temporarily on ice. Events in the insurance industry since 1966 had conspired to vindicate an emphasis on traditional 'mainline' actuarial subjects, and – again, with one eye to recent events – to emphasise that a solid grounding in general insurance was now essential.

A significant change, occurring within the brief span of a generation of actuaries, had now to be faced: more than 90 per cent of those beginning their actuarial training were university graduates. The best of them were capable of qualifying while still very young, and without the maturity of judgement that only exposure to actual situations and decision-making could provide. With the creation of statutory responsibilities for actuaries under the 1973 Act, it became more essential that all FIAs, even the newest, possess a level of experience consistent with the work they were required to do. One means of ensuring this was to raise the level at which actuarial qualifications could be obtained. At the request of the Privy Council, which was concerned about standards across the professions, Students commencing their training after June 1975 could become Associates only when all examinations had been passed, and an experience qualification for the Fellowship was introduced 'to ensure that all Fellows will have had an opportunity to absorb a professional outlook on the duties of an actuary'.[10] The necessary changes in the Bye-laws were passed at a Special General Meeting in June 1975.

The Committee's second Report, accepted by Council in May 1976, dealt with detailed syllabuses and courses of reading. The existing titles of 'Intermediate' and 'Final' examinations were discontinued and the new examinations divided into Group A (six basic subjects, examined twice yearly to give Students extra chances for re-sits) and Group B (four more specialised subjects, studied in greater depth and examined annually).[11] A certificate in Finance and Investment was available to Students and Associates who had passed certain examinations that together covered these areas.[12] Minimum age requirements had been introduced in 1938: the former Associateship could not be gained before the age of 21, or the Fellowship before 23.[13] After the 1975 changes, the age limitations of 21 and 23 were maintained, but new-style Fellows also had to complete four years' practical actuarial work, at least two of which had to be after completing the examinations. (Later, in 1995, four years was reduced to three and the post-examination requirement was abandoned.)

The Committee recognised that the actuary of the future would need better communication skills. Up to now consulting actuaries and those few in 'wider fields' had perhaps had more need for, and had developed to a greater degree, the ability to explain the basis of their advice. From the mid-1970s an actuary assuming the Appointed Actuary role in a life office had an *entré* to its upper echelons (Fred Menzler's dream of greater corporate recognition for actuarial expertise was now enshrined in law) but to fill that position with optimum benefit to the company, the Appointed Actuary had to be able to hold his own with colleagues from other disciplines. In the words of one speaker at an Institute sessional meeting, 'the appointed actuary should be seen as a valuable member of the management team, influencing his colleagues informally, day by day helping to frame the policy of the office'.[14] The actuary in this position was therefore also likely to need a knowledge of financial planning and management techniques, though the Committee considered that such subjects were best taught as post-qualification courses by bodies other than the Institute.[15] In recommending a measure of specialisation in the Institute's own syllabus the Cornwall Committee was reverting to the remedy for student overload first suggested by the Lever Committee a quarter of a century earlier.

While the Institute already collaborated with several universities offering undergraduate courses leading to exemptions from some of its examination subjects, there did not yet exist south of the border a specific undergraduate actuarial degree. (In Scotland, a degree course was established in 1972 at Heriot-Watt University.) In 1973, with funding from the Life Offices Association, the Association of Consulting Actuaries and an anonymous charitable trust, Council established the first Chair of Actuarial Science in England and Wales at the City University, London. Bernard Benjamin was appointed to the Chair, with Steven Haberman (*) as Lecturer, and a three-year course leading to a Bachelor of Science degree in actuarial studies commenced in October 1974. (Jim Pegler succeeded Bernard Benjamin in 1975. On Jim Pegler's retirement in 1979, Steven Haberman took over as Director of what had by then become the Actuarial Studies Unit.) Graduates of the City University course could claim exemption from 'Group A' subjects, but by 1982 the ASU was providing daytime tuition for some of these subjects on behalf of the Institute. This slightly reduced the strain on the ATS, whose shortage of manpower was still acute even though actuarial Student recruitment numbers were in fact dropping.[16] (To give an idea of the ATS workload, in 1978 143 Institute tutors marked over 11,000 test papers and led a total of 230 discussion classes.[17]) This, together with a fee structure that had been left behind by inflation, meant that the ATS's aim of financial independence was becoming ever more difficult to achieve.

Although the experience requirement for Fellows was in principle a response to the Insurance Companies Act 1973, by the time it came into effect in 1978, it was even more relevant since the Social Security Pensions Act 1975 and the new State Earnings-Related Pension Scheme (SERPS) became effective the same year. Under this legislation, the graduated pension introduced in 1961 to supplement the basic State pension was scrapped in favour of an earnings-related pension based on the 'best 20 years' of an employee's working life, and protected against inflation. The basic State pension was also to rise in line with the greater of National Average Earnings (NAE) and increases in the Retail Price Index. Occupational pension schemes, which still covered nearly half the workforce, could contract out of SERPS if they undertook to provide employees with guaranteed minimum pensions of at least the same value as the State earnings-related pension foregone; in return, they received rebates of part of their National Insurance contributions. This signified the acceptance of occupational schemes, and hence of the private sector, by the Labour Government, and the recognition that occupational schemes made 'a valuable contribution to the economy through their encouragement of private saving'.[18] While occupational schemes were funded, the State scheme, operating on a 'pay-as-you-go' basis, would require ever-higher National Insurance contributions in future in line with the general ageing of the population.

SERPS was introduced with a contracting-out facility because of the widespread prevalence of occupational pension schemes by that time: in 1979 there were about 11 million employees (about half of the working population) who were members of such schemes; only 1.3 million were not contracted out.[19] But by 1979, Labour had been ousted by the Conservatives under Margaret Thatcher, and alarm was growing about the spiralling cost of State pensions. Part of this administration's commitment to 'roll back the boundaries of the public sector' was therefore to link State pensions to an index of retail prices, rather than allowing them to remain aligned with NAE. It was claimed at the time that pensions would increase in line with the cost of living and therefore that those dependent on them would continue to share in rising prosperity.[20] The intractable problem of State pensions expenditure, together with those of 'early leavers' (even though those with five or more years of pensionable service now had a measure of protection), the self-employed and employees who remained outside their employer's occupational scheme would lead the Conservatives within a few years to a further, more drastic examination of the whole area of State pensions.

The Occupational Pensions Board (OPB), originally set up to complement the Insurance Companies Act 1973 and including a number of actuaries among its members, was given the responsibility under the 1975 Act for verifying that each pension scheme which was to be contracted out had – and continued to have – sufficient resources to meet its commitments. It relied on regular certificates signed by an actuary to this effect. In March 1977 the OPB issued a Memorandum outlining its requirements, but – just as the requirements of the Insurance Companies Act 1973 had led to GN1 – the Institute and Faculty Councils spoke with one voice to give members of the profession an added gloss on its meaning. One extract from the Notes issued by the two professional bodies in October 1977, which later became GN3, will suffice to indicate the kind of semantic haze through which the actuary was expected to grope in carrying out his statutory duty, and the value of the 'experience qualification' for new Fellows. By signing a certificate testifying to the soundness of an occupational scheme, the actuary was stating that:

4.1   *... in his opinion the resources of the scheme are likely in the normal course of events to be sufficient at all times over the next five years ... to meet in full, in the event of the winding up of the scheme, the priority liabilities. Before he can do this, he must interpret the words 'likely in the normal course of events'.*

4.2   *First, although the winding-up of a scheme is usually regarded as an abnormal event, the wording of the certificate requires that the 'normal course of events' must be qualified by the assumption that a winding-up will actually take place.*

4.3   *Secondly, 'events' include events external to the scheme, e.g. economic and financial developments.*

*4.4   Thirdly, the meaning which the actuary attaches to the words 'likely in the
normal course of events' should comprehend a prudent view of the future without
taking into account every conceivable unfavourable development. He should
regard those words as excluding the possibility of events which he cannot
reasonably be expected to have allowed for in a conservative approach to the
matter taking into account the considerations surrounding signing a certificate
including in particular those set out below ... (the list should not be taken to be
exhaustive).*[21]

Prudence, like the other cardinal virtues, is not a subject that can be examined, but rather a quality that is developed through repeated effort – in this case, through the repeated applications of a young actuary's knowledge in real situations, learning all the while from working with others more experienced. The Institute and Faculty, in addressing the responsibilities placed upon members of the profession, thus tried to provide as supportive a body of guidance as possible. Once issued, this guidance was mandatory and operated as a system of internal regulation backed up by the disciplinary procedures described in a previous chapter. Within a few years 'GNs' were produced on the Employment Protection Act 1974 (GN4), Actuaries Advising Insurers Overseas (GN5), the Policyholders Protection Act (GN6), and the Relationship between the Actuary and the Auditor of a Company Transacting Long Term Insurance Business (GN7). The Insurance Companies Act 1981, which introduced explicit solvency margin requirements in line with the requirements of the EEC First Life Directive, led to the need for further guidance for appointed actuaries which became GN8. Each GN was the product of months of intense work on the part of a designated Joint Committee of the Institute and Faculty, sometimes working closely with the Government Actuary's Department. However much some senior retired actuaries wryly deprecated the need for them as well as the number of them, they were intended as survival kit and quickly came to be appreciated as such.

Concurrently with developments in insurance and pensions, equity investments were recovering from the slump of the mid-1970s. Unit-linking was the common feature of the many new insurance products that were now coming onto the market, some sold by companies that had sprung up to take advantage of improved prospects. With so much current emphasis on verifying solvency, these products were of obvious interest to the profession. The Institute and Faculty Joint Technical Working Party on Valuation Regulations, considering that unit-linked products that offered guaranteed returns at maturity merited closer attention, appointed a Maturity Guarantees Working Party in 1977, chaired by Alan Ford and advised by Sidney Benjamin. Its task was to devise a basis and method for reserving which ensured, so far as possible, that insolvency would not result from the granting of maturity guarantees. Traditional methods of life office valuation were felt to be insufficiently responsive, and the Working Party discovered great variation in the reserving policy of insurance providers. It concentrated on finding a suitable model that would reproduce past movements of ordinary share portfolios with reasonable accuracy, with the idea that the model could be used as a basis for reserving, with modification if it could be foreseen that the future would be subject to different influences than the past.[22] The majority of the work was based on the De Zoete & Bevan Equity Share Index, and a variety of models – from the pure 'random walk' to fluctuations around a trend line – were employed to reproduce the price movements of the past. Simulations were used to produce series of unit prices for the future, the overall conclusion being that maturity guarantees should be backed by specific and generous reserves.

The Working Party submitted its Report in 1980. One of its observations was that although it appeared that the risk attached to maturity guarantees could be greatly reduced by adopting an immunization strategy, significant risk remained, and generous reserves were still a necessity for maturity guarantees. Similarly, the manipulation of a company's investment portfolio to reduce the cost of maturity guarantees had stringent conditions attached.[23] The Working Party's findings led many companies to cease offering maturity guarantees. One important result of its investigations was the emergence of the 'stochastic' asset model – a model involving variables – devised by David Wilkie (*), which models the random behaviour of investments and of various economic series[24] over time. The 'Wilkie model' was novel for, among other features, incorporating 'auto-regressive' behaviour, or reversion to a mean, within its projections of economic series, in contrast to the 'equal likelihood' scenario presented by the 'random walk'. Within a few years the Wilkie model would become the most popular stochastic asset model and an indispensable actuarial tool, and David Wilkie's already international reputation would be much enhanced.

Under the aegis of the Institute two further valuable activities were constantly in progress. The Continuous Mortality Investigation Bureau systematically collected and analysed its data, and from time to time published one of its 'Investigations'. The series was brought up to date with the *1967–70 Tables for Assured Lives*, the *a(90) Tables for Annuitants* and the *PA(90) Tables for Pensioners*. The FT–Actuaries' Share Index was regularly adapted to reflect the changing categories of companies being monitored. Together with the more prominent profile given to the profession in recent legislation, such initiatives added to the Institute's status. The presence of some of its senior members on government committees of various kinds also implied an appreciation of the actuarial perspective on matters of concern. Royal Commissions, as the *Year Book* for 1978–79 pointed out, 'stand perhaps alone in public interest and importance', and actuaries had figured frequently among their members. Most recently, Ronald Skerman had formed part of the Royal Commission on Civil Liability and Compensation for Personal Injury, which reported in 1978. In the developing field of social insurance, the profession's presence on official bodies of

The Worshipful Company of
Actuaries' Installation Dinner,
17 July 1979:
Geoffrey Heywood, in Master's
robes, centre, with (left to right)
George Ross Goobey (Clerk),
Harry Oram (Senior Warden),
Henry Cottrell (Junior Warden)
and Ian Bullen (Beadle).

enquiry extended all the way back to Sir Alfred Watson in 1911, but had been
brought up to date by that of Leslie Brown on the Committee of Inquiry into
Company Law (the Jenkins Committee), and of Gordon Bayley and Peter
Moore on the Committee to Review the Functioning of Financial Institutions
(the Wilson Committee). Actuaries had been members of a host of standing
committees, councils, working parties and boards over the years. Besides the
OPB mentioned above, the Ministerial Advisers on Insurance, the Committee
on Finance for Industry, and the Council for the Securities Industry were
among those on which the Institute was represented in the late 1970s. Similarly,
the Institute and Faculty had supplied evidence at the request of numerous
government enquiries.

One result of the greater self-confidence enjoyed by the profession was the
feeling among some senior actuaries that links with the City of London should
be strengthened. Staple Inn is situated exactly on the City boundary, and the
profession has an obvious affinity with the 'Square Mile' as the hub of the
insurance industry and the home of many of the clients advised by its members. The idea of an actuarial livery company was Henry Cottrell's, and it was
he who probably did most to bring it to fruition. Inevitably it encountered
resistance from others who saw it as an unnecessary – and even presumptuous
– adjunct to the profession. The Worshipful Company of Actuaries, always
recognised as an association of individual actuaries rather than an offshoot of
the Institute, was formed in March 1979, and in September of the same year

became the ninety-first livery company of the City of London, with Geoffrey Heywood as its founder Master. The Worshipful Company of Actuaries was one of several new companies to add modern professions to the roll-call of the medieval trades. Within the Institute the resistance disappeared[25] as the Company's role in advancing the profession's contacts, especially in 'wider fields', became evident. In time it also became an important medium for charitable and educational activity, as it continues to be. At the time of writing it has about two hundred members, each a freeman of the City of London, and represents a cross-section of the profession.

CHAPTER SEVEN

The international dimension

A LESSER-KNOWN aspect of the Institute's history is the role it has played in an international context. By the actuarial bodies of other countries the Institute is generally acknowledged as the pioneer, but it is also regarded – and rightly – as much more than that. As the recognised professional examining body since 1850, it has provided, with the Faculty, the tuition and study materials for aspiring actuaries from abroad and for those in other countries for more than 150 years. It encouraged the formation of national associations of actuaries in many countries, and played a major part in developing the international gatherings that has brought them together at regular intervals for more than a century. Since 1945 it has strengthened its ties with the European actuarial societies, seeking common ground in the new context of the European Community. Recent decades have witnessed the maturing of the profession in most countries of the industrialised world, and it is the developing countries that now look to the Institute for guidance in fields as diverse as actuarial education, professional conduct and standards, life and pensions legislation, general insurance and investment.

Even before the Institute was formed in 1848, individual British actuaries were in touch with others in Belgium, France and the United States, but it was not until the formation of a precursor of the Dutch association of actuaries in 1888 and of the American Society of Actuaries in 1889 that the Institute and the Faculty had counterparts abroad. Over the next twenty years associations of actuaries were formed in France (1890), Belgium (1895), Italy and Australia (1897), Japan (1899), Russia (1900), Denmark (1901) and most of the other European countries in quick succession. In North America, the Actuaries Club of Canada was formed in 1907, and the American Institute of Actuaries (1909) and the Casualty Actuarial Society (1914) in the United States.

The 8th International Congress in 1927 was the second to have London as its venue. A revised Universal Actuarial Notation was adopted for worldwide use.

The 1st International Congress of Actuaries, held in Brussels in 1895 just after the Belgian society formally came into being, was the initiative of Amédée Bégault, who had translated George King's textbook on *Life Contingencies* into French in 1893.[1] Bégault had also prepared an account of the seven existing systems of actuarial notation then in use. The 1st Congress appointed an international committee (on which the British representatives were George King and Thomas Sprague) to propose a universal actuarial notation, and set up the Permanent Committee for International Congresses of Actuaries to ensure that a continuous sequence of similar gatherings would follow. The 2nd Congress, already mentioned elsewhere, was held in London in 1898, with the Institute acting as host. On this occasion, the notation presented by George King, already used by the Institute, was adopted as the universal standard.[2] Further congresses were held in Paris (1900), New York (1903), Berlin (1906), Vienna (1909) and Amsterdam (1912) before the outbreak of the First World War forced the abandonment of the 8th Congress, planned for St Petersburg, in 1915. Momentum was slow to build after the First World War: it was 1927 before a further congress was held; again, the venue was London. Congresses in Stockholm (1930), Rome (1934) and Paris (1937), together with a joint meeting of the American societies in 1938, gave the actuarial community regular opportunities to meet before the Second World War interrupted the sequence again.

During the interwar period societies of actuaries were founded in most of the European countries, and with each of these the Institute maintained a working relationship based on personal contacts. The Scandinavian actuarial societies were particularly keen on research and new developments in actuarial science. The 9th Congress, held in Stockholm in 1930, inspired Sir William Elderton to pay the Scandinavians a return visit in 1931. From this grew a most fruitful dialogue and the programme initiated by Elderton that brought a succession of young Norwegian, Finnish, Danish and Swedish actuarial students to London for a few months each to study and to attend the sessional and Students' Society meetings. These visits were cut short by the war but eagerly revived after it, and were the origin of some personal friendships that have endured until the present day. The war also interrupted the work of the International Committee set up in 1937 to revise the Universal Actuarial Notation. The Institute and Faculty began to use the revised notation in their publications in 1950, well in advance of its general adoption in 1954.

The Fellowship of the Institute was the actuarial qualification *par excellence* in many parts of the world except the United States until well after the Second World War, with the countries of the so-called 'Old Commonwealth' – Canada, Australia, New Zealand and South Africa – providing many candidates for the Actuarial Tuition Service (ATS) and the Institute's examinations. These could be taken at centres around the world, via the system of Institute-nominated supervisors, some of whom were Fellows resident abroad, who administered them under strict conditions. The ATS correspondence courses were supplemented by classes and tutoring in some countries, just as in Britain. The single largest contingent of foreign aspirants between the wars came from India, which contributed some 20 per cent of total Student membership.[3] A few Indian students came to London to study and assimilated well into Institute life. Ensuring the necessary standard of English for those who remained in their native country was a challenge, but one that was considered worthwhile due to the high mathematical ability of so many of the candidates. Distance imposed its own challenges: there were instances when examination papers from both India and Egypt were lost on their long voyages to be marked in London, and the Board of Examiners had to decide whether to require affected candidates to take the exams again.[4]

Apart from the Institute's own centenary celebration in 1948, the first opportunity for renewed international contacts after the war came with the 13th Congress, held in Scheveningen in The Netherlands in 1951, and attended by 650 actuaries from 26 countries. On this occasion, the Permanent Committee was reconstituted as the International Actuarial Association (IAA), still with its headquarters in Brussels, and tribute was paid to Amédée Bégault, who had been President from 1909 to 1946. Many new societies had been established since 1938, and the size of attendance at Scheveningen was a harbinger of the problems that arose three years later at the Madrid Congress in translating for the different language groups. The 16th Congress in Brussels in 1960, to which 1,100 actuaries came, altered the traditional three-year interval between gatherings to one of four. By the time the Institute and the Faculty jointly hosted the 17th Congress in London and Edinburgh in 1964, translations were being made from and into five languages, and the Congress Committee appointed by Council had been working on the organisational aspects since 1961.

This Congress was attended by over 1,200 actuaries and their wives, from 36 countries – an indication of the growing strength of the profession around the world and the degree to which international contacts were valued. The resumption of the congresses in 1951 had been hailed as 'in the best interests of the profession', since 'in this changing world the need for the regular exchange of ideas between those applying actuarial principles in very different political, social and economic environments, is greater than ever.'[5] By 1964, with Europe in the full bloom of post-war recovery and the European Economic Community (EEC) an accomplished fact, the particular benefit to UK actuaries was identified as the overcoming of traditional British insularity. 'Knowledge of European and other overseas countries came to many members of the Institute mainly from attendance at and study of the papers for the International Actuarial Congresses and from the contacts made on these occasions',[6] Kenneth Usherwood commented in a discussion following a sessional meeting. Elsewhere he emphasised that the underlying differences between British and continental actuaries, mainly in the areas of training and the prevailing regulatory background, made understanding these differences essential for Institute members developing contacts abroad.[7]

For the 17th Congress, a variety of events parallel to the working sessions were arranged in London and Edinburgh, and the proceedings were translated into several languages.

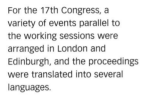

From the early 1960s the Institute's external relations gradually came to be dominated by developments in Europe. Article 57 of the Treaty of Rome, which had brought the EEC into being in 1959, provides for the mutual recognition of professional qualifications by the member countries. From 1962 the Institute was considering the implications for the profession should Britain join the EEC. The qualifications required for becoming an actuary on the continent differed from those in the United Kingdom, and among the European countries themselves there was considerable variation. Links with the universities were greater for the continental associations. A university graduate or post-graduate degree that was primarily mathematical was the most common qualification, although in Spain, for example, State-approved tuition was given at 'commercial colleges'. There was no system of qualification by examination on the continent comparable to that of the Institute or the Faculty. Membership of the European national actuarial bodies was usually granted to those whose employment included actuarial duties and who had reached a certain level of seniority or responsibility in their organisations, not just to those possessing the requisite university degree. In general there was no code of conduct or corpus of professional guidance comparable to that existing in the United Kingdom, but many of the assumptions underlying their calculations were set by State regulators. While in the UK the actuarial profession as such was not regulated by the State, specific actuarial duties were, and performance of them restricted to persons qualified as actuaries. The Institute and Faculty did not award diplomas, as did some continental universities and actuarial bodies; rather, they admitted candidates who had fulfilled certain conditions to a class of membership.

At this early stage, the Institute's first concern was the professional recognition of actuaries from the European countries practising in Britain, a question which the Board of Trade was also beginning to consider. Membership of the appropriate national body was necessary, but not sufficient, for the Institute to grant professional recognition: some evidence of practical experience (not always required in Europe) was also deemed desirable. Secondly, there was the question of mutual recognition in the event of Britain entering the EEC. Before much discussion had taken place, however, the negotiations by which Britain was seeking to enter the European Community foundered, and the matter was temporarily left, not so much in abeyance as in the realm of informal discussions between the Institute's President and his opposite numbers in the European associations.[8]

In 1964 the Council of the Institute appointed a European Relations Committee to strengthen existing contacts, and gather information about the situation of actuaries in the various countries.[9] The Board of Trade encouraged the Institute in this, while the 17th Congress that same year provided the perfect opportunity and setting. Besides the differences mentioned above, perhaps the most revealing divergence from British experience was that fully half of European actuaries worked in areas outside life assurance: as full- or part-time consultants, as managers in industry, in banking, public utilities, forecasting and university teaching. It was also learned that there was much variation in the degree of control exercised by the State over the life assurance companies that employed the other 50 per cent of continental actuaries. There seemed few obstacles, apart from that of language, to impede European actuaries from working in another continental country not their own.[10]

The growing economic collaboration among the European states brought greater emphasis upon the need for security in all the areas of interest to British actuaries. By 1968, the Organisation for Economic Co-operation and Development had working groups dedicated to solvency and reserves in both life and non-life assurance, the British representatives for the life field being Ronald Skerman of the Prudential and Colin Stewart of the Government Actuary's Department. The differences that emerged in the respective continental and British attitudes to solvency margins and reserves, as in the varying degree of freedom companies had in their choice of investments, took some time to iron out. To this process of achieving agreement Ronald Skerman made an outstanding contribution, presenting a paper on solvency margins to the German Actuarial Society in 1968 which outlined what were known thereafter as 'Skerman's Six Principles' for ensuring and verifying solvency. When the European Union Third Life Directive came into being some twenty-three years later, it was seen to be based solidly on Skerman's work.

Despite the lack of uniformity of practice, agreement was reached on some basic principles in the life insurance area that paved the way for future harmonisation. As Harold Purchase, Jim Pegler and Ronald Skerman put it,

While it could not be claimed that the views expressed are exactly what British actuaries would have wished, it is thought that they contain an adequate recognition of the British point of view. In view of the enormous differences between our outlook and conditions and those of our Continental colleagues, there is some satisfaction in this.[11]

Three essential points – the need to combine a high degree of security with a maximum yield on investments, the need to keep the cost of insurance as low as possible, notably by sharing the profits with the assured, and the need to lighten progressively the restrictions on investments existing in some countries – led to a fourth which summarised the purpose and reality of the whole exercise.

Ronald Skerman, President 1970–72 and Gold medallist. He was also one of the UK profession's best-known ambassadors, with strong European connections.

The effort which is being made to set up a European capital market can be successful only if the restrictions and discriminations which hinder the movement of capital are lifted. For life assurance companies it is also from this aspect that a progressive liberalisation of investments proves itself to be desirable. For one must not lose sight of the fact that the important element which is the basis of most life assurance contracts, namely the element of saving, is an action which is by nature both regular and long term, contributing in this way to the development of the economy.[12]

Most encouraging was the willingness of the continental actuaries to seek common ground with their British counterparts. The Institute, realising the importance for the profession of investigating thoroughly the provisions of the Treaty of Rome and the whole question of relations with actuaries in Europe, set up a Working Party in 1973 to act as liaison between Council, external bodies such as the Privy Council, and the European actuarial bodies on matters relating to the profession. The proposal to create an organisation to represent the profession within the European Community was circulated to the actuarial association of the member states by the Presidents of the Belgian and French associations in the same year. It took several meetings to define how this would work, and it was not until June 1977 that the formation of such a permanent consultative body was approved.[13] The first meeting of the 'Consultative Group of Associations of Actuaries of Countries in the European Economic Community' – more often referred to, even by English speakers, as the 'Groupe Consultatif' – took place in Paris on 11 May 1978. It was to consist of two members from each country, appointed for two years and meeting at least once annually, initially under the

Presidency of Max Lacroix of France, with a Secretariat based at Staple Inn. Its brief was to reply to requests for an opinion from the institutions of the EEC on questions of concern, in particular those parts of the founding treaties applicable to the profession. The Institute's representatives were Brian (later Sir Brian) Corby and John Martin (*); the latter was chosen Vice-President of the Groupe and became its President on the retirement of Lacroix in 1988. The Institute also agreed to represent the Society of Actuaries in Ireland.

Sub-committees of the Groupe were set up to consider the provision of actuarial services within the Community (freedom of movement, establishment and services), the presentation of insurance company accounts, and solvency margins. By the time of its second meeting, in Cologne in March 1979, the Groupe had produced reports on these topics, on actuarial training in the various countries, and on the role of actuaries in the EEC.[14] (John Martin's comprehensive overview of 'The Training of the Actuary in Great Britain' was presented as the British National Report at the 21st International Congress in Zurich and Lausanne in 1980.) The Sub-committee on Insurance Company Accounts, chaired by Stewart Lyon, was mainly concerned with the drafting of submissions to the European Communities Commission of the EEC. The Commission had requested the Groupe's views on a draft proposal for a directive on annual accounts of insurance companies. These submissions were well received and the Groupe subsequently worked closely with the Commission in the preparation of the final directive. The International Accounting Standards Committee also sought the advice of the Groupe on the various drafts of the document on retirement benefits that became International Accounting Standard 19. Other actuarial and representative professional bodies exchanged views with the Groupe on subjects of mutual interest. This helped to identify in greater detail the similarities and anomalies in the situation of actuaries in the different countries so that action could be initiated in the various national contexts.[15]

The aim of seeking a common approach at European level was to strengthen the voice of the profession in dealing with the authorities of the European Community. As one Groupe circular noted, 'it would have been disadvantageous for the actuarial profession to have remained aloof' from the general effort on the part of many professions to create a permanent liaison with the EC, partly because of the high level of actuarial competence and responsibility, but also because the profession was only about 6,000 strong in the entire Community.[16] Such a liaison, in the form of the Groupe Consultatif and the relationships it built up, was not something that could be hurried, and required – as the Institute's representatives confided in reporting to Council – considerable patience, due to language barriers and the less formal business methods of some of the European associations.[17] They recognised, too, that the Institute could unwittingly dominate the discussion, given the depth of experience it could draw upon, and wisely sought to 'lead from behind' so as to ensure their European colleagues' greater participation.

The consulting actuaries, through a similar process to that which had brought the Association of Consulting Actuaries into existence, by now possessed their own international association. As before, the idea had arisen in conversation, this time at the 16th International Congress in Brussels in 1960, with Geoffrey Heywood and Max Lander carrying it forward, through a further informal meeting at the Congress in London and Edinburgh in 1964, to fruition in Munich in 1968.[18] This first meeting was attended by sixty-four actuaries, who adopted a constitution and elected Geoffrey Heywood President and Max Lander Secretary, assisted by an international Committee on which the UK was represented by Ronald Abbott (*). The number of consulting actuaries in Europe and indeed the world was still very small; even in Britain and the United States, where most of them were to be found, they comprised a minority more notable for its outspokenness than for its size. Nevertheless, the aim of IACA (the International Association of Consulting Actuaries) was to secure the discussion of issues of concern to consulting actuaries, which, it was felt, were not being addressed by the international congresses. Its guiding spirits considered that four years was too long between gatherings, and that its aim would be better achieved through biennial IACA conferences complementary to the international congresses – which, of course, IACA members would continue to attend. The second meeting of IACA took place in 1970 in Washington DC, and thereafter it has met at two-yearly intervals in locations around the world.

Max Lander, who had been a prime mover of the Association of Consulting Actuaries (ACA) in 1951 and Chairman 1971–73, also promoted the formation of the IACA, the international body, in 1968.

The international congresses, representing the entire profession, continued to be organised by the 'Conseil', or Council, of the IAA at its annual meetings and in the intervals between them by its appointed Congress Committees. The IAA Council (on which the UK was represented by Marshall Field (*) of the Institute and Robert Clarkson of the Faculty) also decided what action should be taken on actuarial concerns at international level. In 1977, for instance, it reconstituted the International Committee on Actuarial Notation. This subject had come up in Tokyo at the 20th Congress a year earlier, since actuaries in several parts of the world were by then considering revisions or alternative notations to take account of changing needs, especially compatibility for computer use, ease of reproduction in print and extensions to other fields. Between the big four-yearly gatherings, contact among the actuaries of various countries went on via other channels. At the time, the Institute and the Faculty were the only two national associations to appoint local representatives abroad (by 2003, they had between them representatives in fifty-four different countries), both to keep abreast of developments and to ensure that actuaries in those countries were similarly informed. The landmark anniversaries of the various national associations – twenty, twenty-five or fifty years – were celebrated by the whole international profession, and brought Presidents and office-holders together with relative frequency. A fairly full calendar of one-day business meetings, colloquia and summer schools – arranged by the Institute, the Groupe Consultatif and other associations and attended by individual actuaries and students – provided opportunities for discussion and gave younger members of the profession a chance to meet. Some national associations, such as that of Switzerland, funded study through meetings and educational grants as part of a commitment to research in actuarial science.[19]

The development of the profession outside Europe during the 1980s, particularly in Australia and North America, led the Institute and Faculty to form an International Relations Joint Committee to reflect this wider reality. It also fuelled the need for the Institute's President to travel more often, and farther afield. This was a trend that would increase in future, and which – while adding to the time each President devoted to Institute affairs – helped to strengthen relations between the Institute and sister organisations abroad. In 1983, for example, Stewart Lyon made a month-long tour of Australia, New Zealand, Singapore and India, conferring with and addressing their national and regional actuarial bodies. The most frequent themes for discussion were education, professional conduct, discipline and guidance on standards, but he was also alert to opportunities for the Institute to assist actuaries in those countries to strengthen their collective position in relation to government and the accountancy profession. The actuarial associations of New Zealand and Singapore were small but flourishing, that of Australia burgeoning and independent (thanks largely to the degree course devised by Alf Pollard of Macquarie University). In India, which had once provided so many students for the Institute's examinations, the situation was radically different; the profession had been in decline since the nationalisation of the insurance industry in 1956 and was all but moribund by 1983. Stewart Lyon's visit gave him the chance to analyse the current malaise and offer the Institute's moral support, although there was little that could be done while the industry remained nationalised. The 22nd International Congress in Sydney a few months later gave the Actuarial Society of India the benefit of additional perspectives.[20]

The Institute continued to house the Groupe Consultatif Secretariat, headed by John Henty, at Staple Inn, and to provide active members for its Standing Committees on Insurance, Finance, Pensions, and Freedoms and General Purposes. Much of the Groupe's work in the 1980s was aimed at facilitating the movement of actuarial labour within Europe, which meant the prior establishment of mutually recognised and accepted standards within the European Community. This goal was only achieved in the 1990s, but in advancing towards it, the Groupe contributed to the Directive on a General System for the

Recognition of Higher Education Diplomas elaborated by the Commission of the European Communities, and fostered the necessary agreement among the national actuarial associations in the European Community. The more recent stage of its work forms part of a later chapter, in which the Institute's involvement in international affairs is brought up to date.

By the mid-1980s a new area of actuarial interest, that of financial risk, was generating much the same desire for more concentrated attention as general insurance had some thirty years earlier. Just as a special interest group was instrumental in the formation of ASTIN, AFIR or Actuarial Approach to Financial Risk was a response, initially French, to the sense among some actuaries directly concerned with this area that it was not receiving the attention it merited at congresses. At first the idea was resisted as likely to remain a purely academic interest, but an international Steering Group, on which the UK was represented by Bill Abbott, adapted the original proposal and this specialist section came into being at the 23rd International Congress in Helsinki in 1988 with the aim of promoting research into financial risks and problems. Its primary function has been to bring together actuaries from different countries, and from newer disciplines such as financial economics and risk management. The first of AFIR's annual colloquia was held in Paris in 1990, and the second in Brighton in 1991. Within the Institute there was some feeling that no international section could be supported without an appropriate national interest group. Bill Abbott took the lead in forming one, which was quickly seen to have filled a need that had barely been recognised, and has done much to encourage interest in financial economics.

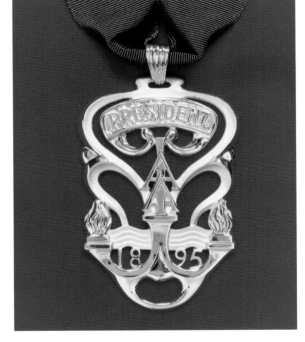

The presidential badge of the IAA, presented in 1970 by the Institute and associations of those countries that took part in the 1st International Congress in 1895.

Not only new areas of investigation, but new involvement in post-communist Europe and the developing world, would provide stimulating international challenges to the Institute and Faculty in the 1990s, about which more will be said shortly. The individual actuaries who exercised their profession in unexpected ways and in parts of the world where actuaries are little known has given a new twist to that well-worn phrase, 'wider fields'. A period of employment overseas in some sophisticated business environment has became more common for younger actuaries, but the need for actuarial skills in developing countries offered the more adventurous the chance to apply their knowledge where it could do immense good. During the same decade, the Institute would undertake a searching review of its own priorities and procedures, so as to be able both to lead and to respond in what was becoming a global sphere of influence.

CHAPTER EIGHT

Looking outwards

THE sense that 'the scope of the profession' – that catch-phrase for generations of actuaries – was taking on new dimensions, together with the impression that the pace of professional life was speeding up, colours actuaries' memories of the 1980s. Actuaries were in a good position to appreciate the impact of new technology. Both the speed and the complexity of calculation made possible by the advent of the individual desk-top machine were revolutionising actuarial work, and increasingly sophisticated techniques and products were emerging from the combination of actuarial skills and technological capabilities. The last of the profession's insularity was eroded as actuaries worked with members of other professions, such as the law, accountancy and university teaching, to resolve matters of common concern. These contacts in turn led to a greater collective self-awareness and a determination to shake off a professional image that was staid and outdated.[1] By the end of the decade, in the radically altered, more open world of 'financial services', the boundaries of the 'wider fields' open to actuaries were fast receding over the metaphorical horizon. New areas such as personal financial planning, long-term healthcare and capital projects have allowed actuaries to contribute their expertise alongside other professionals, and to gain new perspectives through so doing. Ironically enough, the challenges facing the profession in recent years have come, not from any 'wider field' but from the traditional, core areas of life insurance and pensions, operating in a more competitive environment.

Despite the increasing frenetic tenor of working life in the City, at Staple Inn it continued in a relatively unruffled fashion. The Institute passed some milestones, such as the centenary of the granting of the Royal Charter in 1984, and the seventy-fifth anniversary of the Students' Society in 1985. The latter was enthusiastically celebrated with another exhibition of *Landmarks in*

Actuarial Science in Staple Inn Hall, consisting of the historic books and artefacts assiduously collected during the previous few years. The Society brought its published history up to date with Colin Stewart's *The Students' Society Log 1960–1985*, and, as was mentioned earlier, changed its name to the Staple Inn Actuarial Society (SIAS). In the field of research, Institute regulations were changed to permit its Silver Medal to be replaced by a new medal named after its first President, John Finlaison, for individuals who made a significant contribution to the profession.[2] The first recipient of a Finlaison Medal was Rodney Barnett (*), for his work on mortality and contributions to the Continuous Mortality Investigation. No change was made to the stringent rules governing Gold Medals. These were awarded to Ronald Skerman in 1980 and to Sidney Benjamin and Gordon Bayley in 1985, bringing to ten the number of actuaries who had received the profession's highest honour.

The windows donated by the Staple Inn Actuarial Society (SIAS, formerly the Students' Society) to commemorate its 75th anniversary. The quotation (right), from Sir Francis Bacon, continues 'from the which as men do seeke to receive countenance and profit, so ought they of duty to endeavour themselves by way of amends, to be a helpe and ornament thereunto'.

There were losses, too. Frank Redington – past President, Gold Medal winner, 'the guiding spirit of the actuarial profession during our present century'[3] and, some would have said, its best interpreter to the wider public – died on 23 May 1984, leaving a wealth of tantalising lines of enquiry for succeeding generations. The publication by SIAS on 27 October 1986 of Redington's collected writings and speeches, edited by Gary Chamberlin under the title *A Ramble Through the Actuarial Countryside*, was a tribute to their author and a most welcome legacy to the profession. (Marshall Field, who delivered his Presidential Address on the same day, remarked that both events were taking place simultaneously with the 'Big Bang' on the London Stock Exchange, a coincidence that would have appealed to Redington's sense of humour.) Another respected figure departed when Norman Page OBE, leading Secretary since 1963 (termed 'Secretary-General' from 1977) and previously Assistant Secretary to Allan Dale, retired in 1983 after thirty-one years at Staple Inn; he was succeeded as Secretary-General by Clive Mackie.

The period under discussion was one in which the professions were, generally speaking, on the defensive; the Prime Minister, Margaret Thatcher, was known to resist what she saw as privilege masquerading as acting in the public interest, and the professions were – in the words of Stewart Lyon, speaking at an Institute Biennial Dinner in 1983 – 'finding it increasingly difficult to convince a sceptical public that they are entitled to a monopoly of their particular kind of wisdom'.[4] Peter Moore (*), President from 1984 to 1986 – whose Presidential Address was called, appropriately, 'The Necessity for Change' –

Frank Redington receives his Gold Medal in June 1968. As usual, he injected humour into the occasion, as witnessed by the expressions of Bernard Benjamin (left) and Jim Pegler (right).

brought a proactive approach to improving perceptions of the profession. Council commissioned a consultant's report on its external image, and Jim Lagden produced another on 'Marketing the Profession'. The Professional Conduct Committee headed by Brian (later Sir Brian) Corby undertook the revision of the *Memorandum on Professional Conduct* to eliminate any hint of restrictive practice, and clarify the responsibilities and hence the position of the actuary employed by a company *vis-à-vis* his company's clients. The actuary now became directly professionally responsible for advice given via his employer.[5] At the same time, the conclusions drawn from the rulings of the European Court of Human Rights led the Institute in 1985 to alter its bye-laws governing disciplinary procedure, in advance of any actual case that might have led to conflict.[6]

With regard to actuarial training, there was a strong feeling that the periodic reviews which merely reassessed the content of the syllabus were no longer adequate in the light of the changes that had taken place during the previous twenty years. Entrants were now almost all graduates, there were universities offering actuarial degrees, and the computerisation of offices had altered the manner and kind of training students received from their employers. Students had become more aware of the comparative prospects offered by various professions, and the professions more adept at recruiting, making the process of attracting the right candidates more competitive. Some intractable problems remained: low examination scores and pass rates, the time taken to qualify, a qualification rate of less than 30 per cent, and the economic situation of the Actuarial Tuition Service (ATS). A more radical review chaired by Paddy

Kennedy, with a brief to recommend structural, rather than cosmetic, changes to the education provided by the Institute, reported in June 1984. The Kennedy review, emphasising that improved teaching was the way forward, made two major recommendations that were quickly implemented. Post-graduate one-year diploma courses were set up at City and Heriot-Watt Universities, with their first intake of students in October 1985. The venerable ATS was dissolved and a new service employing a handful of full-time tutors – the Actuarial Education Service – was created to provide comprehensive support for students taking the Institute examinations, with ongoing consultation with the Faculty to avoid duplication of effort. The corps of honorary tutors (so called because all now received a symbolic sum) was still overburdened, and it was becoming harder to keep textbooks and course material up to date. An agreement was reached with the two universities that in exchange for financial support for the actuarial departments, additional help with the design of course material would be forthcoming. In the interval since the Cornwall review the material the student was expected to absorb had expanded in both volume and detail. The Kennedy recommendations overturned those of the earlier review in reintroducing specialisation: there was a return to the ordinary and specialist levels for the four final examination subjects, with candidates required to take at least two subjects at specialist level.

The Kennedy review was far from definitive, however, and by the time its recommendations had been put into effect, the pace of change (fresh legislation – the Social Security Pensions Act 1985 and the Financial Services Act 1986 – and the new disciplines and techniques that were emerging from university departments in both the UK and the US) meant that a further review was already under way. This was the altogether more strategically focused undertaking chaired by Chris Daykin (*) under the title 'Educating Actuaries for an Uncertain Future'. It was appointed in 1986 by the Futures Committee, itself set up a year earlier to monitor changes in the environment in which actuaries operated and to consider the extent to which the profession should change or take initiatives in order to respond. This was another example of a newly proactive attitude at work, and reflected an awareness that the impact of change would eventually increase the demand for actuaries. But what kind of training would they need? It was hard enough for a profession to adapt its structures to cope with rapid change. It was harder still 'to handle change when it happens so rapidly that each individual can only keep pace with developments in one limited area of involvement, and where the state of the art moves forward onto an entirely different plane long before any education and training system can be adjusted'.[7]

Daykin's committee, reporting in 1987 and 1988, recognised that it was now impossible for any actuary to be truly expert in more than one field of study. In acquiring a grounding in basic areas and a reasonably detailed understanding in one, the emphasis should be on principles rather than detail, and on absorbing the actuarial concepts and thought processes that would enable the actuary to apply his expertise in a variety of situations. Specialised training beyond this point could be taught through university courses or Institute-run residential courses. The idea was gaining ground that an actuary's education did not stop at qualification, but carried on through his professional life. The desirability of recruiting students from a variety of backgrounds followed naturally from the recognition that not all actuaries would require the mathematical sophistication that up to now had been seen as the hallmark of the profession. Computerisation had made some mathematical techniques redundant, leading to a refocusing of attention on the assumptions underlying the calculations, the design of the programs used, and the scale of answer sought. It also facilitated the design and marketing of new products. The actuaries of the future, whatever their specialised area of study, must be able to make effective use of ever more powerful computing facilities and remain firmly in control of the results. They must also be good communicators, with a thorough understanding of both the technicalities and the practical and commercial issues.

It was intended that the change of direction implied by these ideas should convey a more positive message to students: that actuarial education was not meant to be a long-drawn-out process with an unreasonable number of obstacles to surmount. Progress to qualification should be reasonably rapid given adequate study and a disciplined approach, and to this end the tuition system, the reading lists and the examinations would have to be streamlined to eliminate unnecessary detail. A new spirit informed the Daykin review, one which recognised that the profession would have to work harder at its own presentation, and which recognised that the wider opportunities opening for actuaries required new abilities and a more adaptable outlook.

The importance of improving the communication of actuarial ideas came to be appreciated only slowly by the majority of the profession, mainly through individual Institute members' experience of working more closely with other professionals – legal practitioners, economists, statisticians, accountants, academics. Consulting actuaries prided themselves on being able to explain complex actuarial matters to their clients. (Pension scheme trustees often included trade union representatives and other laymen.[8]) Traditionally, however, there had never been much need for actuaries working in the life offices to acquire this skill. The advent of the appointed actuary system and a statutory role for actuaries in 1973 brought those concerned with life insurance into a closer relationship with members of the sister profession of accountancy acting as auditors.[9] Actuaries had no defined role under the Companies Acts, whereas compliance with them was the auditors' primary concern, and these differing priorities sometimes led to misunderstanding in individual cases. Formal attempts at resolution first came to fruition in the statements issued by the Consultative Committee of Accountancy Bodies (CCAB)[10] in September 1979 and by the Institute and Faculty in January 1980. The latter was GN7 in the series of mandatory guidance notes and was entitled 'The relationship between the actuary and the auditor of a company transacting long-term insurance business'. Tony Ratcliff (*), who was President of the Institute in 1980, paid tribute to the members of both professions who had achieved 'an important understanding' between them.[11]

In 1982, by which time the provisions of the Insurance Companies Act 1982 made the revision of the two professions' guidance opportune, a Joint Working Party of accountants and actuaries was reconstituted at the request of the CCAB. It was a welcome suggestion, since the Councils of the Institute and Faculty shared the CCAB's view that the new law still did not deal fully with the relationship between the two professions in the context of long-term business. The auditor needed to form an opinion as to whether the company's accounts presented 'a true and fair view' of its financial position. 'True and fair' had to keep in mind that life insurance contracts typically lasted for many years, and their outcome in terms of profit and loss remained uncertain until their end. Periodically the liabilities arising from long-term business had to be valued so that the adequacy of the provision made to cover them could be shown and surplus funds identified. While a company's accounts and returns were the responsibility of the directors, the valuation and certification of the long-term liabilities was that of the appointed actuary alone. The returns submitted by him to the Department of Trade and Industry (DTI) were drawn up in accordance with regulations the effect of which was that assets were valued according to prescribed rules, while liabilities were valued according to actuarial principles.[12] In the worst scenario the auditor might find it difficult to decide whether the actuary's valuation did indeed represent 'a true and fair view' and hence might qualify his audit statement, while the Appointed Actuary might regard as intrusive a request that he justify – or even alter – the valuation base he had used.

What was needed was for the members of each profession to appreciate the responsibilities, approach and priorities of the other. While the actuary was expected to appreciate the accountant's concern to form a 'true and fair view', the accountant who acted as auditor

should understand, as a reasonable person but not an expert, the objectives which an actuary will have in mind when making a formal investigation of the financial condition of the long-term business. In particular, he must understand that there is a relationship between the methods used to make actuarial valuations and the bases on which the related assets are valued.[13]

In other words, the process of valuation was neither arcane nor idiosyncratic, but it did involve the actuary's professional judgement. But this measure of individuality was not *per se* easy for some accountants to accept and the onus was on actuaries to explain their principles and procedures. In his

Presidential Address Tony Ratcliff had cited the 'terminological confusion' that actuaries had 'allowed to creep in' as one source of mischief in their relations with accountants.[14]

As with life assurance, so with pension schemes: there was a need for the two professions to determine what each should expect of the other. An Accounting Standards Committee (ASC) working party set up in 1980 included actuaries, and tackled the question 'what information needs to be given for a clear and open presentation of the affairs of the pension scheme?' The replies filled nine hundred pages and formed the basis for an Exposure Draft (ED34), published as a Statement of Recommended Practice in 1986, on the form and content of pension fund accounts. The ASC went on to produce Standard Statement of Accounting Practice (SSAP) 24 ('Accounting for Pension Costs') in 1988, on the treatment of pension costs in the accounts of companies with occupational pension schemes.[15]

The Institute's efforts from the mid-1980s onward to dispel the mystique surrounding the profession derived at least partly from the realisation that other professions sometimes had genuine difficulty in understanding the actuarial position – in modern colloquial terms, 'where the actuary was coming from'. There was a growing recognition that when necessary the actuary had to 'go the extra mile' with those outside the profession, ensuring that they had the information they needed. As Alex Shedden (President of the Faculty in 1983) aptly put it, 'Our professional seclusion, such as it was, is virtually at an end. The actuarial approach no longer goes unchallenged and unquestioned, and we are now expected to expose our principles and practices to public gaze and to defend them if necessary.'[16]

But this process worked both ways, and actuaries also experienced the satisfaction of gradually winning over another profession, the judiciary, to the acceptance of the actuarial argument in the question of damages in personal injury and fatal accident litigation. This is an area in which the perseverance of actuaries in making the case for reform resulted in a notable contribution to the public good. It was a natural field for the application of actuarial skills, since it involved determining the present value of future contingencies, but the actuary's potential role was recognised by few legal commentators: Lord Blackburn, one of those few, writing in 1880, observed that where values had to be determined, 'actuaries had tables, founded on extensive experience … which enabled them to value with considerable accuracy the probabilities of life'.[17] It would be another century before the champions of this view gained a victory; in general, judges and counsel resisted the involvement of actuaries in legal proceedings. Their grounds ranged from the expense of an expert witness to the belief that actuarial calculations were incomprehensible, and the results obtained through using them no more accurate than those from any other mode of assessment.

It was not until the 1960s that both the actuarial and the legal professions experienced a renewal of interest in the question of personal damages.[18] In 1967 a new edition of the standard legal work by David and Sylvia Kemp on *The Quantum of Damages* for the first time contained a chapter on 'Actuarial evidence and related calculations', to which Bill Phillips contributed shortly before his death. In the same year the Institute set up a Working Party on the assessment of damages, which based its deliberations on the work being done by one of its members, John Prevett (*), a consulting actuary from Bacon & Woodrow. His paper, 'Actuarial assessment of damages', delivered at a sessional meeting in April 1968, was a comprehensive analysis of the existing situation and a blueprint for the progress hoped for. Between 1967 and 1973 the Working Party collaborated closely with the Law Commission on its *Report on Personal Injury Litigation – Assessment of Damages*, which included actuarial tables and concrete reforming proposals.[19] Together with the publicity surrounding the thalidomide tragedy and the *Sunday Times* campaign on behalf of some of the affected children, it seemed – according to John Prevett, who acted as an expert witness – that the understanding of how actuaries could help in such cases was increasing. This advance was unfortunately countered by the comments of the judges in *Taylor v. O'Connor* in the House of Lords and *Mitchell v. Mulholland* in the Court of Appeal, the effect of which was to entrench the *ad hoc* calculation of lump sum damages.[20]

The usual method by which a judge arrived at this lump sum was by using a 'multiplicand', being the annual net loss or cost incurred, and a 'multiplier', being a number of years' purchase, taking account of the age, sex and personal circumstances of the plaintiff. The actuarial view was that this method could, and on occasion did, disadvantage the victim. When a number of imponderables had to be allowed for, the result was bound to be imprecise and might be too low to meet the victim's lifelong needs. Statistical projections drawn from the pooled experience of similar claimants would provide a more accurate calculation of the needs of the individual plaintiff, and awarding a 'life annuity' was in any case thought to be a more prudent course than awarding the total sum at once. The latter method was criticised for making no allowance for inflation. Worse still, it placed upon the injured party or carers the responsibility for investing the sum so as to produce an adequate return over an unknowable period. All these objections to the prevailing system had been accepted by the Law Commission, but neither its *Report* of 1973 nor, in 1978, that of the Royal Commission on Civil Liability and Compensation for Personal Injury chaired by Lord Pearson (the Pearson Report, whose recommendations on the assessment of damages were, in John Prevett's words, 'intensely disappointing'), produced any action from the Government of the day.[21]

A setback that seemed to mark the nadir of the whole endeavour came in 1981 with the case of *Auty, Mills, Rogers and Popow v. the National Coal Board*, in which the evidence of an actuary appearing for the plaintiffs was rejected by the Court of first instance and the judgment upheld in the Court of Appeal and the House of Lords. In the Court of Appeal, Lord Justice (now Lord) Oliver expressed the opinion that

as a method of providing a reliable guide to individual behaviour patterns or to future economic and political events, the projections of an actuary could be only a little more likely to be accurate (and will almost certainly be less entertaining) than those of an astrologer.[22]

This comment caused great consternation within the profession, but instead of routing those involved, it spurred them to renew their efforts. A small *ad hoc* committee of actuaries under the auspices of the Institute and the Faculty sought parliamentary sponsorship for the insertion of a clause from the Law Commission's *Report* into the Administration of Justice Bill then passing through Parliament. The clause was duly tabled but was withdrawn on the understanding that the Lord Chancellor would approve discussions between the actuarial and the legal professions.[23] A more formal Joint Committee[24] was established at the end of 1982, forming part of an inter-professional Working Party with representatives of the Inns of Court and the Bar, the Law Society and the Scottish legal system. It was chaired by Sir Michael Ogden QC, at that time Chairman of the Criminal Injuries Compensation Board, and a tireless campaigner for a more equitable system of compensation than that based on conventional multipliers.

The Working Party's brief was to consider and report on 'the feasibility and desirability of issuing authoritative tables for the assistance of the court in assessing an award of damages for continuing pecuniary loss arising out of personal injury or fatal accident litigation' and related questions. In his memoirs Sir Michael Ogden admits that 'It was very hard work, because actuaries are very clever but also very precise people.'[25] His impish humour took some of his legal colleagues aback, but delighted the actuaries:

I said to them, 'The tables themselves are easy and will be prepared by the Government Actuary (who was a member of the working party) but when it comes to the explanatory notes we must make sure that they are readily comprehensible. We must assume the most stupid circuit judge in the country and before him are the two most stupid advocates in the country. All three of them must be able to understand what we are saying.'[26]

This was easier to pronounce than to achieve: 'Consequently, what I had to embark upon – because, being chairman I had to write the explanatory notes – was to translate what could be called actuary language into plain English. This was very difficult indeed.'[27]

The set of tables agreed by the Working Party was published by HMSO in May 1984 as *Actuarial Tables with Explanatory Notes for use in Personal Injury and Accident Cases*, but has always been known, inside and outside the profession, as the 'Ogden tables'. Sir Michael was amused at finding his work on behalf of another profession 'the thing for which I am now best known throughout the Bar'. The tables dealt only with the risk of mortality (though, at Sir Michael's urging, subsequent editions would include other risks such as sickness and unemployment). The introduction described a novel solution to the problems of inflation and the uncertainty of investment return that relieved plaintiffs of the need to 'speculate' with their awards. The issue of index-linked government stocks (a particular cause of David Wilkie's) inaugurated in 1981 provided a

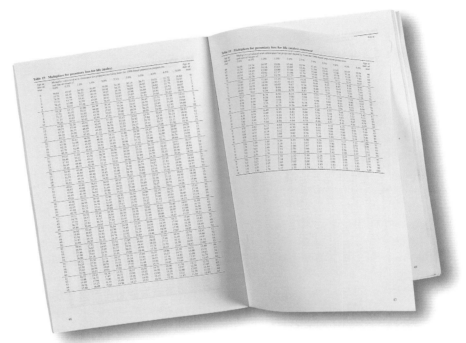

Shortly before his death Sir Michael Ogden QC published his recollections, which include an account of his association with the Institute in the cause of fairer awards of personal damages in legal judgments. The result was the 'Ogden tables'.

risk-free investment which would not be eroded by inflation. On this basis, calculating damages became much more straightforward, since the multiplier used could be based on the rate of discount corresponding to the real yield on such stocks at the date of assessment, producing for the victim a regular income protected against inflation. The Ogden tables at once began to be used, but they gained statutory recognition only in 1995, and will be referred to in a later chapter.

Two concerns dominated the profession during the mid-1980s, as the battle being waged by the Conservative Government to reduce the scope of State control gained momentum. The harsher commercial realities that emerged from this period led to greater competition in the life insurance industry as in every other, with the additional factor that traditional with-profits policies were by now closely rivalled by investment-linked products of various kinds. The first of the actuarial profession's worries, arising from this business context, concerned the degree to which life insurance companies selling new with-profits business, either in their advertising or through their agents, were making it sufficiently clear that the bonus illustrations shown were based upon past performance and were not predictions or promises for performance in the future. Speaking at the Annual General Meeting on 25 June 1984, Stewart Lyon (*) voiced his unease, pointing out that 'the Institute can only lay a professional responsibility on its own members. It cannot require an employer to behave responsibly'.[28] The dichotomy, he said, was nowhere more evident than in the area of new business quotations by life offices selling with-profits policies. In keeping with the custom of the UK market, quotations were illustrated by assuming that current rates of bonus would continue indefinitely, although terminal bonuses were shown separately from annual ones. Some companies did warn policyholders that this might not be the case, but,

however strong the caveat, it will not enable a potential policyholder to understand that the illustration a salesman gives him today is only realistic in the context of a repetition of the economic pattern of the past decade. Bonus rates are historically high following a period when inflation was exceptional, and if it is now going to settle down at a more moderate level there will be disappointment and disillusion when in time there has to be a corresponding reduction in future bonuses.[29]

The Joint Committee on Financial Standards in Long Term Business considered the situation potentially dangerous, favouring instead a solution where past performance was factually reported but future projections were made by reference to standard roll-up rates of interest, as were those for investment-linked contracts.[30] A year after Lyon's address, his successor as President, Peter Moore, reiterated the Institute's deep concern, reporting that he and Alex Shedden, the Faculty President, had conveyed to the chairmen of the Life Offices Association and the Associated Scottish Life Offices their shared view that:

although bonus illustrations are primarily a commercial and not a professional decision, the profession's own reputation and standing is inextricably interwoven with the commercial approaches used. We feel that any industry-led development of a code of good practice for bonus illustrations should satisfy us as to its suitability for general public understanding of the important issues raised by publicity materials which incorporate bonus illustrations and projections of policy yields.[31]

An Institute Working Party was already considering the issue. Its recommendations were presented at the 1st Actuarial Convention in September 1985, a gathering prompted by Council's strong belief that the Institute had to give a lead to the insurance industry on a matter which touched them both. In addition, the guidance given to appointed actuaries in clause 1.4 of GN8 was strengthened.[32] It was still questionable whether it went far enough:

The appointed actuary, or some other actuary, may advise the company on what bonus rates should be declared or illustrated, but the power of decision rests with the company's board and management. They have to reconcile the actuary's advice with the marketing pressures …[33]

The future of pensions was the other issue that was causing alarm. The profession's worry arose from its profound understanding of the demographic and economic realities facing the country. Stewart Lyon had dedicated his Presidential Address[34] to the subject, drawing upon the report produced by Francis Bacon, Bernard Benjamin and Douglas Elphinstone back in 1954 (*The Growth of Pension Rights and Their Impact on the National Economy*, referred to earlier) to illustrate how the prospect they had described was fast becoming a reality. The problem of an ageing population and a declining birthrate – identified as characteristic not only of Britain but of all the developed countries – was now coupled to that of paying for the pensions commitments enshrined in post-war legislation. The resulting transfer of spending power to the retired in the form of pensions, according to figures provided by the Government Actuary (GA) to the Committee to Investigate the Functioning of Financial Institutions (the Wilson Committee) showed an alarming trend. Already in 1979 this transfer was equivalent to $12^{1}/_{2}$ per cent of total consumers' expenditure, and by the year 2000 it would reach 16 per cent. The big question was 'whether the economy would grow sufficiently to prevent the transfer from prejudicing the standards of living desired by the working population? … That is the crunch we cannot escape'.[35] Inflation and recent economic vicissitudes cautioned against complacently assuming perpetual growth:

Changes are likely in the pattern of employment as a result of new technology and our industrial decline: we do not know how far reaching they will be, but already the whole of the goods and services being produced in the U.K. represent the output of 4 million workers fewer than 20 years ago. What we do know is the scale of the pensions promises we have made to ourselves through the state scheme and through occupational pension schemes. And warning signs are clearly visible in our systems for financing them – signs which could become storm signals should our economy not grow sufficiently to sustain so large a transfer of spending power to pensioners.[36]

The most obvious of these signs was the higher rate of contributions that would be needed to fund pension commitments. In July 1982 the GA's Quinquennial Review of the long-term finances of the State scheme revealed that the combined contribution rates falling on employers and employees for State benefits were expected to increase from some 15 per cent of relevant earnings in 1985–86 to around 22 per cent ultimately.[37] The greatest factor contributing to this increasing cost was purely demographic – the number of contributors to pensioners was set to decline from its current ratio of 2.25:1 to

2:1 by about the year 2000, unless circumstances changed, perhaps through a lowering of the rate of unemployment, the reversal of the trend towards early retirement, or through immigration. In addition, employers faced increasing demands for better protection against inflation; and the equalisation of retirement ages for men and women, a policy encouraged by the European Commission, was no longer a remote possibility but a likelihood that in time would lead to increased costs for the working population. The risk was very real that 'at some future date, total contributions will exceed what is felt to be a tolerable level and the level of benefits which present contributors have promised themselves may have to be diminished'.[38]

It is interesting, and not a little sobering, to compare such words with those uttered by Leslie Brown in the Institute's debate on the Beveridge proposals in 1943[39] and those of Frank Redington in *National Pensions* in 1959, and they were only two of many actuaries who over the years had spoken with the voice of Cassandra at the prospects facing the nation on the pensions front. The Institute welcomed the broadening of public debate on pensions in 1983, but lamented that 'much of it has suffered from being ill-informed'.[40] One initiative to combat this state of affairs was to sponsor, jointly with the Faculty, a prestigious seminar on pensions in Staple Inn Hall in November 1983. On this occasion an invited audience that included MPs and senior civil servants heard the major pensions issues discussed by leading actuaries, including Edward Johnston (the GA), Gordon Pepper, David Wilkie and Bernard Benjamin.

David Wilkie is a Fellow and Gold medallist of both the Institute and the Faculty. His redemption yield formula of 1979 (with George Dobbie, also of the Faculty) and stochastic model for investment use of 1984 are two of his outstanding contributions to actuarial method, and gained him an international reputation.

At this point the profession's concern coincided with that of the Conservative Government, but the latter's was motivated by an additional, overriding and ultimately ideological rationale. Now embarking on a second term of office, the Thatcher administration had identified the reform of the pensions system as a key element in its concerted drive to realign the thinking of the nation along entrepreneurial lines. The mounting cost of SERPS, the second-tier earnings-related pension brought into being in 1978, was the prime target. This was less the result of actuarial warnings than on the grounds that, because SERPS was earnings related, it benefited those on higher earnings, and thus offended the Conservative principle of focusing benefits on those most in need and withdrawing them from those able to manage without them.[41] Similarly, the final salary occupational schemes (including those that were the contracted-out alternative to SERPS) were held to discourage job mobility, and hence the initiative and independence the Government sought to foster.

The question of the future role of SERPS – including the possibility of its abolition and replacement with compulsory private schemes – began to be formally debated in December 1983, when the Secretary of State for Social Services, Norman Fowler, announced the setting-up of an Inquiry into Provision for Retirement (the Fowler Inquiry).[42] Three members of the Institute – Marshall Field, Edward Johnston and Stewart Lyon – served on the Inquiry, and the Institute and Faculty were invited to submit written evidence. Individual actuaries – Roy Colbran, Hamish Gillon, Kenneth Smith and John Prevett – represented the profession in giving lengthy evidence in person. The discussions of several sub-committees produced the views contained in two Institute–Faculty Submissions: one on the new concept of 'personal portable pensions', and one on the implications for pensions provision of future changes in the elderly population.[43] The two bodies also prepared a Joint Response to the Consultative Document on Personal Pensions issued by the Secretary of State in July 1984.

The discussions that took place at the Institute and Faculty early in 1985 reveal the profession's dismay at the superficial consideration given by Government to the significant and complex issues raised in all of the joint evidence. While no actuary would ever have said SERPS was perfect, it was generally felt to have served the nation well. It had seemed that there was a consensus on the part of all political parties about the place of both State and occupational schemes in providing secure pensions, and the stability that had reigned since 1975 was valued.[44] Among the questions given detailed treatment were those relating to early leavers and transfer values, the effect of a large-scale move to personal pensions on the funding of occupational schemes, and the danger from inflation inherent in the shift from 'defined benefit' schemes to schemes run on a basis of 'defined contribution' or 'money purchase', such as personal pensions. Most importantly, the profession was sceptical about personal pensions on the purely practical grounds that neither the public nor the economy were ready for them. 'In an ideal world', the Joint Response conceded,

the concept of Personal Pensions has a great deal to commend it. The pre-conditions of this 'ideal world' include:

(i)   *a public well informed in and understanding of financial matters;*
(ii) *a young generation fully aware of and prepared to act upon the need to provide for their own old age;*
(iii) *a stable currency and an investment climate which can be relied upon to provide regular positive real returns;*
(iv) *a stable long-term policy on provision for retirement, including tax aspects.*

Unfortunately we believe that these conditions are unlikely to be met in the foreseeable future.[45]

But the Government was not to be dissuaded. The profession had (as David McLeish of the Faculty put it), 'been through 18 months of public debate and dialogue with Government in the form of both written and oral evidence'[46] yet neither the collective views of experts whose advice had been sought, nor the presence of three senior actuaries as members of the Inquiry were permitted to alter the course already determined.[47] Not all went according to plan, however. The Green Paper published in June 1985 which outlined the proposed abolition of SERPS encountered great resistance from employers on the grounds of cost and had to be modified. The Social Security Act 1986 retained SERPS, but reduced its provisions in such a way that the estimated cost in the year 2033 would be £13 billion rather than the original figure of £25 billion.[48] At the same time, people were to be offered financial incentives to contract out of SERPS and set up personal portable pensions. Although personal pensions were an obvious boon to the self-employed, not even actuaries had any idea how popular they would become: it was suggested at a Faculty discussion that perhaps 10 per cent of occupational scheme members, or about a million employees, would take out personal pensions,[49] whereas by 1993 those opting out of SERPS numbered five million.[50] More will be said in the next chapter about the mis-selling of a large number of these pensions, an unhappy saga which would bear out every earlier actuarial fear about commercial responsibility and severely damage public confidence in the insurance industry.

As the 1980s progressed, in contrast to pensions and other long-term concerns, some novel social problems, mainly to do with health, began to affect the life insurance industry and through it, the actuarial profession. Evidence that smoking was damaging to health, for instance, led life insurance companies to offer preferential terms to non-smokers, and actuaries were faced with the challenge of devising appropriate premium bases before the statistical information on smokers' mortality was fully available.[51] The most important of such problems was related to the feared global spread of AIDS and HIV, and resulted in the setting up of an AIDS Working Party, chaired by Chris Daykin, in 1987. At that time about nine hundred cases of AIDS had been reported in the United Kingdom, of whom about five hundred had died.[52] This was a far lower incidence than in the United States and in some European countries, but it was estimated that many cases in the UK were as yet undiagnosed and that in time the country was likely to face a major health problem leading to an escalating number of deaths. The main aim of

Stewart Lyon, President 1982–84, has the distinction of having received two Gold Medals – one from the Institute in 1991, and one from the British Numismatic Society in 1974 for his studies of Anglo-Saxon coinage.

the Working Party was to help actuaries to assess the potential problems associated with the spread of AIDS, but in order to do this it had to embark on a fairly intensive programme of information-gathering, analysis and projection. The first issue of *AIDS Bulletin* was published in 1987 and explored some of the issues posed by HIV infection and AIDS for the underwriting of life and private health insurance business. It emphasised the importance, both for the security of existing policyholders and for the sake of equity, that insurance companies should operate on the basis of sound underwriting principles.[53] This issue and four subsequent ones, the last published in 1991, provided an overview of the information available, including international comparisons. At the International Congress in Helsinki in 1988, the UK delegation held a session on AIDS at which speakers from various countries were able to air their national experience of the illness and the measures available to insurers.

Despite the relative newness of the problem and the uncertainty surrounding the determination of suitable parameters, the Working Party from the beginning considered it essential to construct a plausible model for the spread of the disease and to investigate its likely impact on reserving, underwriting and mortality. It used a model devised by David Wilkie and based on sound epidemiological principles to provide a series of illustrative projections of the possible spread of AIDS. Each *AIDS Bulletin* also included sets of mortality tables, policy values and premium rates according to each of the several projections, which were adapted as more became known about the disease. The *AIDS Bulletin*s, unlike the discussions of most Working Parties, were intended for the whole profession but were also sent to selected governmental, medical and academic personnel. Given the publicity surrounding insurance restrictions and lifestyle questioning stemming from the prevalence of AIDS and HIV infection in other countries, such as the United States and Australia, it followed that the Working Party's views would attract press interest and the criticism of pressure groups.

In comparison with actuaries working as consultants or in the life and pensions field, those working in general insurance made up only a small proportion of the profession. Most were still largely engaged in premium rating and reserving for personal lines of business, and particularly motor insurance, where the data becoming available seemed to offer the best prospects for using actuarial techniques. (Motor insurance is in fact quite similar to life insurance; data is plentiful, classifiable according to age, gender and geographical area, and easily measured.) The involvement of actuaries with a new area, the London Market, grew out of the wider concern of the GIRO (the General Insurance Research Organisation, discussed elsewhere) that actuaries should eventually assume a significant role in the conduct and supervision of general insurance. It was recognised that if they were to acquire greater influence they would have to involve themselves in all areas of the business, even those where the data was sketchy and the prospects less promising. This meant assessing both the commercial risks taken on by the large composite companies and those found primarily in the London Market, including the associated re-insurance arrangements.[54]

A few actuaries were already working in that area. George Foster and Frank Guaschi (*) at the Mercantile & General did pioneering work in developing an approach to the reserving and premium rating of long-tail (excess of loss) re-insurance liabilities.[55] The short, clear monographs they produced on the application of actuarial techniques to reinsurance were aimed at non-actuarial readers working in the London Market. Another actuary, David Craighead (*), after a decade of setting up accounting systems for reinsurance companies, was asked in 1979 to carry out reserving calculations for some of them. These contacts led to the same kind of work for some of the Lloyd's syndicates holding the strongest reserves. In 1983 – a particularly turbulent time, following the Lloyd's Act 1982 and a spate of natural and man-made disasters – he made contact with the other three actuaries working in reinsurance and several others whom he identified as occupying somewhat isolated positions in general insurance companies. The result was the London Market Actuaries Group (LMAG), which has continued to meet monthly ever since, with Craighead as Chairman until 1989. By then it had 100 members, all connected in some way with reinsurance. Its aim was to develop methods that would enable Lloyd's syndicates to deal with the heavy claims experience of the 1980s in a disciplined way, or that would otherwise improve the financial discipline of Market companies.[56] David Craighead's liaison work with them was instrumental in demonstrating that members of the profession could bring new skills and insights to this process, and he was subsequently awarded a Finlaison Medal.

Tradition and ultra-modern meet in the City of London where Sir Richard Rodgers's Lloyd's Building wears its insides outside. The London Market Actuaries Group seemed almost as unconventional when it began.

In October 1989, the Institute was asked to contribute views to the DTI about the greater participation of actuaries in the supervision of general insurance, along the lines of practice in the life field. A Guidance Note, GN12, on Actuarial Reporting in General Insurance, had been issued in 1987, but the way that actuaries came to have a statutory role in general insurance came about indirectly. Almost at the same time as the DTI talks, and in the wake of the *Piper Alpha* disaster and Hurricane Hugo, members of the General Insurance Joint Committee were invited to confer with the Lloyd's Regulatory Authority regarding regulation for Managing Agents. The result was Lloyd's Regulation 17, issued late in 1989 by the Council of Lloyd's as part of the regulatory control of the Lloyd's insurance market under the Lloyd's Act 1982. The statutory role for actuaries lay in the specification that all syndicates had from then on to obtain an actuarial opinion on their reserves each year. An Institute and Faculty

Working Party worked intensively to produce the Guidance Note issued in April 1990 as GN14 – 'Actuarial Reporting on Lloyd's Run-off Years of Account'. In this they were assisted by advice from accountants already working in the field, underlining once again the understanding between the two professions.[57]

Lloyd's Regulation 17 generated increased opportunities for actuaries, and their work in turn has fostered the better provision of the information on which their opinions must be based. London Market companies followed the lead given by Lloyd's in obtaining actuarial advice and membership of the LMAG grew to 200 by 1992. A further run of natural catastrophes and a wave of claims relating to asbestos, pollution and other health hazards in the early 1990s produced enormous losses at Lloyd's. Members of the LMAG were among the many UK actuaries who became involved in the operations of Equitas, the re-insurance company formed to take over the liabilities of individual Lloyd's syndicates in respect of years of account 1992 and before.[58] The aggregate reserves required for long-tail risks such as pollution and asbestos were extraordinarily difficult to assess for adequacy. Such assessment of the overall and individual liabilities required a variety of approaches, from the basic collection of data to the estimate of claims 'incurred but not reported' and those whose full extent was not yet known. The point was to give the Equitas actuaries a view of the total undiscounted liabilities for all syndicates, so that assets and liabilities could be matched at aggregate level rather than at syndicate level and the amounts to be transferred by the syndicates agreed with their respective actuaries. The DTI eventually approved a formula whereby, included in Equitas's reinsurance policies for accepting liability, there was a provision that if reserves should prove insufficient, cover would abate by as much as was necessary. The actuarial contribution to this process has been much appreciated by the syndicates and their managing agents on one hand and by the DTI on the other,[59] and enhanced the image of the profession in the City.

Following the Lloyd's actuaries into the 1990s has been to explore a tributary, leaving the mainstream behind. A return to it, to resume the narrative in the late 1980s, reveals the pensions system and life insurance industry greatly altered through recent legislation. Reservations about the shift to personal pensions led to some prophetic comment from individual members of the Institute: at the 2nd UK Actuarial Convention in 1987, Marshall Field spoke of 'the risk of some of the less perceptive being tempted, or persuaded, out of their traditional and soundly constructed' occupational pension schemes.[60] In an ironic twist, within a few years the profession would be called upon to help to sort out the mis-selling debacle against which it had cautioned the authorities. This and other, less foreseeable calamities that assailed the life insurance and pensions industries during the 1990s would inevitably have their impact on the profession and the life of the Institute, making this a disturbing and challenging decade.

CHAPTER NINE

Challenges for the profession

I N 1983, after several instances of dishonest securities and commodity dealing had shaken public confidence, the Government appointed a Review of Investor Protection chaired by Professor L. C. B. Gower. The main recommendation of its Report, published in 1984, was for new legislation to regulate investment business, since it had become apparent that major changes were necessary if London were to remain Europe's leading financial centre.[1] The Gower Report was the genesis of the Bill that received the Royal Assent on 7 November 1986 as the Financial Services Act 1986. It was arguably the most significant piece of investment legislation of the century and went much further than consumer protection. Inspired by the need to sweep away outdated and monopolistic practices so as to free up investment business, it overhauled the regulation of the entire financial sector and erected a supervisory framework that would merit investor confidence. Some measures taken in advance of the new legislation were indeed dramatic, such as the London Stock Exchange's elimination of the centuries-old jobbing system and replacement of it by a new market-making system – the so-called 'Big Bang'. The investment field was suddenly open to new players such as banks and building societies, and the way paved for a period of overcapacity and subsequent consolidation in the provision of financial services in the years that followed.

The Financial Services Act had major implications for actuaries, since along with investment business, life insurance and pensions products were brought under its umbrella and from 29 April 1988 it regulated the sale of investment products. The actual regulating was entrusted to a newly created 'designated agency' known as the Securities and Investment Board, or SIB. A person or body concerned with investment business from now on had to be either 'authorised' by the SIB under the Act, or 'exempt'. Exempt bodies were few, and included the Bank of England and Lloyd's; but 'authorisation' could be achieved by several means, one of which was through supervision by one of the 'Self Regulatory Organisations' or SROs set up to oversee specific areas. Among these were LAUTRO (the Life Assurance and Unit Trust Regulatory Organisation), FIMBRA (the Financial Intermediaries Managers and Brokers Regulatory Association) and IMRO (the Investment Management Regulatory Organisation). Alternatively, professional firms whose business was not primarily in the investment field could be authorised if their profession registered with the SIB as a 'Recognised Professional Body' or RPB. After some discussion, this was the course taken by the Institute in February 1987. Letters setting out the pros and cons of RPB status were sent to Fellows, and a vote requested. Given that those whose work involved investment business would otherwise have had to apply for authorisation to the relevant SRO, Fellows of the Institute overwhelmingly approved seeking registration as an RPB. The Faculty vote was against, and thus Fellows of the Faculty of Actuaries in firms seeking authorisation by the Institute as an RPB had to become Affiliates of the Institute.[2] The Institute was granted interim registration as an RPB on 8 February 1988, and final recognition on 16 December 1988, after some necessary changes in the

Deregulation – dubbed 'Big Bang' by the financial press – changed the face of business in the City literally overnight.

Royal Charter and Bye-laws. The 35 firms, which included 350 Fellows, seeking authorisation through the Institute had from now on to demonstrate to the Authorisation Committee that each principal had achieved adequate standards of competence and relevant experience in financial services. They were also obliged to have suitable professional indemnity cover and to subscribe to a compensation fund for the protection of investors.[3]

An important concept introduced by the SIB was that of 'polarisation', according to which persons authorised to give investment advice had either to represent a particular company or to be independent. This contrasted with previous practice, in which many intermediaries occupied a kind of 'middle ground', being nominally independent but actually linked to one or more life insurance companies. Polarisation sought to eliminate conflicts of interest: clients had to be clear about the status of persons giving advice, whether they were company agents, who could only recommend the products provided by their own companies; or independent advisers, who had to offer the client 'best advice' after assessing the products available in the market. The SIB provided a code of conduct for companies, their representatives and independent advisers. One of its stipulations, significant in the light of subsequent events, was that life offices and unit trust companies were permitted to reward external sellers of their products only by way of commission.[4] The independent professional firms regulated by the Institute in its capacity as an RPB were obliged, in recommending the most suitable product of those available, to inform the client of costs and risks, as well as future benefits and the consequences of early surrender. Commission received had to be disclosed and offset against professional fees.

The scene was now set for one of the most painful episodes in the history of the pensions industry. It was a more complex scenario than the casual references to 'pensions mis-selling' still bandied about today would suggest. Under the Social Security Act 1986 employers could no longer compel employees to join or remain in their occupational pension schemes. It also became mandatory for such schemes to provide transfer values for early leavers, or employees who opted out of the scheme, and such transfer values could now be paid to a personal pension scheme as an alternative to an occupational pension scheme. The actuarial profession had recently introduced guidance, in the form of GN11, which actuaries were to follow when calculating these values, known as 'cash equivalents'. These were to be worked out on a basis which had regard to the rates of return on, say, government bonds, but which also allowed for the higher rates of return available from equities, which some actuaries considered it appropriate to include.[5] As an indirect result of these minimum standards, transfer values generally fell. The significance of this did not become clear until some time later.

The Financial Services Act came into effect at almost the same time as the Social Security Act 1986 which – as was mentioned in an earlier chapter –

provided for limited index-linking for early leavers' pensions left in occupational schemes (colloquially but erroneously known as 'frozen pensions'). It also introduced the new 'personal pensions' that could be set up by those wanting to contract out of the State earnings-related pension scheme (SERPS), now readjusted to represent only 20 per cent of average annual earnings during the whole of employment, rather than 25 per cent over the best twenty years, as before. The aim was to prompt individuals to save for retirement while ultimately reducing the cost of State pensions. Between them, the two Acts contained all that was necessary to produce a major shift in pension provision, away from the State and occupational schemes, and into individual arrangements.

With hindsight it is relatively easy to trace how the resulting mis-selling debacle came about. What is dismaying is the realisation that it was predictable, long before it took place, and that it stemmed primarily from a determined and naïve Government policy that gave every encouragement to commercial opportunism. It was not that advice was lacking, or that the pitfalls had not been identified. The National Association of Pension Funds (NAPF), for example, like the Institute and the Faculty, had voiced its misgivings about the sweeping nature of what was proposed during the Fowler Inquiry. The argument that saw personal pensions as a key component in creating greater individual self-reliance was promoted by the Centre for Policy Studies, and largely based on MORI and Gallup polls purporting to have revealed a high level of discontent on the part of early leavers. In contrast, the NAPF and the profession drew upon an intimate knowledge of existing pensions provision, both State and occupational, to show that supplanting SERPS and occupational schemes by personal pensions would not in the long term achieve Government aims. If future returns were poor, many personal pensionholders might become dependent on supplementary benefits. Personal pensions might be appropriate for some – the self-employed, for instance, although it was pointed out that the retirement annuities available since 1956 were very similar – but they were certainly no substitute for membership of an occupational scheme offering both greater security and defined benefits.[6]

But while the expert advice given in 1984 did induce Government to modify some provisions of the proposed legislation, it had little effect overall on the course already determined. Perhaps the evidence of the NAPF was discounted because its exposition of the virtues of the occupational schemes and the potential threat to such schemes posed by the introduction of personal pensions was perceived as self-interested. If that were the case, then the advice contributed by the Association of Consulting Actuaries, the Institute and the Faculty may have been similarly regarded, and perhaps these professional bodies themselves were perceived simply as resistant to change. Within the profession the worry was that personal pensions would be sold to people with little understanding of what they were taking on. Individual actuaries continued to air their concern. Marshall Field's speech at the 2nd UK Actuarial

Convention held in Harrogate in September 1987 has already been cited as having a prophetic ring in the light of subsequent events:

Much as one might wish to bring into being a Nation of mini capitalists, each able to stand on his own financial feet, it had to be recognised that many under such a regime would come to grief ... Personal pensions (as we now know them) will appeal to many employees. Rightly so in some cases, but there remains the risk of some of the less perceptive being tempted, or persuaded, out of their traditional and soundly constructed schemes.[7]

This was not meant to suggest that the life office agents were less than honest; on the contrary, with their close association with the life offices, actuaries knew well the degree to which the British life insurance and pensions industry traditionally relied on the work of life office agents. But they worked to targets set by managers, who sometimes paid too little attention to the rules about switching laid down by LAUTRO. The undue speed with which personal pensions were introduced meant that it was difficult to provide adequate training for selling them in the time available, or to create sufficient controls. Many of the new class of 'Independent Financial Advisers' (IFAs) created by the Financial Services Act were similarly poorly prepared – but the facility with which they could sell personal pensions meant that this lack of knowledge often went undetected.

The scenario thus far was ominous enough, but it was compounded by the inducements offered by Government to leave SERPS and take out personal pensions. From 1 July 1988 it provided non-age-related rebates which were much more generous, in the case of young people, than the value of the benefits given up. In addition, there was the incentive of an outright gift of 2 per cent of relevant earnings to get new personal pensions off to a good start. Given that this made the new pension products easy to sell, and that for each one sold the agent or IFA received commission, it was hardly surprising that they were recommended strongly, without always drawing attention to the risks involved, especially when the client was opting out of an occupational pension scheme. Prior to this, life company agents had needed to work hard to obtain business; now, it poured in, even without promotion.[8] Among the self-employed, some already had the old-style retirement annuities. For those who had as yet made no pension provision, embarking on a personal pension was a positive step. Younger people who enjoyed the stimulus of frequent job changes were similarly attracted by the feeling of being in control of their own financial future that personal pensions gave them.

For the employed who already belonged to occupational schemes, it was a different matter. Besides the many people who were persuaded to abandon perfectly sound company pension schemes for personal pensions, many early leavers who took out personal pensions were later persuaded to transfer into them the 'frozen pensions' left behind in company schemes. Otherwise these would increase only by the rate of inflation, while the likely future return on a personal pension could be illustrated perfectly legally – indeed, as prescribed by the regulators – by unrealistic projections showing rates as high as 13 per cent per annum up to retirement age, much higher than the discount rates used by actuaries in calculating transfer values. Those who chose personal pensions in preference to company schemes were however assuming the risk hitherto shouldered on their behalf. It is unlikely that many of them realised the implications of this, perhaps because few of their advisers did either. The prevailing climate militated against the objective assessment of the client's options. Urged on by frequent press comment making the erroneous comparison between 'frozen pensions' and 'future investment returns', and Government-sponsored television spots depicting the removal of the 'hand-cuffs' of company pension schemes, some 5.7 million people exchanged SERPS and company schemes for personal pensions in the period up to 1993.

By then, LAUTRO and FIMBRA, the regulatory authorities, had begun to investigate the way the selling of personal pensions was carried out. They had sought the Institute's help during 1992 when attempting to compare the benefits under company schemes paying transfer values with the benefits from personal pensions. An Institute Working Party developed some suitable comparisons, and a number of simple Pension Transfer Analysis Systems were devised to try to filter out inappropriate transfers and monitor the flow of them still taking place. The subsequent analysis of a body of transfers, reported to the SIB in December 1993, revealed the alarming fact that some 91 per cent of them failed to comply with the rules concerning proper advice and documentation.[9] The SIB initiated a thoroughgoing review of the business to date, and on discerning the scale and implications of the problem, enlisted the further help of the Institute and Faculty to provide technical support for what became a collaborative regulatory effort to rectify the damage. Through a Joint Committee (somewhat whimsically named 'The 18 February Group' after the date in 1994 of its first meeting), the two professional bodies helped to design the financial terms for the complex set of calculations that would put investors back into their original pension schemes or top up their personal pensions. At the time, however, the profession requested that the SIB be seen as the entity responsible for the work.[10] John Martin, Roy Brimblecombe (*) and Peter Tompkins were members of SIB sub-groups that were particularly involved in this initial process, but literally hundreds of actuaries took part in reviewing and assessing cases and in making the calculations for financial compensation.[11] Such was the demand for their services that some actuaries emerged from retirement, while specialist firms arose to offer outsourcing facilities to the beleaguered life offices.

The clean-up has lasted a decade and to June 2002 had cost insurers and advisers more than £11.5 billion. Pensions mis-selling was a commercial problem; continuing powerful incentives to agents and advisers without a system for checking the suitability of their advice, especially in the case of transfers, was surely questionable. The life offices, as the major personal pensions providers, have accordingly taken the brunt of the blame, as much for the slowness of the rectification process as for this original misjudgement.[12] Life office actuaries may also have been at fault for having permitted projections to be made in a way that led to spurious comparisons between a personal pension and a company pension. Some members of the profession hold that the Institute should have warned them to take a firmer stand on this, or spoken out publicly to clarify matters. The loss of public confidence in an industry that had otherwise served the nation well was one deeply regrettable effect of this whole affair. Yet the roots of the situation lay deeper, in the insistence of the Conservative Government then in office on introducing such sweeping changes in the face of much sound advice and without proper preparation.

Although the actuarial profession was only indirectly involved, it does not emerge untarnished from this unfortunate episode. The simplistic calculations that were being produced by companies and their agents showing transfer values accumulating at high rates of interest, compared with expected values of pension scheme benefits, may have contributed to many decisions to go down the personal pensions route. Perhaps too the lack of information that could be readily understood by policyholders and advisers alike can be laid at the door of the profession. How many advisers understood that in suggesting to clients that they transfer out of company schemes and into personal pensions, they were counselling them to trade relative certainty for uncertainty, with no remedy should the much-vaunted 'high investment returns' shown in projections based on rates of return laid down by the regulator not materialise? As a prime source of information in life companies – overwhelmingly the biggest providers and sellers of personal pensions[13] – actuaries should perhaps have perceived the need for the kind of information that would have clarified such choices.

The review of personal pensions sales was one focus of the insurance industry's attention during 1993, but it was far from being the only one. In the previous several years the Occupational Pensions Board (OPB) had produced a series of reports addressing issues affecting scheme members. Most recently, and arising from the investment conditions of the 1980s, the question of surpluses and such measures on the part of employers as 'contribution holidays' and withdrawals from surplus had focused attention on the ownership and control of pension funds. Then, following the death of Mirror Group tycoon Robert Maxwell in 1991, concern about the workings of occupational pension schemes was heightened when it emerged that the assets of several pension funds within the two groups of companies he chaired had been seriously depleted. Investigation revealed total misappropriations of some £700 million, which were used to shore up the Maxwell financial empire. None of the transactions had been authorised by the trustees, and they would in any case have involved such breaches of trust as to make them unlawful. They were made possible because control rested with a very small number of individuals holding overlapping appointments, and because an in-house entity, Bishopsgate Investment Management Ltd, had custody of the assets of all the funds.[14]

These revelations had been made public at about the same time that the House of Commons Select Committee on Social Security was examining the implications for occupational pension schemes of the Barber decision (which outlawed retirement-age sex discrimination) by the European Court of Justice. The Select Committee recommended a thorough review of the law and regulation of occupational pensions. The Pension Law Review Committee, chaired by Professor Roy Goode QC, was established in June 1992 and published its Report fifteen months later. During that time it collected a substantial body of evidence on issues raised in a widely circulated consultation document, including the appointment and accountability of trustees, the adequacy of existing trust law and the security of pension scheme assets.

The Institute and Faculty were among the many professional bodies that contributed evidence, with a lengthy written submission in December 1992 and a number of Fellows giving oral testimony during January 1993. The written response to the eighty questions was prefaced by a number of recommendations, beginning with the need for disclosure in all major issues relating to pension funds and the clearer recognition of the rights of scheme members under employment law. With specific reference to the profession, the appointment of a 'Pension Scheme Actuary' to every defined benefit scheme was suggested, to be responsible for monitoring the scheme's running and to have a wider remit that included the power to report improprieties to an external body. In addition to existing valuation and reporting responsibilities, the Scheme Actuary should provide an annual statement to scheme members, indicating the solvency level for the accrued liabilities, and it should be binding upon the employer to rectify matters if this level were shown to be below 100 per cent. Such provisions as a compensation fund to cover fraud and theft, and a single regulatory body for pension funds, were obvious responses to the Maxwell scandal.[15]

Members of the Institute were gratified to see, on the publication of the Goode Committee's Report in September 1993, that many of its recommendations had been accepted, particularly those designed to enhance the security of pension scheme members, and that the Committee allocated a central role in achieving this to the actuarial profession. Perhaps the most notable recommendation adopted was that concerning trustee-appointed Scheme Actuaries for all funded schemes, producing annual solvency reports for members and empowered to 'whistle-blow' if necessary. The idea that scheme members should receive an annual statement based on a minimum solvency standard which employers would have to maintain[16] was also accepted, as were the proposals for a compensation scheme and for a stronger pensions supervisory body. These recommendations in due course found their way into the Pensions Act 1995 and its subsequent Regulations, which gave scheme members the right to choose at least one-third of their scheme's trustees and laid down the responsibilities and compliance procedures for trustees. (These included the appointment of Scheme Actuaries who, where necessary, could have recourse to the new Occupational Pensions Regulatory Authority (Opra), which would succeed the OPB in April 1997.) The minimum solvency requirement was renamed the Minimum Funding Requirement in the Act; setting minimum standards for the funding of defined benefit schemes which had previously been left to the discretion of the sponsoring employer.[17] On the face of it, this measure increased the security of benefits, but by the law of unintended consequences, in restricting schemes' investment policy it led to a degree of employer unwillingness to continue providing such schemes. The already noticeable trend away from defined benefit schemes and towards defined contribution schemes, to which the employer generally contributes less and which shifts the burden of risk onto the employees, was thus encouraged.

Duncan Ferguson (left) (Chairman of SIAS, who would be President in 1996–98) and John Martin (right) President 1992–94, with Professor Roy Goode, about to deliver the Institute's 1993 Jubilee Lecture.

The Maxwell scandal, despite the measures that were taken relatively quickly to reduce the likelihood of such abuses in future, sowed further mistrust in the public mind. The considerable success in recovering the moneys taken from the Maxwell pension funds, and ensuring that the impact on members and pensioners was much less than had at first been feared, unfortunately did not receive as much publicity as the original scandal. The disillusion resulting from the Maxwell affair, combined with the reaction prompted by the emerging revelations about pensions mis-selling, had a strong influence on the media coverage of financial matters and pensions in particular. It was hardly surprising that the tone of some of it grew more cynical and the tendency to allocate blame more pronounced. At the same time, in response to the greater interest and financial sophistication of readers, the discussion of such subjects could assume greater knowledge and introduce more technical detail. From these tendencies emerged the generalised demand for accountability in business dealings, disclosure of information and transparency of operation that gained strength throughout the 1990s – perhaps the one positive aspect, besides the remedial legislation, of the otherwise dismal legacy of the mis-selling and Maxwell affairs.

But the last years of the old millennium had more calamity in store for the life and pensions industry and its policyholders. The Equitable Life, dating from 1762, was the oldest surviving British insurance company and a well-trusted mutual: one of the most revered names in the industry. There is a wide gap between the unassailable image enjoyed for most of its long life and its closure to new business in December 2000, and the sequence of events that led from one to the other has given rise to intense speculation. Every forum from the House of Commons to the corner pub has seen impassioned debate about the causes, the rights and wrongs, and what could or should have been done to avert a catastrophe that has affected some half a million policyholders to varying degrees. The affair has of course aroused strong feelings within the actuarial profession, and has provoked some widely diverging views. Given that the origins of the Equitable's difficulties may to some extent lie several decades in the past, what follows can be no more than a summary that suggests the affair's significance for the actuarial profession. Reports already in the public domain[18] provide more information should it be sought. They, together with other material such as the Minutes of Evidence given to the Treasury Select Committee investigating the matter, naturally prompt many questions, to which it is hoped that the Government-sponsored independent inquiry conducted by Lord Penrose will be able to supply some of the answers.

The Equitable not only had an aura of invincibility, it was singular in the way it conducted its business. This was known throughout the industry, and explained in the paper given by two of its actuaries, Roy Ranson and Chris Headdon, at an Institute sessional meeting in March 1989.[19] The company was unique in not maintaining an 'estate', and had a bonus philosophy, complementary to this, that held that each generation of policyholders should receive its own 'asset share', and neither inherit from the past nor give to the future.[20] The lively discussion that followed the paper reveals that this approach – enthusiastically aired with the evident desire to share it with a peer audience – had its admirers and its critics. Later, the Government Actuary (GA) would recall, of the Equitable actuaries, that 'there was quite an active discussion because other members of the actuarial profession felt they were carrying on in a way which was different from what most other companies were doing', and attribute this to the company's singular philosophy and in part to the fact that the Equitable was a mutual, although there were other mutuals which conducted their business with material estates being carried forward.[21]

A certain favourable situation flowed from the approach adopted by the Equitable. Since it did not retain profits to build up reserves proportional to the fund, it was able to declare higher bonuses than any other company. The volume of business that resulted meant lower administration costs: a winning formula as long as no unforeseen adversity occurred that exposed the lack of a cushion of free reserves. Finally, a large part of the Equitable's liabilities consisted of individual and group pension plans carrying guaranteed annuity rates, or 'GARs', which had been set somewhat below the market rates then prevailing. In order to provide flexibility to policyholders to fund their pension when they had moneys available, some contracts contained open-ended options to invest further sums on the same terms as the original investment carrying the GAR, a particularly advantageous offer that was not made so extensively by any other UK company.

GARs were a common and popular feature of pensions policies sold in the 1970s and early 1980s and were certainly not unique to the Equitable. In 1997 an Institute Working Party was set up at the request of the Insurance Division of the Department of Trade and Industry (DTI), prompted by the GAD, which was aware that with interest rates falling, annuity guarantees maturing in any numbers might represent a problem for some companies. It canvassed the industry to ascertain the extent of them, and found that forty-six of the sixty-six companies that responded, including almost all the larger pension offices, had contracts with annuity guarantees.[22] Most of these, the Equitable's among them, had come into being in response to the pension legislation of 1956, and were mainly intended for the self-employed. The difference between other companies, which employed various methods of reserving for GARs, and the Equitable, was that the latter envisaged the terminal bonus as a fully flexible instrument, the adjustment of which (depending on circumstances and on the policyholder's choice at the time of turning a policy into an annuity) would provide for the full cost of meeting each guarantee at the time it was invoked. A form of differential bonus allocation was in fact practised, without attracting adverse comment, in the 1970s, when the annuity rates available elsewhere exceeded those guaranteed by the company; policyholders choosing the GAR were compensated by an additional final bonus, which those who took part of their benefit in cash (a measure made possible by the 1971 Finance Act, and which facilitated the purchase of an annuity at the higher market rate) did not receive.

With the introduction of personal pensions in 1988, superseding the 1956 legislation, the Equitable redesigned the terminal bonus and dropped the GARs for new contracts. It thus created a new class of with-profit contract, different from preceding ones. With hindsight, it was evident that, as the Institute's own official inquiry noted,

a new with-profit product should not be allowed to join a common bonus pool unless it can be demonstrated that there are unlikely to be circumstances when this could cause a problem … As an alternative to a new bonus series, the Appointed Actuary could have insisted that policyholders understood what would happen if the past guarantees became of real value because of a reduction in interest rates leading to reduced market annuity rates.[23]

But the Equitable did not start a new bonus series or alert its policyholders. Although the latter course was apparently considered, it was not taken because three assumptions seemed to render it unnecessary: that the guarantees were unlikely to be invoked; that even if they were, any cost associated with them could be recovered by adjusting the terminal bonus; and that, with the implicit mandate of the policyholders, the directors had absolute discretion over individual terminal bonuses.[24] (This last assumption might not seem unreasonable, considering the wording of the relevant article of the company's Articles of Association (Article 65). But as the House of Lords' ruling later confirmed, the wording of Article 65 was not the only factor relevant to the legality of the bonus policy.)

In 1991, the Equitable again went against prevailing practice in allowing its Appointed Actuary to combine his post with that of Chief Executive. In 1988, the then GA, Edward Johnston, had set out the arguments for and against the practice, current in a number of leading mutuals, of combining these roles, and had concluded that the arguments against such combination were strong.[25] While there were numerous instances of these positions being held sequentially, it was thus by 1991 a departure from the norm that they be held at the same time. The actuarial profession's guidance did not specifically prohibit such dual appointments, perhaps because its emphasis on the Appointed Actuary's independence seemed sufficient. Later, the profession's own inquiry into the lessons to be learned from the situation of the Equitable would comment nonetheless that it was 'hard to understand how the important role assigned to the Appointed Actuary can be made to work in the way intended if the holder of that post is also the Chief Executive, or indeed any other role with the potential for a conflict of interest'.[26]

In 1993, with interest rates having fallen below 7 per cent, the GARs promised to Equitable policyholders began for the first time to exceed current annuity rates. In accordance with its philosophy concerning asset shares, the company sought to equalise the benefits to policyholders who took advantage of the GAR with those who did not, or whose contracts did not contain this option, by reducing the terminal bonus allocated to the first group. Alarmed by the fall in interest rates, the Equitable also estimated the liabilities arising from GARs on the basis of its differential bonus approach and set aside £50 million against them. It is believed that the company debated sending out a circular to policyholders explaining its bonus policy, but dropped the idea when interest rates rose back above the critical level in 1994. Interest rates declined again, however, and by 1997 they were low enough to leave the GAR 25 per cent above current market annuity rates, with the result that more of the guarantees were being exercised. At the same time the company began to use the annual bonus documentation to inform policyholders of the reduced terminal bonus for guaranteed annuities. This led to queries about whether this policy was permissible and, in particular, whether policyholders had been made aware that the choice of the GAR would result in any reduction in terminal bonus. It was policyholder discontent on this point that eventually led to legal proceedings.

By June 1998, the decline in interest rates and the volume of contracts bearing GARs revealed by the Working Group mentioned above had prompted the GAD to investigate the provision each company was making in line with the solvency regulations. The GAD argued that reserves should be established assuming that nearly all policyholders with valuable GARs were likely to exercise them, while the Equitable had assumed that only a minority would do so. A reinsurer was prepared to shoulder the risk that the number of GAR options exercised might exceed the Equitable's estimate. This reinsurance was 'in effect, an asset to set against the Equitable's statutory liabilities and was a necessary arrangement if the Equitable was to continue to be allowed to write new business'.[27]

In 1999, after with-profits policyholders holding policies containing GARs disputed the right of the Equitable's directors to use their discretion to apply the differential terminal bonuses, the Equitable, with legal advice, decided to support a policyholder in bringing a representative case against it, to clarify its own position. The later evidence to the Treasury Select Committee investigating the Equitable supplied by Sir Howard Davies, Chairman of the Financial Services Authority (FSA) (which assumed responsibility as the life insurance industry's prudential regulator from 1 January 1999; up to then the prudential regulator had been the Insurance Division of the Treasury, advised by the GAD), suggests that the company was still being run on lines very different from the rest of the industry. According to this evidence, the supervisory authority was not informed about the legal action until after the proceedings had been issued. Sir Howard Davies's characterisation of the Equitable as 'a company which had an arrogant superiority', and one which 'did not deal with the regulator in the way we would expect'[28] sums up the impression conveyed by much of his own and other evidence supplied to the Treasury Select Committee concerning the way the Equitable conducted its business.

In seeking a declaration that it had exercised its discretion properly, the Equitable board apparently fully expected to have this confirmed by the judgment of the High Court. That this was what happened therefore came as no surprise and was naturally regarded by the Equitable as a vindication. The subsequent decision of the Court of Appeal in favour of the policyholder, however, was viewed as an aberration rather than a serious threat, so that the judgment of Lord Woolf, the Master of the Rolls, did not appear to receive the serious consideration that might have signalled caution in mounting a counter-appeal in the House of Lords.[29] Lord Woolf ruled that a differential final bonus was not a permissible exercise of the discretion conferred by Article 65 of the Society's Articles, on the grounds that such differentiation was intended to negate a benefit which a policyholder was otherwise reasonably entitled to expect under the terms of the policy. (The Equitable's interpretation of its own powers was not disputed by the supervisory authorities, however great their concern about other aspects of its situation.) That Lord Woolf's judgment did not cause as much consternation as it might have done seems also to have been due to the ruling of his fellow-judge Lord Waller, who agreed that the company was not entitled to award differential bonuses to those taking up the guarantees and those who did not, but also indicated that the company could allay the effects of this judgment by employing the differential bonus approach in a different way, to give different bonuses to those with GAR policies and those without (the 'ring-fencing' approach). It seems that it was not until literally days before the case came before the House of Lords that the possibility that the judges might interpret Article 65 along the lines of Lord Woolf's judgment and also reject the ring-fencing approach was regarded as a serious possibility by the Equitable, or by the regulator. The unexpected judgment of the Law Lords in favour of the policyholder was given on the grounds, echoing Lord Woolf – but here simplifying the argument greatly – that to pay policyholders with GARs a lower rate of terminal bonus contravened their reasonable expectations under the policy. A further blow came when the Lords ruled that the Equitable could not allay the effects of the adverse judgment by employing the ring-fencing approach, since the object of so doing would again be to eliminate any benefit of having a GAR included in a policy.[30]

Marshall Field (left), President 1986–88, who warned the insurance industry against the dangers inherent in the indiscriminate selling of personal pensions, and Roger Corley, President 1988–90, who would later head the Institute's own inquiry into the Equitable Life Assurance Society's closure to new business in December 2000.

The Lords' decision spelled doom for the Equitable; the reinsurance that might have provided a safety-net had to be renegotiated, and the Equitable was obliged to make provision for the possibility that many holders of GARs would exercise them, including those with options to make further investments at the same GAR, without being able to assume that the cost would be set against terminal bonuses. The cost of offsetting this risk meant that no reversionary bonus could be paid in the first half of the year 2000. Immediately following the Lords' judgment the Equitable put itself up for sale. Through the summer and autumn the troubled company unsuccessfully sought a purchaser; then on 8 December it closed its doors to new business. Within days the Institute and Faculty had set up a Committee of Inquiry, chaired by past-President Roger Corley (*), to consider the implications for actuaries of the closure. In particular, the Inquiry was to focus on the key issue of professional guidance – whether the Guidance Notes issued to the profession[31] needed 'amending, strengthening, extending or rewriting' – rather than to attempt to chart the history of events or reach conclusions with the aim of allocating responsibility for what had happened.

Its findings and recommendations were published by the profession in September 2001, supported by the written comments of thirty actuaries who had experience relevant to the inquiry. The first two recommendations originated in the Committee's perception of the Equitable's strangely isolated position in the life insurance industry: it did things – most things – differently from any other company, and hence its manner of operation had not been readily comparable with any other. It was suggested that from now on, an external peer review of the work of the Appointed Actuary should be a requirement, together with an annual Financial Condition Report. The other recommendations aimed at making existing Guidance Notes more explicit: specifically, by tightening up procedures for reviewing communications with policyholders, making the formulation of bonus policy more rigorous, and ensuring that the Appointed Actuary presented his or her board with 'reasonable alternative courses of action' along with the recommended ones. One important recommendation appeared in paragraph 68 of the Corley Report, where it was suggested that 'the Guidance Notes should require that an actuary resist holding the dual roles of Chief Executive and Appointed Actuary or any role which compromises his or her ability to fulfil the duties of the Appointed Actuary'.

The Equitable saga is of course far from over, and even though new management has been working to stabilise the position of the company, the outcome for its present and former policyholders is uncertain. The FSA commissioned its own internal Report (the Baird Report) to examine the background to its assumption of responsibility for the supervision of the Equitable on 1 January 1999 and the action taken between that date and the company's closure to new business in December 2000. The Baird Report identified a number of weaknesses in the way the FSA had responded to the Equitable, the only company to be transferred to its authority with an explicit warning from the Government Actuary's Department (GAD), yet towards which it seems to have shown a tolerance bordering on indulgence.[32] Many of the Baird recommendations are being implemented as part of a 'new regime' emphasising proactive rather than reactive regulation. The FSA has also conducted a thorough review of with-profits business. The Treasury Select Committee's own series of Reports on the Equitable Life and the life assurance industry have provided periodic summaries of the conclusions and recommendations drawn from Minutes of Evidence. Its Tenth Report suggests that future investigation of the role of the prudential regulator – the Insurance Division of the DTI and, later, the Treasury, both of which were advised by the GAD – in the period between 1993 and 1998 may provide the answers to some of the many questions still outstanding concerning the supervision of the Equitable. If the Equitable's singular approach did not in itself alert the supervisory authority – perhaps because, as one of the industry's most respected companies, it seemed to require only a modicum of active supervision – it still seems strange that exercising the differential terminal bonus scheme in 1993 did not cause sufficient complaints to attract supervisory attention. On the basis of the evidence given to the Treasury Select Committee, the implication for the company's communication with the regulators, and with policyholders, of its Appointed Actuary holding at the same time the position of Chief Executive between 1991 and 1997 seems to have been tolerated by the GAD and the DTI. Perhaps too the combination of the Equitable's well-attested tendency to pursue its own path without seeking regulatory approval and a shortage of staff at supervisory level was enough to produce a more arm's length monitoring than was the case with some other companies.[33] The Penrose Report may illuminate many aspects of the regulatory system as well as much about the Equitable that at present is less than clear.

The implications for the actuarial profession and the Institute are gradually emerging, not only as the recommendations in all the various reports become public, but also as themes such as Policyholder's Reasonable Expectation or 'PRE' (replaced in the latest legislation, the Financial Services and Markets Act 2000, with the phrase 'treating policyholders fairly') and the future of with-profits business are discussed and any resulting recommendations enacted. Meanwhile, the Equitable's downfall continues to be a subject of intense interest within the profession, with a wide range of opinions being held. Some hold that the conclusions of the Maturity Guarantees Working Party, which considered the not dissimilar problem of reserving for maturity guarantees on unit-linked policies between 1977 and 1980, should have suggested the need for clear guidance from the Institute and Faculty on GARs. Some believe that the Institute should have protested in whatever way was open to it about the potential conflict of interest posed by the appointment as Chief Executive of the Equitable's Appointed Actuary, on the basis that such a dual appointment risked compromising the actuarial independence that is the aim of so much professional guidance. To its credit, the profession is rapidly implementing the recommendations of the Corley Report, especially in the area of strengthening the guidance issued to appointed actuaries, whose position is likely to be affected in any case by new external supervisory measures. The insurance industry has experienced a series of chastening incidents that should act as spurs to improvement, and since many actuaries are employed in that industry, the profession and the Institute have likewise been given much food for thought.

Time present and time past

T HE last decade of the twentieth century would be one of radical self-appraisal for the actuarial profession. By 1990 developments in legislation had taken place in almost every area with which actuaries were concerned and there was now an unending stream of documents, many seeking the profession's views, emanating from government, the European Community, the supervisory authorities and other professions. It was not only to maintain the high regard in which the profession was held, but in the public interest, that the actuarial perspective – often a unique one – be represented when important issues were considered and decisions taken. Part of the difficulty in responding adequately to this obligation stemmed from the fact that the resources of the still largely volunteer and committee-based Institute were badly overstretched.[1]

Partial remedies would not suffice. Something more sweeping was needed, a programme to enable the Institute to give a lead on issues that were important for the profession and the public interest, rather than simply reacting to them as they arose. The perception of actuaries by those outside government circles and the City financial institutions was felt to be outdated, and their role in insurance, pensions and investment less well known than it deserved to be. As if the personal pensions mis-selling debacle were not enough to contend with, the profession suffered along with the whole financial sector as the Maxwell scandal, the Barings collapse and other instances of fraud or mismanagement wrought havoc with investors' confidence and expectations. As the 1990s neared their end, the decline of equity values spelled danger for with-profits business, and the Equitable Life saga delivered its devastating blow to the reputation of life assurance institutions. The consequence of all this for actuaries, through the medium of the Institute, was a certain amount of soul-searching. In part this revolved around whether the profession should, or could, have done anything to mitigate some of these events. There was also concern about what was meant, for actuaries in widely differing modern circumstances, by 'acting in the public interest' – a principle that had always been central to the profession's identity. Out of this emerged a bolder vision for the future, a restatement of the identity forged during more than 150 years, in a vigorous modern guise.

By 1990 the Institute and Faculty were working together more closely than ever before, with many joint committees on matters of common interest. This was a process which was fostered by Roger Corley, President from 1988 to 1990, and furthered, especially in the field of education, under Hugh Scurfield (*), President from 1990 to 1992.[2] The original 'Strategy for the 1990s' was a document prepared by the first Planning Joint Committee of the Institute and Faculty, chaired by Chris Daykin, then recently appointed Government Actuary. It embodied the objectives agreed at a historic meeting of the Institute and Faculty Councils at York on 4 March 1991,[3] and consisted of a 'Mission Statement', expressed in the phrase (echoing the Royal Charter) 'To develop the role and enhance the reputation of the actuarial profession in providing expert and relevant solutions to financial and business problems, especially those involving uncertain future events', followed by a statement and aims in each of five key areas. 'Standards' dealt with the achievement of professionalism, discipline, professional guidance and the promotion of high standards in these areas among actuaries in other countries as well as in the United Kingdom. 'Standing' focused on the promotion of a more positive image of the profession, especially in schools and universities, and on achieving better communications with target audiences such as the press and the financial sector. 'Influence' sought a place for actuarial opinions wherever they might be of value, especially in the development of legislation. Both in the United Kingdom and in the European Community this would require greater effort to identify important issues, and the creation of the means within the profession to address them and communicate the actuarial viewpoint effectively. It is interesting to observe, finally, a specific outreach to journalists, who although they 'do not create policy or take decisions regarding legislation and other developments' nonetheless 'can be very influential in determining the direction in which matters develop'.[4] 'Education' and 'Professional Development' were of course closely allied, one being the natural outgrowth of the other throughout the actuary's practising life. A 'modern and effective' system of education to qualification that maintained high – but not artificially high – standards, and the provision of high quality continuing professional education, were the major aims in these areas.

The 'Strategy' was not greeted altogether uncritically; in the discussion that followed its presentation, some felt that it merely reiterated things that had been said many times, while others pointed out important things left unsaid – such as the need for any advertising to reflect that actuarial advice was not just given to corporations, but to individuals, and in their interests. These were out-numbered, however, by those who considered that clearer objectives would be beneficial, and so the 'Strategy' was approved. Some decisions that pre-dated it were already in motion, as the Institute sought to keep ahead of rising student numbers and spiralling London rents. By the time Bill Truckle retired as Director of Education in 1989, the tuition service involved more than five hundred volunteer tutors, examiners and markers and occupied four sites in Holborn. Under Ken Gardner, the first non-actuary to serve as Director of Education, the newly established Actuarial Education Service (AES) and the library resources that supported it moved to premises in Oxford early in 1990. The new building, known as Napier House (after John Napier (1550–1617), the inventor of logarithms, 'Napier's bones', and other calculating devices fundamental to early actuarial science), became the administrative centre for the profession's educational programme, including continuing professional development. Publications, including that of the *JIA*, were also produced from Oxford.[5] In June 1990, replacing *Fiasco*, the first issue of *The Actuary* appeared. This was a new monthly magazine intended to provide an increasingly dispersed profession with topical articles and a forum for discussion. It was also

The great seventeenth-century mathematician John Napier (left) was honoured in the naming of Napier House, Oxford, in 1990.

something of a showcase: an accessible, quality publication that could communicate actuarial ideas to other professionals as well as to Institute members.

By the time 'Strategy for the 1990s' was set in motion in 1992, there was space at Staple Inn for the expansion of activity and new staff that implementing it required. Arthur Tait, who succeeded Clive Mackie as Secretary General in 1991, remained in that post until 1997 and was primarily responsible for modernising the administration of the Institute. Annual Institute subscriptions went up sharply in both 1990 and 1991 (from £270 to £400, then to £528 for Fellows, proportionally less for other classes of members) to pay for a sudden leap in rent at Staple Inn, the Oxford premises and the implementation of 'Strategy'; they would not rise again until 1998.[6] Promoting an awareness of actuarial services, the task of the Public Relations Committee since its creation in 1972, was felt to need more focus, and late in 1992 a government relations consultant was retained for the first time. The significant overlap between the Public Relations Committees of the Institute and Faculty led to the formation of the first Joint Public Relations Committee in 1993, so that from then on the actuarial profession in Britain did indeed speak with one voice. Two further measures reinforced this. In 1995 the *Journal of the Institute of Actuaries* and the *Transactions of the Faculty of Actuaries* were merged to become the *British Actuarial Journal*. A year later a joint website was launched and continues to provide a steadily updated source of information for members of the profession and various other audiences – government, actual or potential students, and the financial community.

Education and professional development were areas where there was already much constructive ferment at the time the 'Strategy' was introduced. A new syllabus-based approach to the examinations recommended by the 1987 Daykin review (which had stressed 'principles rather than detail') was scheduled to commence in 1992. At the momentous March 1991 meeting in York, however, the Institute and Faculty agreed to adopt a joint education syllabus and examination system, and the Institute offered to delay the introduction of its new programme for a year, to enable the necessary dialogue to take place. Following the untimely death of Ken Gardner, Lis Goodwin was engaged in 1992 as Chief Education Executive, assuming responsibility for education and continuous professional development (CPD). From 1993, the AES no longer set courses of reading or produced textbooks, but rather, produced new 'objective-based' course material. This marked a significant change of approach, defining courses more exactly than before, setting objectives and then breaking these down into specific topics. Distance learning, tutorials and short courses remained the main teaching methods. Closer liaison with the growing number of universities offering actuarial studies would make exemptions from the first group of examinations (subjects A to D) possible for many students entering the system. With the introduction of intermediate qualifications in 1995 it would soon be possible to obtain a Diploma in Actuarial Techniques after the 'foundation' stage. The second, or 'applications' stage (subjects E to

H), dealing with current areas of professional involvement, and the third – the 'fellowship paper' – allowing for a focus on one area and communications skills, were intended to be supplemented, after qualification, by CPD.[7] The process was further refined a few years later; as Duncan Ferguson (*) (President from 1996 to 1998) observed, there was still much to improve in a system in which only 40 per cent of the intake qualified. There had to be a balance between the student expectation that 'hard work plus structured tuition will guarantee success' and 'the examiners who want to be satisfied that students can think laterally and demonstrate their ability to apply their structured knowledge to the solution of relevant problems'.[8] More universities were encouraged to offer courses which would allow the examinations to be completed by students in full-time education. This was intended to appeal to employers who were thought to be cutting back on graduate recruitment.[9] By this time the traditional 'self-study' system, whereby actuarial students studied while employed, was under considerable pressure. Paul Thornton (*), who became President in the Institute's 150th anniversary year, 1998, saw it as the underlying reason why employment prospects for actuaries were still so dominated by the life and pensions sector. In contrast, in most of continental Europe and in Australia, Canada and South Africa, university education was the standard means of actuarial qualification, and graduates viewed the whole financial employment spectrum as their oyster.[10]

The prompting for a formal programme of CPD grew out of the work of the profession's Joint Actuarial Working Party with the Government Actuary's Department (GAD) and the Insurance Division of the Department of Trade and Industry (usually known as the JAWP). It found formal expression, through a DTI publication entitled *Strengthening the Appointed Actuary System,* in the proposal that 'practising certificates' be introduced for the appointed actuaries of life offices. The actuarial profession had never imposed formal requirements in this area, although there had always been plenty of opportunity for its members to exchange ideas. As a learned society that promoted research and made known the results through sessional and other meetings,[11] the *Journal,* summer schools and so on, the Institute had always helped members to further their knowledge. The DTI's proposal, however, echoed the belief of many Fellows that the pace of recent change in the UK had made it almost impossible to keep abreast of current issues and new techniques. Beginning in March 1992, as part of the

In 1993 the Institute was delighted by the phenomenon of two sets of twins qualifying together. John Martin, President 1992–94, congratulates Paul and Graham Fulcher and Edwin and Simon Sheaf.

'Strategy', a programme of CPD was initiated that required each actuary to undertake fifteen hours of formal CPD (such as courses and meetings) and fifty-two hours of informal CPD (such as reading) each year. Although this was unregulated, some indication of having complied was a mandatory requirement for obtaining an Appointed Actuary's practising certificate and also for members of the Institute authorised by it in its capacity as a Recognised Professional Body.[12] Short courses aimed to help actuaries work most effectively in their current situations, or to transfer into new practice areas – even to prepare them to work in fields where as yet actuaries were few. 'Professional development' progressively came to mean more than just attendance at courses and seminars. The attitudes and new skills – from management techniques to a second language – that could make the most of previous training were also part of it, as was the interchange of views with other actuaries, including those from other countries. These were strands in an approach that aimed at keeping each member of the profession moving forward and extending his or her capabilities.

The Institute took seriously its international status in the field of education and CPD, and sought wherever possible to assist actuarial developments in other countries. This became particularly relevant during the early 1990s, following the collapse of the Soviet system and the rise of new insurance industries in the former communist countries. There was an urgent need, to which the Institute and Faculty were well placed to respond, for actuarial training to improve the financial health and ethical conduct of such industries and to create (or recreate) an actuarial profession in each country. An eastern Europe sub-committee led by Chris Daykin established contacts in each of the eastern bloc countries. The first project was a one-week introductory seminar in Budapest in January 1991 on the role of actuaries in insurance. This led to the formation of the Hungarian Actuarial Society in February 1991 and then to a one-year diploma course in actuarial science at the University of Economic Sciences in Budapest. This took place in the academic year 1991–92, and was financed by the Know How Fund of the UK's Department for International Development, with the lecturers supplied from UK universities, from the Institute staff or from other volunteers from the UK profession. This was followed by a more advanced diploma course in Budapest and then by a 'training the trainers' course held at the Institute of Actuaries in Oxford. Running short courses and supplying books and study materials were other ways in which the profession lent a hand during the next few years, aided by funding from the Foreign Office. In addition to Hungary, activities took place in Poland and Bulgaria.[13]

In the 1990s the Institute, following the initiative of the Society of Actuaries from North America from 1988 onwards at Nankai University, Tianjin, fostered the establishment of actuarial education in China by setting up training programmes at the Central University of Finance and Economics in Beijing in 1993 and subsequently at the Shanghai University of Finance and Economics in 1998. The idea of helping to support the development of the profession in these new countries was proposed to the Council of the International Actuarial Association (IAA) in 1991. This led to the formation of the International Promotion and Education Fund, which promotes seminars for those who might be influential in establishing (or re-establishing) the actuarial profession in the different countries of eastern Europe (and later on in other areas of the world).

In 1994 the Institute and Faculty set in motion some further administrative changes. The balance between the short-term detail required on matters of professional significance and the time needed to deliberate long-term strategy led the Joint Councils to create six main Joint Boards – Life, Pensions, General Insurance, Wider Fields, Professional Affairs, and Education and CPD – under which were gathered some thirty existing committees. The Boards reported to the Institute and Faculty Councils, but there were a few activities, such as the Continuous Mortality Investigation, that remained outside the Board structure. In 1996 a Faculty and Institute Management Committee (FIMC) was created at an intermediate level between the Boards and the Councils, and a seventh Board, dedicated to Finance and General Purposes, was formed. A further change took place in 1997, with the distinction between 'Practice Boards' (Life, Pensions, General Insurance and Wider Fields) and 'Business Boards' (Professional Affairs, Education and CPD, and Finance and General Purposes) servicing the whole profession.

Back in 1992 when the 'Strategy' was launched, there had been a degree of uncertainty about the future demand for actuaries, due to the consolidation of the life insurance industry following the 'Big Bang' and the anticipated gradual decline of final salary pension schemes. John Martin, President of the Institute from 1992 to 1994, whose Presidential Address put great emphasis on

CHAPTER TEN

TIME PRESENT AND TIME PAST

Past Presidents, 1992:
Back row, left to right:
Arthur Tait (Secretary-General),
Roger Corley,
Mike O'Brien,
Peter Moore,
Gordon Bayley,
Stewart Lyon,
Marshall Field and
Tony Ratcliff.
Front row, left to right:
Jim Pegler,
Bernard Benjamin,
John Martin (President-Elect),
Hugh Scurfield (President 1992),
Sir Herbert Tetley,
Geoffrey Heywood and
Ronald Skerman.

future developments and the need to venture boldly into 'wider fields', was concerned about the novel problem of unemployed actuaries and about the knock-on effect on recruitment of any narrowing of actuarial employment prospects. John Martin was only the third consulting actuary to have served as President (the previous two were John Gunlake and Geoffrey Heywood). Under his successor Chris Daykin (President from 1994 to 1996) a study was undertaken, chaired by Peter Nowell (*) and issued in September 1995 with the title of 'The Future of the Profession', perhaps as a deferential nod to the Students' Society consideration of the same subject, published exactly fifty years earlier. (Much of the study was carried out by Gregor Campbell, who would succeed Arthur Tait as Secretary General on the latter's retirement in 1997.) The 1995 paper's analysis of the current and likely future employment situations was more positive than had been expected, and revealed some interesting trends. For all the references to 'wider fields' in actuarial literature since the 1920s, in 1995 only 2 per cent of actuaries actually worked in them. This included those in healthcare, which had been designated a 'wider field' since 1992. The life insurance and pensions sectors still accounted for more than 80 per cent of actuaries, whether they were employed by the life offices or acting as consultants. Breaking down the profession by employer, it was evident that consulting actuaries, at 40 per cent of the total, were fast overtaking their life office colleagues at 47 per cent.[14]

While the demand for actuaries in life insurance was momentarily flat, demand in pensions was growing steadily, and in general insurance rapidly. It was nonetheless true that consolidation and financial constraints were resulting in some loss of actuarial positions. It had long been assumed within the Institute that if employers in businesses outside the traditional life and pensions areas were made more aware of the value of actuarial training, more opportunities would arise. This did happen, but to a very modest extent. But it was also assumed that new Fellows would be eager to use their actuarial training as a 'stepping stone' to careers in the 'wider fields'. In practice, relatively few chose to do so – perhaps because the traditional areas of work represented a security that was highly desirable after the five or six years of post-graduate study. All the indications were that by 2005 there would be slightly less demand for actuaries in life insurance and pensions and somewhat more in management, investment and in 'wider fields' such as healthcare, capital projects and project management. The challenge would be to produce actuaries who were either flexible generalists, able to apply actuarial techniques to a variety of problems, or actuaries who had acquired additional capabilities to meet the needs of a specific sector.[15]

Actuaries working in the financial, business and 'wider' fields just mentioned (usually by deliberate career choice but sometimes through what one has wryly called 'accidental drift') were the thin end of what was becoming a somewhat more substantial wedge by the mid-1990s. The presence of actuaries in the universities, as teaching staff and researchers, is sometimes overlooked by the practising majority of the profession. Since the war academic actuaries have played a prominent part in the advances in actuarial science that have eventually been adopted by the rest of the profession, the obvious example being stochastic modelling. The fact that the profession embraces both academics and practitioners is not without its challenges, for although the Institute and Faculty have always been well supplied with stimulating material,

where papers are generated by academic or research actuaries rather than by practising actuaries, the practising actuaries among us will freely admit that they have some difficulty following the mathematics! So there is a gap … between the actuaries who are pushing forward the boundaries of actuarial knowledge and the practitioners who need to take those advances and use them to solve the practical problems that their clients have.[16]

Perhaps this has been best illustrated by the controversy surrounding financial economics, which has divided opinion within the actuarial profession since the early 1990s. Financial economics, the application of economic theory to financial markets, is according to some 'the science that aligns itself most closely with the perpetual concern of actuaries' in that it attempts to model and price financial risks.[17] The antecedents of the subject go back to the early twentieth century and the work of the French mathematician Louis Bachelier. It evolved slowly and was only seriously developed, mainly but not exclusively in American academic circles, from the 1950s, beginning with the work of Henry Markowitz on the basic principles of portfolio construction. By the 1980s, the scientific study of financial markets had found a place in many American MBA courses and the corresponding theory was being exported to London and other financial centres by the American investment banks.

This is not to say that British actuaries had made no contribution to investment theory up to that time. Such names as Dennis Weaver, George Ross Goobey, Leonard Hall and Peter Moody (*) (the initiator of stockbroker

research) come to mind, for their pioneering roles in serious institutional investment in equities and in the formation of the Society of Investment Analysts.[18] During the 1960s Gordon Pepper produced important papers on the mathematics of the fixed-income market and on the importance of monetary economics. In the 1970s, however, with new openings for actuaries in pensions consulting and the large-scale emergence of unit-linked contracts, attention had shifted away from investment and back to traditional fields. Little was done to further the study of financial economics during the 1980s except by two prominent actuaries, Robert Clarkson and David Wilkie, who held opposing theories. Through the 1990s a group of younger actuaries who had avidly embraced financial economics remained at odds with those as yet unconvinced of its blanket applicability, while the majority, holding moderate views, 'tended to keep their heads down for fear of being shot at by the committed idealogues from either extreme'.[19]

Whether actuaries espouse financial economics wholeheartedly or with reservations, there is no longer any doubt about the subject's influence. For some years, following the example of actuarial studies in the United States, it has been included in the actuarial training given by British universities. Several specific models to which it has given rise have come into widespread use. They and the subject's theoretical applications have led to what Bill Abbott has called 'wholesale changes in the nature of the products traded on the market and the ability to manage funds in an apparently more structured fashion':[20] that is, the development and trading of derivative products such as futures, options and swaps. Given the danger of an improper assessment of the risk being run, the prudent influence that can be exercised by a fund manager who is also an actuary can be valuable. The extent to which the principles of modern financial economic theory should influence actuarial science and practice continues to give rise to lively discussion. It is generally accepted that some aspects of the theory can provide useful insights into complex situations. Another welcome aspect is the emphasis placed on the need for transparency, including assessments based on current market conditions. The emphasis on up-to-date market values as the best available measure of worth is less welcome to many actuaries, who point out that the market value of shares on a particular day may be influenced by considerations of marginal supply and demand, liquidity and short-term 'sentiment' as well as by more fundamental considerations.[21] Different ideas of the role of actuarial judgement and about the degree to which logic and long-term views inform investors' decisions have provoked disagreement, but recently a more balanced view that holds that financial economics and actuarial methodologies are complementary has gained and seems to be holding the middle ground.[22]

The work of some 7 per cent of actuaries can be categorised as falling under the general heading of investment. Some are concerned with aspects of institutional investment, while others work as consultants, perhaps helping to determine an overall investment strategy for their clients. Despite the growing presence of actuaries in other types of investment work, it is still likely that most people have heard of them in the context of investment indices, with which they have been associated since the 1920s. From 1992 Richard Pain was the profession's representative on the Steering Committee overseeing the management of the new indices created to supplement the original 'Footsie' 500 and All-Share compilations: the FTSE 350 Index of the top 350 companies, the FTSE Mid 250 Index covering the next 250 companies after the top 100, and the Stock Exchange's Eurotrack Index. The profession has continued to be involved in the construction of share indices in conjunction with the *Financial Times*, mentioned earlier, notably the expanded FTSE All-Share Index in 1997. Actuaries have imposed rigorous criteria for the inclusion of companies in an index that ensure quality and reliability. Experience with index construction has drawn actuaries into the related fields of performance measurement, passive fund management and investment strategy. The measurement of past performance, an essentially statistical task, has become a significant industry owing much to actuarial input.[23]

There have always been a few actuaries who have had a more direct involvement in the investment markets, working for firms of stockbrokers, or as portfolio managers and investment analysts. Others have provided the tools and theory underlying such activity. David Wilkie, for example, has designed investment models for the stock market, and Andrew Wise has developed the theory of optimising portfolios. Fund management and investment management are activities to which actuaries are well suited, since their training equips them not only to measure performance but to involve themselves in investment strategy and the calculation of any associated risks. They can often provide useful insights into the relationship between risk and reward, illustrating them with statistical models for long periods of past performance. With the development of more sophisticated quantitative investment techniques actuaries have had a definite edge thanks to their understanding of risk and probability. As consultants, their involvement can assist decision-makers by clarifying the implications and possible outcomes of alternative courses of action. The long-term perspective they bring to the investment of institutional funds, where different future scenarios may lead not only to distinctive investment returns but also to changes in the value of the institution's liabilities, is of particular benefit.[24]

In this context, one of the actuary's basic tools since the late 1980s has been asset liability modelling, specifically as applied to the problem of asset allocation. The practical work was stimulated by papers published by David Wilkie and Andrew Wise (*) on the matching of assets to liabilities and on portfolio selection. The technique is basically an updated version of the immunization and matching theory of the 1950s, and involves the projection of assets and liabilities through a range of possible economic scenarios. This may be done to test a fund's solvency, or to evaluate and compare alternative financial strategies.

Through today's vastly increased and much cheaper computer power, multiple simulations of the future funding levels emerging from a variety of investment policies can be produced. Future liabilities can be 'hedged' through the construction of an appropriate portfolio, taking into account the risk tolerance and desired level of future surplus of a given fund. There are a number of methods of valuing assets and future liabilities, the crucial point being that the method used to value both should be consistent. (Asset liability modelling is also frequently applied in other fields outside that of pure investment: for example, in reinsurance. It has become a major area of work for the consulting actuarial partnerships, which use it to help clients – pension fund trustees, for instance – towards a better understanding of the options arising from a variety of investment strategies and asset allocations.)

A further investment field that has been much influenced by asset liability modelling is the corporate finance area of investment banking, where actuarial skills and understanding of derivatives can be used in the construction of complex products tailored to the needs of corporate clients. The work of actuaries in corporate finance usually combines risk and finance and often requires reassessment over periods extending many years into the future. Some have become involved in structured finance, alternative risk transfer, credit derivatives and other relatively esoteric financial instruments, while others have taken up risk management. One has started a commercial on-line bank for a large insurance company.[25] A few – too few, according to Paul Thornton, who created a Working Party to address the situation – have gone into banking.[26]

Corporate finance has been one route – but not the only one – to another of the profession's 'wider fields', the appraisal of capital projects. These are large-scale projects, often of long duration, that involve the initial investment of a capital sum on the basis that the project will generate returns on the initial investment during its lifetime. Actuaries can add a great deal to such endeavours through analysing the risks and calculating the costs involved over long periods, the skills needed being similar to those developed in the context of life assurance and pension funds. Despite the obvious usefulness of such advice to decision-makers, a survey conducted by the Confederation of British Industry in 1994 revealed that only one-quarter of British manufacturing companies were using any form of quantified risk assessment in appraising projects.[27] There are numerous examples of projects that have exceeded their anticipated time and cost and which might have benefited from such appraisal: Concorde, the Channel Tunnel, the Jubilee Line Extension and the British Library are only a few of the most notorious. The cost of the new British Library, for example, rose from an initial estimate of £116 million to an eventual £511 million, while its completion time was double the original estimate of ten years. More recently, as an appreciation of the value of risk assessment has grown, actuaries have assisted in the appraisal of, among other projects, the Scottish Air Transport Control System, the Nottingham Light Railway and the Derbyshire Health Project.

Some of the first capital projects involving actuaries stemmed from the Government-sponsored Private Finance Initiative. These projects – often social ones such as hospitals or schools – represent partnerships between the public and private sectors. In a public sector project, the private sector participates by funding and delivering a service (for example, a proportion of the beds in a hospital) for which the public sector then makes repayment over a period of years. Risk is thus redirected from the public to the private sector and the private sector's incentive to deliver on time and to an agreed standard is harnessed for public benefit. Not all such projects run smoothly, however, and it was partly to improve the process that a team from the Institute and Faculty of Actuaries led by Chris Lewin (*) worked closely with the Institution of Civil Engineers to devise a risk management methodology for capital projects. Launched in July 1998, 'Risk Analysis and Management of Projects' was published as *The RAMP Handbook* and aims to enable users to identify, evaluate, reduce and control any kind of risk and uncertainty during the life cycle of a project. One key aspect is that it facilitates the assessment of a range of possible financial outcomes from the project, allowing for risk. Detailed risk analysis can also help businesses to draw up plans to mitigate risks and so reduce potential liabilities. The RAMP method has applications to other kinds of projects than construction – trading operations, loans, privatisations and product launches come to mind – and a potential usership that could include government and local authorities as well as companies and banks. The elimination of costly and wasteful misjudgements is of benefit in any situation, but in large-scale projects such as these, the dispassionate and objective analysis that actuaries can contribute is surely an essential basic ingredient. RAMP is continuing to attract widespread interest as a useful and practical framework for managing project risks and a second edition of *The RAMP Handbook* was published in 2002.

Some actuaries working in the capital projects field assert that the starting point for any participant in the appraisal process – whether actuary, accountant, engineer or legal practitioner – is an approach that is flexible, prepared to learn from others and able to forsake a degree of security for the chance to do something different. A capital project involves the participating actuary in a team effort that draws upon the skills of other professions in a way that is both demanding and stimulating. He or she must be cognisant of a variety of factors that may impinge on decision-making: national and local tax, environmental issues and social legislation, for example, as well as the purely technical factors that will determine how and where a capital project is situated and develops. Those who have worked on capital projects have found it satisfying to bring into being something beneficial and lasting. This is particularly true of projects in developing countries, where they create infrastructure and employment opportunities.[28]

Another 'wider field' for actuaries has been health and care, with some actuaries working for private health insurance providers and others for the National

Health Service and its associated trusts, purchasing authorities and general practitioner fundholders. The demographic trends prevailing in the UK and the rest of the developed world ensure that health and care will continue to be a growth area in which actuaries will be greatly in demand. The actuarial skill-mix is particularly well suited to the design and funding of healthcare systems, including retirement homes and long-term healthcare facilities. In developing countries, where healthcare systems have only recently come into being, regular monitoring by actuaries contributes to the likelihood that the systems will be able to meet the demands made upon them over time. Similarly, the necessary interaction between the actuary, emphasising the long-term view, and local authorities responsible for policy development can assist in creating greater stability.

The Institute and Faculty have backed up the penetration of the 'wider fields' by members of the profession through the work of the Board which from 1994 was dedicated to these areas. By 1997 the Wider Fields Board encompassed the work of four Committees: Investment, Capital Projects (soon to be renamed Corporate Finance), Health and Care, and Personal Financial Planning. In addition the Board coordinated the profession's participation in dialogue with other organisations seeking to formulate policy on the question of genetic testing and insurance. Personal damages was a further area in which the profession continued to be involved. The long struggle to gain acceptance for the Ogden tables came to a jubilant end when the Civil Evidence Act 1995 enshrined them in legislation. They could now be used as admissible evidence in proceedings for damages without requiring further expert evidence. The growing acceptance of actuarial evidence in the courts had already led to the issue of a specific guidance note on 'The Actuary as Expert Witness' (GN24) a year earlier. (In July 1999 would come the landmark ruling of the House of Lords in the case of *Wells v. Wells*, which established the principle of using the yield on index-linked gilts for assessing damages in personal accident cases. Sir Michael Ogden lived to see the fourth edition of the tables, published in 2000.)

Some of the social issues included in the profession's 'wider fields' were the subjects of an increasing level of public interest and debate. In the belief that the profession could contribute greatly to the development of policy on these issues, and that a stronger focus was needed on investment matters, the Wider Fields Board was later (in 1999) divided into two new Boards. The Finance and Investment Board, with its Banking Group and Risk Management Task Force, now works closely with academic actuaries in encouraging research in the theory and methodology of finance and investment. It also makes its own contribution to the profession's education, CPD and public relations effort, with the aim of adding to the number of actuaries whose work lies outside life assurance, pensions and general insurance.

The other new Board was concerned with social policy and took over some historic areas that required monitoring as well as some recent ones that had captured public attention. All of them – the ageing population, damages, the environment, genetics, health and care, pension provision and personal financial planning – require long-term perspectives and the clarity that soundly based projections can provide. The promotion of research in all these areas plays a major part in the Board's objective of contributing to government social policy and increasing the profession's involvement in issues of public interest. In January 2002, for example, it mounted in Edinburgh the profession's first conference on ageing ("The Ageing Population – Benefit or Burden?"), with an international array of speakers on demography, economics, social policy and personal finance, and former BBC Reith lecturer Tom Kirkwood, Professor of Gerontology at Newcastle University, as the keynote speaker.

CHAPTER TEN
TIME PRESENT AND TIME PAST

Genetics will have an increasingly important role in the future. Here, for the cover of *Nature* magazine, the human genome is represented by a composite photograph showing the array of humanity that incorporates the image of the double helix.

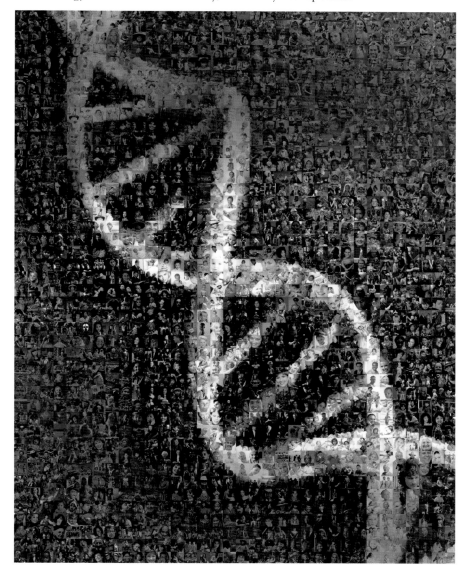

While all of the issues considered by the Social Policy Board are topical, the one which has perhaps attracted most attention is genetics, thanks to recent developments in genetic science and the confusion that has arisen about the impact of genetic testing on the insurance industry. As a paper presented to the Institute and Faculty in February 2003 expressed it, there existed 'a commonly held and deep-seated fear that increased knowledge of any genetic mutations may render individuals uninsurable'.[29] Insurers, for their part, were concerned about 'adverse selection', a term designating situations in which people have more information about their level of risk than they are prepared to divulge to the insurer, and use this to their advantage by purchasing insurance, or more of it. Public discussion of the questions arising from the advent of genetic testing in the early 1990s resulted in a polarising of views: to insurers, it seemed a point of principle that applicants should disclose all the relevant information, whereas civil liberties and other groups held just as strongly the opinion that people should not be penalised for their genetic inheritance.[30]

In 1997, following the adoption by the Council of Europe of a convention stating that genetic testing may only be carried out for purposes of health-care or research, in the United Kingdom the Human Genetics Advisory Commission issued *The Implications of Genetic Testing for Insurance*. This Report limited the insurers' requirement for disclosure while concluding that a permanent ban on the use of genetic tests in insurance would be inappropriate. Instead, it recommended a moratorium which was agreed to by the Association of British Insurers (ABI). This was the first of three moratoria; the most recent is set to last until 2006. The Institute and Faculty have contributed to the clarification of the points at issue in several ways. During several years when the subject was becoming widely discussed, submissions were made to public bodies and public lectures held. The Institute also coordinated support from, among others, the Royal Society, the ABI, the Wellcome Trust, the Nuffield Foundation and the Consumers' Association to establish the UK Forum for Genetics and Insurance (UKFGI) in 1998, and it continues to provide the secretariat to the UKFGI. Since speculative views about the financial implications of genetic testing lacked quantitative evidence to support them, actuarial research was directed towards beginning to supply such evidence. Through statistical modelling, it has been possible to portray a variety of possible outcomes and suggest a range of interpretations and responses to each. This information has been made widely available, both to the public and to policy-makers such as the Human Genetics Commission and the Department of Health. The whole complex field of genetics is evolving rapidly. Future developments are likely to lead to improved mortality rates and reveal more about genetically caused predispositions to illness. The pricing of insurance products may be affected, while counselling may come to be widely used in conjunction with genetic testing. Insurers will very probably be faced with more potential conflicts between their traditional freedom in underwriting, designed to avoid financial strains that could endanger solvency, and practices that are considered fair and socially desirable.

The monitoring and response to developments in life insurance, pensions and general insurance have been the responsibility of the Boards dedicated to these areas since 1994 and reporting to the FIMC. Like all the Boards, they are the profession's interface with the relevant organisations in the wider world, whether at a given moment this means the Treasury or the Inland Revenue, the GAD or the Financial Services Authority (FSA), or other bodies – the Accounting Standards Board, the ABI, Lloyd's or the Institute of Chartered Accountants. The 1990s brought a great deal of new legislation, as well as the amendment of existing law, related to pensions and to insurance in all its forms. There were also important changes in regulation and supervision, and the extension or alteration of actuarial responsibilities, as in the creation of the role of the Scheme Actuary under the Pensions Act 1995, and the requirement, effectively a statutory one,[31] that from year-end 1997 all Lloyd's active syndicates obtain an actuarial opinion on their reserves. Such changes have been anticipated or reflected in professional guidance. One aspect of the work of the Life, Pensions and General Insurance Boards is the preparation and periodic revision of Guidance Notes; well over half the existing ones (thirty-six at the time of writing) date from 1990 or later. Some of the earlier ones have gone through repeated updates as the relevant legislation has altered, with GN11 ('Retirement Pension Schemes – Transfer Values'), first applied in 1985, currently in its eighth version.[32]

The work of the Boards at a given moment encompasses a range of topical issues on which the profession wishes and is expected to contribute a view. Many of the requests for such opinions come from government and regulatory bodies. Besides the 'demographic timebomb' about which the Institute has been warning successive governments since the 1950s, and the genetic issues currently the focus of attention, the topics considered in recent years have included fair value accounting, permanent health insurance costs, Individual Savings Accounts (ISAs), the simplification of private pensions and the creation of Stakeholder pensions, the proposed raising of State pension age, motor insurance premiums, retirement options (including annuities), environmental change and equity release schemes. The decline of stock market values since the late 1990s, after a seemingly endless bull market, is challenging the future of with-profits business, the two most publicised issues arising from this being endowment mortgage shortfalls and the lack of transparency of with-profits contracts. These and other issues have been the subjects of position statements developed by Board working parties. Once approved by the FIMC, they are made available to government, the financial community and the media and appear on the profession's website.

More detailed responses are on occasion requested by government, sometimes with reference to Green Papers or as evidence to Select Committee inquiries. There have also been submissions to the major inquiries into current issues, mainly relating to insurance and pensions. There was significant input to the Myners Review of Institutional Investment, and Mike Pomery (*) and Wendy Beaver represented both the Faculty and the Institute in the broadly based Consultation Panel set up under the auspices of the Department for Work and Pensions to explore the options for replacing the Minimum Funding Requirement. Substantial contributions were also made to the Government-appointed review of the financial services industry chaired by Ron Sandler and the review of pension provision chaired by Alan Pickering. The profession has also launched its own independent inquiries. Sir John Banham was asked to lead a Committee of senior people from outside the profession to consider the Provision of Financial Information and Advice, and reported in March 2001. In December 2000, as has already been mentioned in connection with the Equitable Life, the Corley Inquiry into the adequacy of the professional guid-

ance given by the Institute and Faculty was set in motion, reporting in September 2001. (This was the profession's first purely internal inquiry and among its five members were two non-actuaries.) In September 2002 the profession submitted to HM Treasury some extensive comments on the draft of a new edition of the Government's 'Green Book' on the appraisal of public-sector projects.

The Institute continues its support for the international development of the actuarial profession. The actuarial education initiative begun in Hungary, Poland and Bulgaria has been extended to Slovakia, Russia and almost every other country of the former

Institute President Jeremy Goford presents Chinese actuarial students of the Shanghai University of Finance and Economics with their diplomas.

Soviet bloc. The basic actuarial diploma course was well established in most of the eastern European countries by 1997 and the advanced course somewhat later. Both in these countries and in China, senior members of the profession have been invited to present the diplomas – a happy experience for all concerned. Seminars and courses for students and for teachers of actuarial studies continue to be run. The International Promotion and Education Fund continues to support – and the Institute to provide the organising power for – the meetings that have taken place in almost every year since 1994, in such widely separated venues as Minsk (1995), Accra (1999) and Kuala Lumpur (2001). The ambassadorial role of Chris Daykin has been a key element in furthering not only the manner and substance of actuarial studies abroad, but in spreading respect for the profession at every level.

In Europe, by 1992 the work of the Groupe Consultatif resulted in an agreement concerning reciprocal recognition of actuarial associations within the European Community, and a shared code of professional conduct. The Groupe, composed of representatives of fifteen associations from twelve countries, had also achieved harmony on recommended practice guidelines in life insurance, pensions and general insurance. In Europe, perhaps more than in most parts of the world, the professional role for actuaries was increasing rapidly, but the trend towards a truly international profession was notable almost everywhere. Neither the Groupe nor the IAA was felt to be an adequate vehicle for dealing with international problems in a coordinated way, or at least this was the conclusion reached by some who discussed the matter informally at the 24th International Congress in Montreal in 1992. The Groupe Consultatif was a permanent committee of individual representatives of European associations, while the IAA was an association of nearly seven thousand individual members drawn from forty-seven actuarial associations. A small group headed by Paul McCrossan, at that time President of the Canadian Institute of Actuaries, agreed to work towards the establishment of a new international body to coordinate standards for an increasingly global profession. The progress towards its formation was not without controversy, but the 'McCrossan Group' completed the planning in the comparatively brief time of two years and presented the idea to the IAA Council meeting in 1994. At the 25th International Congress in Brussels a year later – coincidentally, the year of the IAA's centenary – the IAA Council approved the formation of the International Forum of Actuarial Associations (IFAA) as a 'section' of the IAA. It was the third such section, after ASTIN, the Association for the Actuarial Study of Non-Life Insurance, and AFIR, Actuarial Approach to Financial Risk, and had the stated aims of promoting high standards of professionalism and scientific development on an international level, adhering to a common code of conduct, sharing common standards of practice, and working towards a unified core of actuarial education.

At the IFAA's first meeting, at which Paul McCrossan was elected Chairman and Chris Daykin Deputy Chairman, thirty-nine national associations were represented. Institute and Faculty representatives at once started a debate within the IAA Council which resulted in the appointment of a Committee of six, with Hans Bühlmann as chairman and Roger Corley as a member, to consider the future relationship between the IAA and the IFAA. During the next two years the potential advantages of allowing the 'section' to take the lead in discussions with other international bodies representing associations became more apparent, particularly in responding to proposals from the International Accounting Standards Committee (IASC) for revised versions of international accounting standards. Deliberations along these lines eventually led to the 'reverse takeover' at the 26th International Congress in Birmingham in 1998, whereby the IFAA's constitution was adopted by the IAA and the IFAA was dissolved. The IAA now concentrates on cooperation among the various national associations, which represent some 98 per cent of the world's actuaries. Its old tasks of organising congresses and maintaining membership contacts are continued by its Committee for Services to Individual Members.[33] Membership of the IAA has continued to increase, and it takes a special interest in assisting newly formed associations to develop appropriate standards. Its interaction with other international organisations has extended to include the International Association of Insurance Supervisors, the International Accounting Standards Board, the Organisation for Economic Co-operation and Development, the World Bank and others.

The Institute and Faculty remain leading members of the international actuarial community. One telling indication of this is the success with which aspects of the UK profession's mode of operation have been exported to other countries. It is natural that the English-speaking Commonwealth countries – at least until they became well established – derived much of their education and examination systems from the British models. (The Actuarial Society of New South Wales, for example, from which today's Institute of Actuaries of Australia is descended, was founded by William Day, the son of Archibald Day, an early President of the Institute.[34]) Although these countries later adopted systems better suited to their own requirements, the old affinity remained and it is not surprising to find that the Appointed Actuary system has found fertile soil abroad. Much of the credit for this again must go to Chris Daykin, whose tireless advocacy has aided the transplanting process. Hong Kong, Singapore and Malaysia have Appointed Actuaries, as do South Africa and Australia; Canada has adapted many features of the system to a different legal and regulatory environment and applied it also to general insurance. Ireland operates on almost the same basis as the UK, while a number of the continental European countries follow the example of Germany in having 'responsible actuaries' with some of the same functions as the Appointed Actuary. Japan has introduced

These striking commemorative windows, now in Staple Inn Hall, were gifts to the Institute on its 150th anniversary in 1998 from (left to right) the American Academy of Actuaries, the Canadian Institute of Actuaries, the Society of Actuaries and the Faculty of Actuaries.

appointed actuaries, and issued guidance which is strongly influenced by GN1. It is hoped that, as a culture of professionalism is created in the countries of eastern Europe where actuarial education is proceeding apace, newly trained actuaries will assume some responsibilities from the supervisory authorities, and so place the nascent insurance industries on a steady course.[35]

The 26th International Congress, held in Birmingham from 7 to 12 June 1998, was the fourth to be held in the UK. It was also one of a series of events held to mark the Institute's 150th anniversary. Its theme, 'Unity and Diversity', became a living reality with the attendance of nearly a thousand actuaries from around the world. The growth of the actuarial family since the previous Congress held in the UK (the 17th) in 1964 was very marked: whereas delegates from twenty-two countries had attended the earlier occasion, on this one, sixty countries were represented. More than 160 scientific papers and national reports were given in a week-long schedule of plenary and specialist sessions. The patron of the Congress was HRH the Duke of Edinburgh, and the Institute – via Her Majesty the Queen's representative, the Lord Lieutenant of the West Midlands – sent Her Majesty a Loyal Address reaffirming the aims of the Royal Charter. A range of other events was held. An exhibition devised by Sally Grover (the Institute's Senior Librarian) in conjunction with the Axiom Design Partnership and entitled 'Modelling the Future' was displayed in Staple Inn Hall before travelling around the country, ending at Maclaurin House, the Faculty's new home, in time for the Edinburgh Festival. The publication of *Life, Death and Money*, edited by Derek Renn, brought together eleven specialist essays covering the breadth of the actuary's work. The revival of a 300-year-old tradition in the form of the now annual 'Staple Inn Reading' connected the Institute firmly to the history of the area around Staple Inn, and especially to Gray's Inn, to which it had been affiliated in centuries past when it was an Inn of Chancery. On 12 May, Charles Sparrow QC, Master of Gray's Inn, was received by Duncan Ferguson and senior members of Council and escorted to the Hall, where he duly read aloud Sir George Buck's 'The Fayrest Inn', written in 1631. The Institute's birthday, the date on which it had been founded 150 years before – 8 July 1848 – was commemorated by an evening garden party at Gray's Inn, attended by members of the Institute and Faculty and complete with fire-eaters, men on stilts and other amusements.

Such celebrations served to underline the unifying quality of the Institute, 150 years after the events

CHAPTER TEN
TIME PRESENT AND TIME PAST

The revival of the Staple Inn Readings has renewed the ancient links with Gray's Inn and brought some enjoyable pageantry into the life of the Institute. Here, in July 1999, Staple Inn Reader Dame Mary Arden and Institute President Paul Thornton follow Vic Maddocks (Beadle of the Worshipful Company of Actuaries) bearing the mace. In procession are Fraser Low (Faculty President 1998–2000), Sos Green (Master of the Worshipful Company), David Paul (Faculty of Actuaries Council member), Jeremy Goford (Institute Vice-President, later President 2002–04) and Masters Sparrow and Butcher (Utter Barristers of Gray's Inn).

– only in retrospect seen as momentous – that had brought it into being. This has, however, been challenged by the continuing trend since the 1970s for the life insurance companies to move out of London. Actuaries have become widely dispersed around the country and regional actuarial societies have been established in a number of major cities. The regional societies facilitate the exchange of ideas and social contacts through their own programmes and dining clubs, and provide CPD locally. The dispersal of the profession has reduced the numbers at Institute sessional meetings and dining club events,[36] but generally speaking these still enjoy a respectable turn-out.

Far more important than geographical proximity is the fact that members of the Institute remain bound by common ideals, expressed in its founding documents and Royal Charter, and also by a corpus of Bye-laws and professional guidance. Howard Webb (*), whose twenty-five years on Council have led to close involvement with both, sees control of its own governance and guidance as central to the cohesiveness of the profession, and to its very identity. (The price of this independence is, of course, to administer it well and in the public interest.[37]) The qualifying process, and after it, CPD, creates a sense of common endeavour and high standards among Fellows. Despite the opposing social trends, the Institute continues to draw members together, beginning with the Staple Inn Actuarial Society or SIAS, formerly the Students' Society, at whose general meetings many young actuaries first cross intellectual sabres with an audience of their peers. Then there are sessional meetings, at which the latest investigative findings are opened up to informed debate. Transcripts appear promptly in the *BAJ*, which (like *The Actuary*) is received by every member. The need to keep an ever more widely dispersed membership in touch

Chris Daykin President 1994–96 presents Howard Webb with his Finlaison Medal, in recognition of his outstanding contribution to professional guidance for Members of the Institute.

has been met by the creation of a website providing exceptional support, as well as extensive information about the profession. Similarly, the Library at Napier House provides a postal loans service to members, while both it and the Library at Staple Inn handle members' – and particularly Students' – requests for information.

Its past has always been important to the Institute, but so too are its links to the wider community. Occasions such as the Biennial Dinner, the Staple Inn Readings, the President's Dinner and, more recently, the creation of Honorary Fellows drawn from outside the profession, celebrate the Institute but also emphasise the wider context in which actuaries operate. The educational and

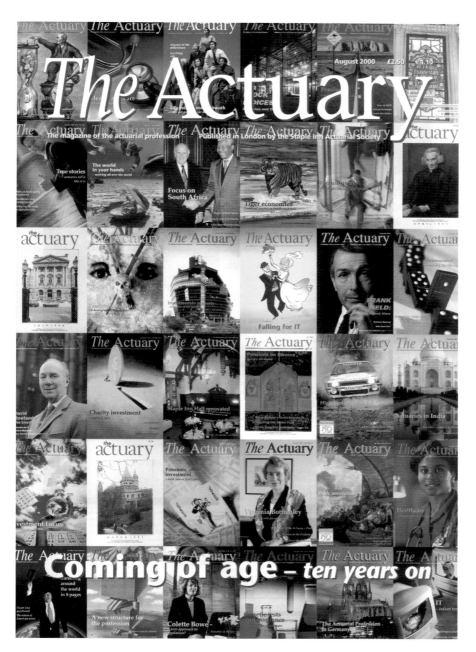

Ten years of *The Actuary*
magazine are recalled by this
lively cover showing a selection
of past issues.

charitable activities of the Worshipful Company of Actuaries have given the
profession a recognised collective presence in the City of London. And, finally,
there is Staple Inn itself: one of London's more enchanting corners now as in
1887 when the Institute took up residence there. The profession remains quiet-
ly proud of its presence in Staple Inn, and what the place has meant to generations of actuaries is probably beyond expressing in words. Frank Guaschi, who

was born nearby and bears the distinction of having been pushed to the Staple Inn garden in his pram, speaks for many in describing his deep respect for his profession as somehow mirrored in the dignity of the Institute's surroundings. Yet far from being some museum setting lost in medieval or eighteenth-century reverie, Staple Inn is daily recalled to a place in the modern world as major issues are analysed and debated within its walls. Few buildings with a history as long as Staple Inn's could say as much, if stones could speak.

Within the Institute the effort to raise the profile of the profession and to improve actuarial education was ongoing. The financial services industry was experiencing rapid change and there was a sense within the Institute that the position of actuaries within life insurance companies was gradually being diminished. Actuarial skills were being put to excellent use by Appointed Actuaries; the unique perspectives they possessed were often brought to bear on mergers and acquisitions or on financial management. Only those with demonstrated management skills continued to fill senior posts, however, in contrast to the situation in the 1970s, when a good number of chief executives and senior managers were actuaries. (There was later a certain amount of debate about whether this represented a loss of influence in the management of life insurance companies, but that is how matters were seen in the mid-1990s.) Computer advances were observed to be changing the nature of actuarial tasks, and closer cooperation with other professions was becoming a reality for more actuaries at a time when bancassurers were entering the marketplace. To some practitioners it appeared that actuaries were losing ground, both in these new entities (there were few actuaries working in the banking sector) and in relation to money purchase pension schemes that were becoming more common.

In addition, by the end of 1998, its anniversary year, the Institute was having to field unfavourable press comment arising from the problems of the insurance and pensions industry referred to in an earlier chapter, and with which actuaries were – correctly or not – identified to varying degrees. The economic downturn that began slightly later took its toll on with-profits business, with negative results for pension schemes, endowment mortgages and any other financial product dependent on equity values. As the insurance industry was widely criticised, the actuarial profession came in for its share of the opprobrium. The old charge of incomprehensibility, of hiding behind a mystique, returned as suspicion, and actuaries found that their profession had indeed become better known, but not in the way that the 'Strategy for the 1990s' had ever intended.

It would have been surprising if the profession had not experienced something of a crisis of confidence when financial products began to perform badly, and indeed, this does seem to have happened. The criticism, however exaggerated or misplaced, could neither be ignored nor taken overly to heart, although two things appeared indisputable. One was that despite all the Institute's efforts, the press and public still did not understand the profession. The second was that the profession had to be the agent of change in improving this, as well as in repositioning itself so that the value of its strengths was evident. Together with the feeling that some fresh thinking was in order as the century drew to a close, these conclusions led Paul Thornton, President from 1998 to 2000, to put in motion a major reappraisal of the profession, its strengths, roles and aims, which was carried forward jointly with the President of the Faculty, Fraser Low. The shift in thinking brought about by this exercise envisaged the profession some twenty years in the future – and then identified what it must do and be to arrive there from where it presently was. The resulting document was called 'Vision and Values', and represented the views of actuaries from all over the country, not just London, about the future direction the profession should take.[38] 'Vision and Values' begins from the basic premises above. The 'Vision' defined the actuary of 2020 as working in a wider range of businesses than at present, and equipped by training for a career in finance, with a special capability for work involving uncertainty and risk. From the vantage point of that future date, what actuaries are and do, how they are educated, how they serve the public interest both individually and as a professional body, are clearly set out. The 'Values' reaffirmed are expertise, integrity, professionalism, serving the public interest, and adding value.

The phrase 'Making financial sense of the future', conceived during Duncan Ferguson's Presidency and introduced early in Paul Thornton's, was part of an extensive preliminary public relations and marketing plan that was a novel initiative for the Institute. The six words encapsulated the profession's problem-solving approach: as a later President has said, 'If we had wanted to say only that actuaries make financial *models* of the future, we could have done so.' Rather, the 'highly practical, innovative, versatile, and numerate' people who make up the profession specialise in providing solutions to problems involving financial risk and contingent events, especially where quantitative theory can be applied.[39] The consensus achieved around this bye-line and around the principles and aims of 'Vision and Values' allowed for some significant shifts of emphasis in the work of the Institute. The division of the Wider Fields Board into the Finance and Investment and Social Policy Boards has already been mentioned: this gave Board prominence to the profession's corporate finance and investment activities, while the range and importance of the topics remaining as 'wider fields' then received the greater focus they merited. The Professional Affairs Board was encouraged to develop a more proactive outlook and a greater sensitivity to public interest issues. Actuarial education was considered in an international context, and is discussed below.

'Vision and Values' sought to move the thinking about the profession going on within it into a longer time-frame with wider horizons. It has provided the excellent basis from which the profession has moved forward since it was launched. The continuing test will be the means by which, over the next several years, the 'Vision' is realised. At the time it was conceived there was still

Alan Fishman FIA presented the Institute with the splendid tapestry that today hangs in Staple Inn Hall, as a way of expressing his gratitude to the profession. Designed and woven by Jennie Moncur, the tapestry contains symbolic references to the actuarial profession and the Institute. Some echo the Institute coat of arms, while others – the oak leaves, representing the dominant wood in Staple Inn Hall, and the owl from the Faculty crest – draw from the Institute's closest historical associations.

much to be done, not only to change public perceptions but to change the actuarial reality. Since 1999, the issues raised and the action required have been given concentrated attention from designated steering groups or committees, and where appropriate their conclusions have been published. Successive Presidents Peter Clark (*) (2000–02) and Jeremy Goford (2002–04) have carried on the process begun by Paul Thornton. Each has identified specific aspects of the 'Vision' as priorities, but broadly considered they can be reduced to three: improved communications, the need to broaden the profession, and the need to be seen to act in the public interest.

Chief among these has been improved communications. In an age in which advanced mathematical study is declining, when the technological and information revolutions have created a more widespread but still superficial financial literacy, it is unlikely that many people today, apart from those working in contiguous fields, really understand what actuaries *do*. In an earlier age – in 1949, perhaps – this would have mattered less, because actuaries could take a justified pride in the trust reposed in them as professionals and in their judgement as experts. The preservation of educational standards was, to successive Councils, far more important than the question of whether other professionals, the press, or the general public understood the value of actuarial work. Fifty years later, that scenario has changed completely. In the consumer-oriented society of the third millennium, trust has been replaced by the demand for openness. Lines of responsibility are expected to be clear, and mistakes rectified, possibly by some form of compensation. Not only is what is done scrutinised, but how, by whom and with what effect. Operating in a business context in which these conditions are assumed has made the need to accommodate them important to every profession.

For those professions involved in financial matters the need is greater because public disillusion, arising out of recent events, is also greater. The need to communicate clearly with the public is matched by the need to communicate clearly with members of other professions. Considering the future, with its likely further convergence of financial services, possible regulatory changes, and 'wider fields' inviting greater actuarial penetration, it may be that the actuarial profession will have to make a greater communications effort than some others. Peter Clark has suggested that without the ability to communicate ideas to a variety of audiences, the actuary of 2020 is less likely to be 'working in a wider range of businesses than at present' than to be confined to technical financial work.[40] Actuaries must make that greater effort because unless they do, they cannot fulfil the responsibility that is an intrinsic part of their identity. As Clifford Sharp (*) recently reminded the profession,

We do not want to be regarded merely as highly efficient technicians ... but rather as those with a broader view of the realities of life who can be relied upon to provide a grasp of the wider, and often more important, features of the major problems arising

from the need to see [that] a reasonable degree of financial security is available for members of our community.[41]

Jeremy Goford (*) has pointed out the link between communicating ideas well, extending the profession's influence, and putting its knowledge at the service of society. Actuaries are, as he put it, 'the thinkers and interpreters of complex financial systems. We need to find ways to ensure that what we know is made more available for the benefit of our employers and clients and the public at large, and not left in the back room'.[42] While on an individual level the acquisition of communications skills falls within the remit of actuarial education, the Institute has set in train various initiatives to refresh the collective image and the external perceptions of the profession. In 2000 a Communications Committee was established with a brief to undertake a fundamental review of the way the profession markets and promotes itself to the media, government, the regulators and consumers, as well as to its own members. This has led to a new house-style and image and greater and more perceptive press coverage. The Committee was elevated to the status of a Board in 2002. Its role is proactive, in that it works with the other Boards to identify and anticipate issues on which the profession can usefully contribute an informed view, often in the form of position papers.

Much will depend on the education of future actuaries, which lies at the heart of the aim of broadening the profession. Among the external forces that may affect the design of future education are the roles that actuaries are likely to play in the business world, the globalisation of the actuarial profession, and competition from other professions for the best students. Arising from 'Vision and Values', a Working Party was appointed in 1999 to consider the development of an international education strategy. For the first time a global perspective was attempted, which involved consultation with the Society of Actuaries in the United States and the Institute of Actuaries of Australia, the IAA and Groupe Consultatif. In May 2000 an international education conference was held at Staple Inn and a set of principles developed that both retained the unique characteristics of actuarial education and introduced new emphases to equip future actuaries for a variety of emerging roles. The principles were seen as an overarching framework extending towards 2020, but within this a more proximate education strategy was devised, to be introduced in 2005. Recognising that actuaries needed both technical and applied knowledge, the new route to qualification will consist of 'core stages' in each, which will include a stronger focus on financial economics and new subjects such as business awareness and communications, and 'specialist stages' allowing considerable choice. Notable contributions to actuarial method, such as the concept of the actuarial control cycle developed by the Institute of Actuaries of Australia,[43] have been incorporated, and there is a refreshing awareness of the business and regulatory context in which actuaries work. The time needed to qualify should be four or five years, depending on whether entry comes at undergraduate or post-graduate level and whether study is pursued full- or part-time. While high standards will be upheld, there will be a shift in emphasis from knowledge *per se* to 'what actuaries know how to do', with the demonstration of actuarial skills being required at every stage. Whereas before, a large proportion of actuarial work had been based on established methodologies, the new programme seeks to provide a solid foundation which will prepare actuaries for positions in a broader range of environments, with further specialist study and CPD as needed.

Broadening the profession also implies broadening its appeal, its membership, and the thinking that drives it. Ways to achieve these goals are evolving from the communications and education initiatives. On the principle that thinkers from outside the profession can enrich its own thinking and assist in promoting the same objects as the Institute, in each of the past several years it has invited a number of outstanding scientists and academics, leading figures in the professions and a number prominent in insurance and the public service to become Honorary Fellows. This has injected new life into a custom that has existed since the Institute's earliest days. New perspectives on public issues are valuable, as are views of the profession itself as seen from other vantage points. Another measure has been to make it possible for members of other professions working in the same fields as a growing number of actuaries to become Affiliates of the Institute or Faculty. Part of the broadening process, as Jeremy Goford sees it, lies in actuaries adopting a more confident view of their own capabilities that is solidly based on competence, professionalism and the willingness to meet others – regulators, clients and experts from other disciplines – on a basis of mutual understanding.[44] Actuarial thinking can add value to almost any financial situation or analysis, and actuaries should not leave it to others to say so. In this, as in so much else, the proactive approach will serve both the profession and society best. As the late, revered Frank Redington affirmed, the actuary's real strength lies, not so much in techniques as in

a broad training whose firm roots are in mathematics and statistics, but whose branches reach out into commerce, investment, administration and all the bustle of humanity. It is not the tools he uses which make a great craftsman. It is the way he feels and thinks.

And while the actuary cannot (as some believe) foretell the future, 'What he can do and does is to sense the wide-ranging possibilities that the future may have in store and then to make them a living part of the present where decisions are made.'[45]

The principle that the Institute act 'in the public interest, to promote knowledge and research in all matters relevant to actuarial science and its application' is enshrined in its Royal Charter. This, however, refers to actions

MIND OVER DATA

AN ACTUARIAL HISTORY

Peter Clark, President 2000–02, presents a silver salver named for Thomas Bond Sprague to Professor Peter Goddard at the Centre for Mathematical Sciences at the University of Cambridge.

initiated by the Institute, rather than to the traditional assumption that as members of a profession, actuaries would always act in the public interest. It has always been part of the profession's ethic that the public interest also be served by the individual actuary's work or advice, in that this has been expected to be competent and trustworthy, independent, and performed or given with the best interests of the client in mind – in a word, *professional*. In fulfilling their statutory roles, which exist to ensure the protection of policyholders or consumers, and in following professional guidance, actuaries act in the public interest. In placing its expert knowledge and often unique perspective at the service of government and regulators to assist in the development of desirable policies, the profession also has a long and honourable record. Individual members of the Institute who have served on Royal Commissions and on government, public and external bodies of every kind, have clearly added to this public interest role. More recently, however, the ideal of acting *always* and *entirely* in the public interest has not been entirely free of perplexity for some individual actuaries, especially those wishing to develop the entrepreneurial skills necessary for senior management positions, and some who are employed by institutions. In 2002 a Working Party was appointed to consider the public interest stance of the profession and its interpretation.

Reaching an appropriate interpretation of what is meant by 'acting in the public interest' is one of the issues recently highlighted as being of particular importance for the actuarial profession in the immediate future. Achieving a measure of equilibrium in the debate about financial economics, and making the most of the opportunities presented by the advent of fair value accounting, are other matters which need to be settled. Perhaps the most problematical issues of all, at the time of writing, result from the dismal condition of the equity markets, and the effect of the decline in share values on the life insurance, pension and investment fields with which the profession has always been so closely associated. The events of the 1990s in all these areas – some little short of cataclysmic in their consequences for policyholders – have brought in their wake the likely restructuring of the regulatory system; the FSA now operates as the lead regulator under the Financial Services and Markets Act 2000, and the future of self-regulating entities, the Institute among them, is uncertain. The significance for the actuarial profession, and especially for the appointed actuary system, of the FSA's review of with-profits business is similarly unclear.

Current thinking within the Institute engages with this gamut of challenges and uncertainties, but endeavours not to be bound by them. The fulfilment of the Institute's obligations on a multitude of fronts – to Fellows and Students, to its international colleagues, to government and the regulatory bodies, to the industries with which the profession is intrinsically allied, and to the wider public – does not obscure the vision for the longer term, nor the ways in which the profession can put its values into practice in the more immediate future. Central to the latter is the emphasis placed on the profession's stance on public issues where its contribution is likely to be among the most expert available, and its voice, as a result, one of authority. The long-term objectives for 2020 set out in 'Vision and Values' will be well served by this focus at every intermediate stage by identifying consumer needs, and ensuring that the profession's views give a lead in any related public forum. The essential aim, whether short term or long, is that the thinking done within the Institute results in action – publications, conferences, research, or collaboration with other organisations – that not only repositions the profession in the public mind, but genuinely serves the public interest.

The world in which the Institute exists today may have altered out of all recognition from the one its founders knew, but they would recognise and claim that hope of placing their knowledge at the service of society as their own. It is the hallmark of all professions, and all professionals, whatever the individual qualification. The actuarial profession, as its earliest spokesmen often reminded Institute gatherings, had important things to say, and enjoyed an influence out of keeping with its numbers. That is no less true for today's profession, in a business context and a society that has even more need of independent and informed judgement. The difference is that the public trust that once went with influence now has to be earned, over and over again. That this applies on the personal as well as the collective level is so obvious as to be hardly worth stating: the actuarial profession's strength is every member of it, from the oldest Fellow to the newest Student. In the past, integrity was held to be the essence of the professional character. Today, that commitment to maintaining the highest ethical standards is no less present, but must in addition find expression in the ongoing acquisition of

MIND OVER DATA

competence, the willingness to communicate and share, and the ability to demonstrate an understanding of affairs from the standpoint of others. These attitudes are among the fundamentals that young actuaries absorb along with the latest modelling techniques. They are part of a commitment to the public interest that will be the Institute's priority as it moves towards 2020, but though they are phrased in the language of the new millennium, they are recognisably among the aims of the Institute's founders. Tomorrow's actuary will be no less a debtor to the profession than the most respected of its many great names have been. There is always, of course, the possibility of becoming as worthy an ornament.

The garden of Staple Inn, which won the City of London Best Kept Small Garden Award in 1995.

Notes to the chapters

ABBREVIATIONS

BAJ   *British Actuarial Journal*
JIA   *Journal of the Institute of Actuaries*
JIASS *Journal of the Institute of Actuaries Students' Society*
TFA   *Transactions of the Faculty of Actuaries*

CHAPTER ONE

1   Letter from Oliver D. Cumming to Harold F. Purchase, 23 June 1969. Institute of Actuaries Archives. Duncan Ferguson in his Presidential Address, 7 October 1996, cites a quotation from Suetonius's *De Vita Caesarum*: 'Pro Quinto Metello non inmerito Augustus existimat magis ab actuaris exceptam male subsequentibus verba dicentis quam ab ipso editam.' ('Augustus said that the "Defence of Quintus Metellus" could hardly have been published by Caesar himself, and that it appeared to be a version taken down by shorthand writers who could not keep up with his rapid delivery.') Gaius Suetonius Tranquillus, *The Twelve Caesars*, translated by Robert Graves, 1957, 33. T. E.Young's address to the Institute, 'The origin and development of scientific and professional societies', *JIA* 33 (1898), 453–485, has an appendix dedicated to the title of actuary.

2   Maurice Ogborn, *Equitable Assurances* (1962), 100–104.

3   *ibid.*, 85–97.

4   See Philip Gosden, *The Friendly Societies in England* (1961), 11.

5   *An Act for the further Protection and Encouragement of Friendly Societies, and for preventing Frauds and Abuses therein* … [60 Geo. C3], better known as the Friendly Societies Act 1819, specifies, concerning 'Restrictions upon dissolution of Society or Division of Funds', that the consent of the trustees is necessary for dissolution, and that this can not be given 'unless and until it shall have been certified by two or more professional actuaries or persons skilled in calculation'.

6   'Memoir of the late John Finlaison Esq., Actuary of the National Debt, Government Calculator, and President of the Institute of Actuaries', *Assurance Magazine and JIA* 10 (1861), 147–169. See also 'Memoir of the public services of the late John Finlaison Esq., Actuary of the National Debt, Government Calculator and President of the Institute of Actuaries', separately published and different.

7   D. O. Forfar, 'History of the development of the actuarial profession and of actuarial thought in Scotland', *Transactions of the 26th International Congress of Actuaries*, 7–12 June 1998, vol. 2, 451–479.

8   Quoted in G. H. Recknell, *The Actuaries' Club 1848–1948* (1948), 10.

9   *ibid.*, 16–18.

10 'Memoir of the late Griffith Davies, Esq.', *JIA* 5 (1855), 337–348.

11 Recknell (1948), 18.

12 R. C. Simmonds, *The Institute of Actuaries 1848–1948* (1948), 6.

13 On apprenticeship, see W. J. Reader, *Professional Men: the Rise of the Professional Classes in Nineteenth-century England* (1966), 116–126.

14 Simmonds (1948), 10–14.

15 Quoted in Recknell (1948), 33–34, and Simmonds (1948), 30. A further commentary on the formation, made by John Francis, the editor of *The Athenaeum,* in the issue of 22 July 1848, points to the wider view of actuarial work, which 'though at present it principally relates to *life* contingencies, yet must be held to include all *contingencies* to which calculation of probabilities can be applied'.

16 Quoted in Simmonds (1948), 31–32.

17 From 1866 it was known simply as the *Journal of the Institute of Actuaries*.

18 Simmonds (1948), 66–77. It should not be forgotten that attending a Council meeting in London involved a lengthy day's travel and possibly an overnight stay for someone coming from Edinburgh.

19 Quoted in R. C. Simmonds, 'The work of George King', *JIA* 64 (1933), 247.

20 Simmonds (1948), 88.

21 Simmonds, 'King', 247.
22 Simmonds (1948), 288, 291.
23 George King, 'Memoir of Dr Thomas Bond Sprague MA LLD', *JIA* 52 (1921), 241–259.
24 *ibid*., 245.
25 *ibid*., 247.
26 D. F. Renn, 'The road to Windsor: centenary of the Royal Charter of 1884', *JIA* 111 (1984), 224.
27 G. J. Lidstone, 'Memoir of Sir George Francis Hardy KCB', *JIA* 49 (1915), 8.
28 *ibid*., 10.
29 *Institute of Actuaries Year Book 1939–1940*, 5–6.
30 Simmonds (1948), 163.
31 H. J. Tappenden, 'Sir William Palin Elderton, KBE, PhD (Oslo)', *JIA* 88 (1962), 247–248.
32 Geoffrey Marks, 'Opening address by the President', 16 December 1918, *JIA* 51 (1919), 185–210.
33 See J. H. Gunlake, 'Memoir of Frederick August Andrew Menzler', *JIA* 95 (1969), 177–181. On the dinners, soon made biennial and moved to May to coincide with the President's election, see Simmonds (1948), 204. There was an interesting sequel to the first Dinner mentioned above, at which Sir Joseph Burn and Geoffrey Marks had both spoken of the actuary's rightful place in 'wider fields'. Two weeks after the Dinner, at which the President of the Institute of Chartered Accountants had been a guest, an anonymous article appeared in *The Accountant*, effectively warning actuaries off the turf already occupied by the accounting profession. It was left to E. W. Phillips and C. R. V. Coutts, on the occasion of the former's paper to the Institute in February 1927, 'The actuary in commerce and industry', to repair the damage by restating the view that the activities of actuaries and accountants were distinct and complementary. See Chris Lewin, 'Breaking into wider fields', *The Actuary*, September (1998), 32–33.
34 Charles Florestan Wood, 'Address by the President', 22 October 1956, *JIA* 83 (1957), 5–12.
35 *ibid*., 8.
36 *ibid*., 9.
37 *ibid*., 13.
38 *Institute of Actuaries Year Book 1939–1940*, 167.
39 General Meetings Minute Book, May 1943 – December 1950 (Special meeting of 1 September 1944), 49. For eyewitness impressions of the blast, see Arthur Tait, *A Story of Staple Inn on Holborn Hill* (2001), 75–77. Frank Guaschi was one of the first to see the destruction, which occurred when he was a 13-year-old playing football nearby. He recorded his memory of the event in 'The Old Staple Inn', *The Actuary*, September (1994), 30.

CHAPTER TWO

1 *Institute of Actuaries Year Book 1945–1946*, 147.
2 *ibid*., 211.
3 *ibid*., 151.
4 Dennis Gilley, for example, wrote his in a ruined castle at Predappio, Italy. Interview with Dennis Gilley, 7 September 2001. Gordon Bayley was one of several who qualified before being demobbed in 1946.
5 Fred Lloyd, 'Air Force actuary', *The Actuary*, November (1997), 24–25.
6 S. S. Townsend, 'Interlude in Whitehall', *Fiasco*, June (1990), 11–13. See also the section 'Actuaries at war', which includes essays by Jack Plymen and Max Lander, in *Proceedings of the Centenary Assembly of the Institute of Actuaries*, vol. III (1950), 291–334.
7 Life Offices Association. Scrapbooks containing material circulated to members (hereafter referred to as LOA Papers). Guildhall Library MS 28376/44, General Purposes Committee, 25 January 1943.
8 'Social insurance and allied services': verbatim report of discussions of Sir William Beveridge's proposals at Staple Inn Hall on 29 January, 5 February and 12 February 1943.
9 *ibid*., 4.
10 *ibid*., 20. The Government Actuary, Sir George Epps, had indicated to Beveridge that, taking demographic trends into account, the likely future cost of the universal scheme would be much greater than anticipated. Better pensions could be achieved through means testing or delaying retirement. See John MacNicol, *The Politics of Retirement in Britain, 1878–1948* (1998), chapter 4, 'The Beveridge Revolution', where the GA's highly technical calculations are considered to have 'expertly muddied' the waters of the debate on pension funding, which was less about eradicating social ills than redistributing income between the social classes (403).
11 *ibid*., 46.
12 *ibid*., 54–55. Frank Gardner pointed out that the GA's Memorandum did not form part of the shorter, popular version of the Beveridge Report, and thus even financially knowledgeable members of the public who might have been able to understand it had no access to the figures that would enable them to judge the true implications of the proposals.
13 Institute Council Minute Book (May 1943 to December 1950), 29 September 1943, 12–28; 3 December 1943, 18–49.
14 LOA Papers. Guildhall Library MS 28376/48. Pensions and Life Assurance Schemes (Arising out of Nationalisation) Committee, 24 February 1947.
15 On the ILOA's attempt, in conjunction with the Prudential, to save the approved societies, see Laurie Dennett, *A Sense of Security: 150 Years of Prudential* (1998), 294.

16   Council Minute Book (May 1943 to December 1950), 11 February 1946, 128, 127.
17   LOA Papers. Guildhall Library MS 28376/50. Special Committee on Nationalisation, 7 May 1948.
18   Faculty of Actuaries. LOA/Associated Scottish Life Offices Joint Standing Committee minutes, 24 February 1949, Appendix A. The charges against the life offices were that their large funds gave them undue power in the economy; that their expenses were higher than they would be under a State-controlled system; and that their profits were made at the expense of the insuring public. All of these charges were vigorously countered during the 'doorstep campaign' later in the year.
19   LOA Papers. Guildhall Library MS 28376/52. Memorandum dated 21 March 1949.
20   Interview with Colin Stewart, 10 October 2001.
21   F. A. A. Menzler, *The Institute of Actuaries Students' Society: the First Fifty Years 1910–1960: an appreciation* (1960), 72.
22   'Report by the Committee of the Institute of Actuaries Students' Society on the Future of the Profession' (1945), 21–24. Seven members of this Committee dissented from the general recommendations about part-time study and proposed that the Institute run its own full-time course to cover part of an actuary's training.
23   *ibid.*, 13.
24   Sir Andrew Rowell, 'Address by the President', 28 October 1946, *JIA* 73 (1947), 3. David Purchase, in his 'Seven years hard – a review of the examinations of the Institute of Actuaries', *JIASS* 27 (1984), 31–66 (also published separately by the Students' Society in 1984) claims on page 46 that the median qualification time was 8½ years.
25   Institute of Actuaries. Report of the Examination Sub-Committee on the Institute's Examination System (Lever Report) (1946), 21–30.
26   *ibid.*, 32–38.
27   Menzler (1960), 70.
28   See Menzler (1960), 80, where a letter from a bewildered 'Fellow under forty' is reproduced.
29   See Menzler (1960), 81, for the text of Hilary Seal's 'Apologia'.
30   The gift of £500 to found the lectures was made anonymously, but was later revealed to have been made by Reginald Maudling (father of the politician of the same name and Sir Alfred Watson's successor at R. Watson & Sons).
31   The first of these receptions was a dinner at Guildhall, at which the guest of honour was the youngest-ever President of the Board of Trade, Harold Wilson. Gordon Bayley, who was deputised to receive him, reminded him of the occasion some thirty years later. 'That's why,' Wilson replied, 'I arranged for you to join the Wilson Committee when it was formed.' (Anecdote supplied by Gordon Bayley to the Institute History Steering Group, 24 July 2002.)
32   Miscellaneous Committees Minute Book (November 1945 to December 1950), 57 and 99, and Council Minute Book (May 1943 to December 1950), 143–183.
33   Sir George Maddex, 'Address by the President', 25 October 1948, *JIA* 75 (1949), 1–11, 6.
34   D. F. Gilley, 'The past and future development of the consulting actuary's work', *JIA* 100 (1973), 73.
35   Maddex, 'Address by the President' (1949), 10.
36   Gilley (1973), 72.
37   Miscellaneous Committees Minute Book (November 1945 to December 1950), 162, 27 January 1948.
38   Hunter Devine (with Ronald Abbott), *50 Years on: a History of the Association of Consulting Actuaries* (2001), 2.
39   *ibid.*, 3.
40   *ibid.*, 1.

CHAPTER THREE

1   *Institute of Actuaries Year Book 1952–1953*, 209. The Public Relations Committee was set up by Geoffrey Heywood, President 1972–74. Marshall Field was its first Chairman and the Institute's first Press Officer.
2   *ibid.*, 210.
3   Dennis Gilley, letter to the author, 10 September 2001. Institute of Actuaries Archive.
4   R. F. Harrod, 'Savings and inflation', *JIA* 78 (1952), 3.
5   W. F. Gardner, 'Address by the President', 27 October 1952, *JIA* 79 (1953), 1–13, 3.
6   H. E. Raynes, 'The place of ordinary stocks and shares in the investment of life assurance funds', *JIA* 59 (1928).
7   H. E. Raynes, 'Equities and fixed-interest stocks during twenty-five years', *JIA* 68 (1937).
8   J. B. H. Pegler, 'The actuarial principles of investment', *JIA* 74 (1948).
9   A. H. Bailey, 'On the principles on which the funds of life assurance societies should be invested', *Assurance Magazine and JIA* 10 (1861–1863), 142–147.
10   G. H. Recknell, 'Insurance against inflation', *TFA* 19 (1950).
11   T. R. Suttie, 'Equity in bonus distribution', *JIA* 73 (1947).
12   A. T. Haynes and Robert J. Kirton, 'The financial structure of a life office', *TFA* 21 (1953), featured in Institute of Actuaries Students' Society exhibition, *Some Landmarks in Actuarial Science* (1985), 40.
13   F. M. Redington, 'Review of the principles of life-office valuations', *JIA* 78 (1952).
14   Correspondence between Maurice Ogborn and Gordon Bayley, 29 May, 3 June, 13 June and 15 June 1946.
15   Frank M. Redington, *A Ramble Through the Actuarial Countryside. The Collected Papers, Essays and Speeches of Frank Mitchell Redington*, edited by Gary Chamberlin (Institute of Actuaries Students' Society, 1986), 67.
16   *ibid.*, 68.

17 Gordon V. Bayley and Wilfred Perks, 'A consistent system of investment and bonus distribution for a life office', *JIA* 79 (1953).

18 Geoffrey Heywood, 'George Henry Ross Goobey', *The Actuary*, July (1999), 20.

19 Redington, *Ramble* (1986), 234 *et seq.*

20 The lecture rooms were given the names of Lidstone (George Lidstone) and Phelps (William Phelps).

21 Maurice Ogborn, *Staple Inn*, Institute of Actuaries (1964; reprinted 1980), 23. Part of one of the ancient timbers had been used to make the beautiful gavel and block in a presentation case given by the Institute to the Society of Actuaries of the United States on its formation in 1949. The gift was recalled on the Society's fiftieth anniversary in 1999, at which members of the Institute were present.

22 *Institute of Actuaries Year Book 1954–1955*, 202; *1956–1957*, 19–22. Also Institute of Actuaries, *Return to Staple Inn* (1955).

23 See 'The presidential badge', *JIA* 82 (1956) and 'The Institute's coat of arms', *JIA* 83 (1957); also Harold Merchant, 'Arms and actuaries', *Fiasco* 112, February (1989), 4–5.

24 *JIA* 83 (1957), 1–4. An interview with John Bunford, *The Actuary*, September (1991), 38–39.

25 F. W. Bacon, M. D. W. Elphinstone and B. Benjamin, 'The growth of pension rights and their impact on the national economy', *JIA* 80 (1954), 201.

26 Redington, *Ramble* (1986), 169.

27 W. F. Gardner, 'Address by the President', *JIA* 79 (1953), 1–13, 4.

28 'Memorandum of evidence submitted by the Councils of the Institute of Actuaries and the Faculty of Actuaries in Scotland', *JIA* 80 (1954), 282–283, ix.

29 *loc. cit.*, xi.

30 *loc. cit.*, xii.

31 R. W. Abbott, 'Pension schemes, aims and achievements', *The Accountant*, 29 January (1955), 115.

32 The discussion of the 'Report of the Committee on the Taxation Treatment of Provisions for Retirement' (Cmnd 9063) was published in *JIA* 81 (1955). The joint 'Memorandum of Evidence' produced by the Institute and Faculty appears in *JIA* 77 (1951).

33 *Some Landmarks in Actuarial Science*. Catalogue of an exhibition in Staple Inn Hall, November 1985, 40.

34 Councils of the Institute of Actuaries and of the Faculty of Actuaries in Scotland, *National Pensions: an Appeal to Statesmanship*, May 1959, 2.

35 Institute of Actuaries, Miscellaneous Committees Minute Books, vol. 13 (1955–1957); Minutes of the National Superannuation Joint Committee, 25 January, 8 February, 14 February, 1 March, 14 March, 22 March, 5 October, 8 November (all 1955).

36 Redington, *Ramble* (1986), 144.

37 *National Pensions*, 11.

38 *ibid.*, 6.

39 *ibid.*, 9.

40 *ibid.*, 10.

41 R. W. Abbott, 'Growth of state pensions and their effect on occupational schemes', *The Accountant*, 4 June (1960), 688.

42 Redington, *Ramble* (1986), 147.

CHAPTER FOUR

1 See *Institute of Actuaries Year Book 1956–1957*, 242; Supplemental Royal Charter, clause 1. The £8,000 per annum rent was good value, but according to Roger Corley, no provision was made for a possible rise at the end of the lease and thus no one was prepared for the shock of having the rent go up to some £250,000 per annum in 1989.

2 Education Committee Report, April 1958, 4, clause 18.

3 *op. cit.*, 2, clause 9.

4 *op. cit.*, 3, clause 12; 4, clause 16.

5 In 1960 subscriptions stood at £15 per annum for Fellows, £10 for Associates and £5 for Students; overseas rates were £12, £8 and £5 respectively.

6 There has never been a limit on the number of years a Fellow may serve on Council, although since 1919 he or she must stand down for a year every five years. The redoubtable Fred Menzler stepped down in 1956 after serving on Council, with the required breaks, for thirty years, but there have been many others with similar records. The two longest-serving Fellows to date have been Thomas Sprague, thirty-eight years (1863–1901) and Augustus Hendriks, thirty-seven years (1866–1903).

7 *Institute of Actuaries Year Book 1963–1964*, 21–22.

8 M. E. Ogborn, *Staple Inn*, 1964.

9 F. A. A. Menzler, *The Institute of Actuaries Students' Society: the First Fifty Years 1910–1960: an appreciation* (1960). Colin Stewart, *The Students' Society Log 1960–1985* (1985).

10 Standing Resolutions adopted by Council on 17 April 1941, and amended 17 March 1944, 8 March 1948, 11 July 1949, 8 February 1954 and 12 March 1956. Miscellaneous Committees Minute Book, vol. 13, 1955 to 1958. At any one time there were four Vice-Presidents, each serving for three years, with at least one being replaced each year.

11 The MPC was supplemented by a note on the specialist subject of Reversions and life interests in 1967, following concerns about actuaries with limited experience operating on a part-time basis, who, it was feared, might bring the profession into disrepute. (Later, this note was included in what had by then become a series of Institute professional Guidance Notes as 'GN10'.)

12 Peter R. Cox, Untitled memoir of the GAD, in chapter 'At the Treasury', 2. Institute of Actuaries Historical Archive.

13 R. L. Michaelson, 'Large-scale electronic digital computing machines', *JIA* 79 (1953), 274–322.

14 Miscellaneous Committees Minute Book, vol. 12, 1951–1954, 201, 242, 301; Reports of Committees to Council, vol. 13, 1955–1958: Report 634.

15 W. T. L. Barnard, 'Some changes in actuarial methods arising from the use of a small computer in a medium-sized office', *JIA* 91 (1965), 108–146.

16 *JIASS* 17 May 1963, 93–153; *JIA* 92 (1966), 134–192.

17 *Institute of Actuaries Year Book 1956–1957*, 27; Reports of Committees to Council, vol. 14, 1959–61: Reports 780, 813; vol. 15, 1962–1964: Report 885.

18 H. W. Haycocks and J. Plymen, 'The design, application and future development of the Financial Times–Actuaries' index', *JIA* 90 (1964), 267–324.

19 J. V. Evans and K. P. Kelly, 'From death to immortality', *Transactions of the 22nd International Congress of Actuaries*, Sydney, Australia, 21–27 October 1984, 4, 271–279.

20 *ibid.*, 278.

CHAPTER FIVE

1 The Casualty Actuarial and Statistical Society of America was formed in 1914 and changed its name in 1921 to the Casualty Actuarial Society.

2 Miscellaneous Committees Minute Book, January 1951–December 1954, 320; Reports of Committees to Council, vol. 12 (1951–55): Report 618, to which is attached a note by R. E. Beard and correspondence between him and Dr Paul Johansen of Denmark.

3 Reports of Committees to Council, vol. 12 (1951–55): Report 640.

4 Reports of Committees to Council, vol. 16 (1964–65): Report 994 (Report by Colin Stewart on the Arnhem Colloquium).

5 'The diversification of insurance products in recent years and anticipated future development in Great Britain', in *Transactions of the 20th International Congress of Actuaries*, Tokyo, 25 October to 1 November 1976, 1, 165.

6 Peter Johnson, 'Actuaries and general insurance'. Note prepared for the Institute of Actuaries History Collection, 4 June 2001.

7 My thanks to Frank Guaschi for his recollection of a contemporary BIA television advertisement featuring a character called 'Fred', ensconced in a tower, advising people to 'get the strength of the insurance companies around you!' This proved something of an embarrassment when the Fire, Auto & Marine insurance company crashed, since there was a degree of public expectation that policyholders would be compensated on account of its membership of the BIA.

8 C. D. Daykin, 'The developing role of the Government Actuary's Department in the supervision of insurance in the United Kingdom', *JIA* 119 (1992), 313–343; 313–334.

9 There were also important papers given at Institute sessional meetings, such as P. D. Johnson and G. B. Hey, 'Statistical studies in motor insurance', *JIA* 97 (1971), 199–249.

10 See J. A. Jolliffe's review, in *JIA* 98 (1972), 276, of the 'Report of the Tribunal appointed to inquire into certain issues in relation to the circumstances leading up to the cessation of trading by the Vehicle and General Insurance Company Limited', London, HMSO, 1972.

11 Daykin, 'Developing Role' (1992), 334.

12 Reports of Committees to Council, vol. 19 (1970–71): Report 1202 (Non-life Insurance Committee) with a memorandum on the V&G collapse by Sidney Benjamin; vol. 20 (1972–73): Report 1271 (V&G Affair Ad Hoc Committee) with memo to be sent to the DTI attached; Report 1275 (General Insurance Committee), with correspondence between Geoffrey Heywood, President of the Institute, and the DTI; Report 1390 (Legislation Committee); Report 1404 (General Insurance Study Group).

13 *GIRO Bulletin* 1 (February 1975), 2.

14 C. D. Daykin, 'The regulatory role of the actuary', presented to the Institute of Actuaries, 22 February, *BAJ*, 5 (1999), 529–574.

15 Daykin, 'Developing Role' (1992), 332–333.

16 Daykin, 'Regulatory Role' (1999), 530–531.

17 Some which were rescued, besides the London Indemnity & General, were the Lifeguard, the Capital Annuities, and the Vavasseur Life.

18 Daykin, 'Developing Role' (1992), 336.

19 Daykin, 'Regulatory Role' (1999), 531.

20 C. M. O'Brien, letter to David Raymont, 5 October 2001. Institute Historical Archive.

21 Daykin, 'Regulatory Role' (1999), 532–533; 'Developing Role' (1992), 336–337.

22 Reports of Committees to Council, vol. 22 (1976): Report 1496 (Professional Conduct Investigating Committee); Report 1505 (General Purposes Committee); circular and agenda dated 31 March 1976 regarding the Special General Meeting of 26 April 1976.

23 Reports of Committees to Council, vol. 22 (1976): Report 1519 (General Purposes Committee).

24 *Institute of Actuaries Year Book 1977–1978*, 93.

25 *Institute of Actuaries Year Book 1978–1979*, 105–106.

26 This paper was prepared at the request of Council by J. K. Scholey and M. T. L. Bizley.

27 See Francis Bacon, 'The economic and financial impact of state and private pension provision', presented to the British Association on 1 September 1964. Institute History Archive, Pensions file.

28 See C. S. S. Lyon, 'Social security and occupational pension schemes', *JIA* 94 (1968), 173–253.

29 William Phillips, 'Private pension scheme developments since 1944' in *Transactions of the 17th International Congress of Actuaries*, 26 May – 3 June 1964, vol. 2, 713–723.

30 This was one of Stewart Lyon's conclusions in 'Social security and occupational pension schemes', *JIA* 94 (1968), 173–253.

31 The sessional meeting held on 24 March 1969 was devoted to a discussion of the Government's White Paper, 'National Superannuation and Social Insurance'; the discussion was published in the *JIA* 95 (1969), 369–392.

32 *ibid.*, *JIA* 95 (1969), 390.

33 Reports of Committees to Council, vol. 18 (September 1968 to December 1969): Letter attached to Report 1091 (Report of the President), dated 14 April 1969.

34 Reports of Committees to Council, vol. 18 (September 1968 to December 1969): Report 1078 (ad hoc committee on Pension Schemes).

35 Reports of Committees to Council, vol. 18 (September 1968 to December 1969): Report 1099 (Legislation Committee); Report 1107 (Legislation Committee).

36 'Pension rights when you change your job', a speech given by Richard Crossman to the Institute of Actuaries, 19 November 1969.

37 See Redington, *A Ramble Through the Actuarial Countryside* (1986), edited by Gary Chamberlin, 510–517. Also Leslie Hannah, *Inventing Retirement: the Development of Occupational Pensions in Britain* (Cambridge, 1986), 60: 'Thatcher and Joseph were contemptuous of the moderate, diplomatic liberalism of the actuaries and other professionals at the Life Offices Association', preferring advice more favourable to building up the private sector.

38 'State and occupational pension provision' (Report of discussion only), *JIA* 102 (1975), 18.

CHAPTER SIX

1 See *Institute of Actuaries Year Book* for the relevant years. In 1986, twenty years on from the first figures cited, active UK Fellows numbered 1,486, of whom 876, or roughly 52 per cent, were employed by the life offices.

2 Conversation with Dennis Gilley, 20 December 2002. His 'The past and future development of the consulting actuary's work', *JIA* 100 (1974), 71–107, is an excellent overview.

3 Conversation with Dennis Gilley, 20 December 2002.

4 Table showing the ratio of men and women members of the Institute, 1895–2000, compiled from Institute *Year Books*. See also file on Mrs Dorothy Spiers.

5 As several articles written for *The Actuary* during the 1990s have: see Jennifer Lang, 'Attracting women to the profession' (September 1993) and 'Women in the profession II' (March 1995); Jillian Pegrum, 'Women in the profession' (November 1993); and Deborah Cooper, 'Life's little difficulties' (November 1998).

6 A. R. Davidson was speaking in 1956 and is quoted in Cooper, above.

7 Of the first eleven women actuaries, beginning in 1923 with Dorothy Davis Spiers, two left full-time employment on marriage, while the other nine remained single.

8 Frank Gardner, President of the Institute 1952–54, encouraged the Institute's recruitment officers to arrange visits to girls' schools as well as boys', something that until then had not been done. See his comments at the Institute AGM, 8 June 1953, in *Institute of Actuaries Year Book 1953–1954*.

9 All of the information regarding the Students' Society is taken from C. M. Stewart, *The Students' Society Log 1960–1985: Twenty-five Years of Enterprise* (1985).

10 *Institute of Actuaries Year Book 1974–1975*, 5.

11 The new arrangement of subjects, replacing the old 'Intermediate' and 'Final', was as follows: Group A: A.1 Probability and Elementary Statistics; A.2 Compound Interest; A.3 Life and Other Contingencies; A.4 Investment: Principles and Economic Background; A.5 Further Statistics; A.6 Mortality and Other Actuarial Statistics. Group B: B.1 Institutional Investment; B.2 Life Assurance; B.3 General Insurance; B.4 Pension Funds.

12 *Institute of Actuaries Year Book 1978–1979*, Examination Handbook, 17. Students or Associates who had passed A.1, A.2, A.4 and B.1 were entitled to this certificate on application to the Institute.

13 On the basis of a recommendation from the Education Committee (Reports 352, 353) Council moved (minutes of 13 October 1936) that the minimum age for the granting of the Fellowship be raised from 21 to 23, since 'in view of the very important statutory duties which a Fellow may be called upon to perform … the present age of twenty-one is too young'. The relevant bye-law was altered in 1937, with effect from 1938. See also Report of the Bye-laws Committee to Council (Report 355), 8 December 1936.

14 'Actuaries and long-term insurance business', *JIA* 103 (1976), 137–166. G. E. Barrow's contribution to the discussion, 163.

15 In practice this would prove hard to realise and various formulae were adopted, but this was the genesis of the Institute's current requirement that all active Fellows participate in Continuous Professional Development. *Institute of Actuaries Year Book 1977–1978*, 4; Examination Handbook 1967, 2–4.

16 *Institute of Actuaries Year Book 1976–1977*, 105. See also P. R. Goddard, 'The education and examination of actuaries', *JIA* 106 (1979), 201–206. By 1982, 158 students had obtained the City University degree, of whom 73 were subsequently admitted to the Institute.
17 *Institute of Actuaries Year Book 1978–1979*, 74.
18 *Better Pensions*, Cmnd 5713, HMSO, 1974, quoted in Nicholas Timmins, *The Five Giants: a Biography of the Welfare State*, 2nd edition (London: HarperCollins, 2001), 347.
19 C. S. S. Lyon, 'Occupational and personal pensions' in *Life, Death and Money: Actuaries and the Creation of Financial Security*, edited by D. F. Renn (1998, 110), drawing upon the Sixth Occupational Pension Scheme Survey, 1979, produced by the Government Actuary.
20 Timmins (2001), 374, citing Roy Jenkins's speech in the Commons, *Hansard*, 13 June 1979, col. 439.
21 Reproduced in *Institute of Actuaries Year Book, 1978–1979*, 52, and subsequent editions.
22 'Report of the Maturity Guarantees Working Party', *JIA* 107 (1980), 105.
23 *ibid.*, 113. Paragraph 7.2 sets out the conditions that would have to apply as '(a) the office would have to have complete discretion with regard to investment policy and the fund could not, for example, be designated an equity fund or a property fund, (b) the publicity material and the policy would have to make it clear to the policyholder that the office may follow an investment course designed to avoid payments being made under maturity guarantees rather than to optimise investment performance, and (c) the directors of the office would have to undertake to the actuary that they would take an appropriate course of action when the threat of maturity guarantee payments materialised'.
24 Such as price and wage inflation, short- and long-term interest rates, exchange rates, share yields and dividends. See David Wilkie, 'A stochastic investment model for actuarial use', *TFA* 39 (1986), 341–403.
25 Marshall Field, President of the Institute 1986–88, and Roger Corley, President 1988–90, were the first two Presidents who were already liverymen.

CHAPTER SEVEN

1 Until the edition of 1963–64, the *Year Book* carried a fairly detailed account of how the International Congresses came into being; this was scaled down in 1963. Apparently in June 1894 a reference in a Bill on friendly societies being debated by the Belgian Parliament caused a member to enquire what an actuary was. This so aroused the indignation of the newly associated Belgian actuaries that they called a conference, thereafter regarded as the 1st International Congress, in September 1895.
2 *Transactions of the 2nd International Congress of Actuaries*, London, 1899.
3 The Institute *Year Books* give a complete list of Students and their addresses, from which it is possible to arrive at this percentage. In 1935, for instance, of the 672 Students listed, 149 had addresses in India.
4 Miscellaneous Committees Minute Book, January 1951 to December 1954, 233, 246, 273. Minutes of the *ad hoc* committee appointed by Council on 14 December 1953 to consider all matters relating to Indian membership.
5 *Institute of Actuaries Year Book 1951–1952*, Fred Menzler's review of the year, 219.
6 A. R. N. Ratcliff, 'State and private pension schemes in the European Economic Community and the United Kingdom', *JIA* 89 (1963), 157–225, 207.
7 Kenneth Usherwood, 'Address by the President', 22 October 1962, *JIA* 89 (1963), 12.
8 P. R. Cox, 'The European actuary – the nature of his work', a Memorandum attached to Reports of Committees to Council, vol. 17 (1967–68): Report 1004 (European Relations Committee), 9 January 1967.
9 Reports of Committees to Council, vol. 15 (1962–64): Report 918, 13 April 1964.
10 Cox, *op. cit.*
11 Reports of Committees to Council, vol. 16 (1965–67): Report 1045 (European Relations Committee), 8 January 1967.
12 'On the choice of investment of life assurance companies operating in the European countries', a Memorandum attached to Report 1045 above.
13 Reports of Committees to Council, vol. 23 (1977–78): Report 1646, 10 July 1978.
14 Reports of Committees to Council, vol. 24 (1979–80): Report 1702, 9 July 1979.
15 Groupe Consultatif des Associations d'Actuaires des Pays des Communautés Européennes, 'Communication to the Presidents of the National Associations of Actuaries in countries of the European Communities on improvements of the recognition of the role and responsibilities of actuaries in each of these countries', 28 June 1982.
16 Groupe Consultatif, 'To the Presidents of the National Associations of Actuaries of the Countries of the European Communities', November 1984.
17 *ibid*.
18 Maxwell Lander, 'IACA' (the text of a speech, n.d. but suggested date 1999).
19 Reports of Committees to Council, vol. 25 (1981–82): Report 1877, 11 October 1982.
20 Reports of Committees to Council, vol. 26 (1983–84): Reports 1956, 1959, 12 December 1983.

CHAPTER EIGHT

1 *Institute of Actuaries Year Book 1985–1986*, 113.
2 The award of a Finlaison Medal did not preclude the later award of a Gold Medal.

3 Gary Chamberlin, editor of Frank M. Redington, *A Ramble Through the Actuarial Countryside. The Collected Papers, Essays and Speeches of Frank Mitchell Redington, MA* (Institute of Actuaries Students' Society, 1986), xv.

4 *Institute of Actuaries Year Book 1983–1984*, 79–85. Sir Douglas Morpeth, who delivered the Watson Memorial Lecture in 1983, and Professor Ralf Dahrendorf, the Director of the London School of Economics, who addressed the Institute's Biennial Dinner in the same year, both spoke about the rising distrust of the professions and the need for the latter to regulate themselves effectively.

5 *Institute of Actuaries Year Book 1984–1985*, 82. The wording was summarised as: 'the actuary will have to be personally identifiable as the source of the advice, and he will be giving it on his own professional responsibility'.

6 A Special General Meeting was held to discuss this before the Annual General Meeting on 24 June 1985. See *Institute of Actuaries Year Book 1985–1986*, 106–107.

7 Report of the Education Working Party of the Futures Committee. 'Educating Actuaries for an Uncertain Future' (1988), 6.

8 Dennis Gilley's *How to be a Happy Pension Fund Trustee* (Ringley Communications, 1987) was written for such people. Despite its light-hearted title it is a mine of solid information, seasoned with the author's extensive consulting experience as a partner in R. Watson & Sons.

9 A small group of members of the Institute had in fact been meeting with representatives from the Institute of Chartered Accountants since 1971. Initially this was prompted by Insurance Companies (Accounts and Forms) Regulations 1968 and the successive Companies Acts, from which arose the need to clarify the extent to which the auditors of a life office had to concern themselves with the work of actuaries (and after 1973, appointed actuaries) in carrying out actuarial valuations.

10 The CCAB consisted of the Councils of the Institute of Chartered Accountants of England and Wales, the Institute of Chartered Accountants of Scotland, the Institute of Chartered Accountants in Ireland and the Institute of Certified Accountants. Its statement was called 'Auditors' relationship with actuaries concerning actuarial valuations of long-term business funds of insurance companies'.

11 A. R. N. Ratcliff, 'Address by the President', 27 October 1980, *JIA* 89 (1981), 9–18, 12.

12 CCAB, 'Auditors' Relationship', clauses 6 and 7.

13 'The Relationship between the Actuary and the Auditor of a Company Transacting Long-term Insurance Business' (GN7), 1980. The version of GN7 issued in 1991 in response to the Auditing Guideline *Life Insurers in the United Kingdom* made it compulsory for the actuary to familiarise himself, not only with that guideline, but also with the auditor's new responsibilities under the Companies Act 1985. It also enjoined upon him a willingness to discuss with the auditor 'any relevant reports he has made to the directors of the company, including his valuation of the long-term liabilities, to enable the auditor to form the opinions on which he bases his audit report'.

14 Ratcliff, 'Address by the President' (1981), 5.

15 See Ian Hay Davidson, 'Do actuaries need standards?', *JIASS* 28 (1985), 43–52. The title of this 'Jubilee Lecture' was acknowledged by the author (an accountant) to be 'provocative', since clearly actuaries, like other learned professionals, 'both need and enjoy the highest standards'. But in his view, there was not yet 'a full recognition within the actuarial profession of the need for a codification of professional practice so that we laymen may know and understand what you professionals are saying' (51). Actuaries' perception of this need was, if not 'full', then definitely on the rise.

16 A. D. Shedden, 'Address by the President', 17 October 1983, *TFA* 39 (1984), 2.

17 *McDonald v. McDonald* (1880) 5 A.C. 519, cited in J. H. Prevett, 'Actuarial assessment of damages', *JIA* 94 (1968), 294. The classical legal principle underlying the assessment of personal damages is that of *restitutio in integrum*, or compensating the victim of an accident (or his dependants, if he had been killed) so as to restore him to the same financial position he would have enjoyed had the unfortunate event not occurred. Without the possibility of divining the future this is clearly an unattainable ideal, but the problem of how best to approximate it had attracted the attention of actuaries even in the nineteenth century.

18 The publication in 1962 of Professor Harry Sweet's *Principles of the Laws of Damage*, which contained a chapter entitled 'The utility of actuarial calculations', brought greater recognition of the need for reform. The Report by Justice (the British section of the International Commission of Jurists) in 1966, commenting on the trials of motor accident cases, acknowledged that 'Problems of this kind which are to a large extent statistical in nature are within the special competence of the profession of actuaries and are capable of actuarial solutions which have a high degree of precision and reliability.' Cited in Prevett (1968), 298.

19 See Reports of Committees to Council, vol. 18 (September 1968 to December 1969): Reports 1089 and 1118 (Reports of the Working Party set up to consider the assessment of damages); vol. 19 (January 1970 to December 1971): Report 1227; vol. 20 (January 1972 to December 1973): Reports 1325, 1335; also vol. 23 (January 1977 to December 1978): Report 1640 (Report of the Joint Committee on the Assessment of Damages); vol. 25 (January 1981 to December 1982): Report 1872 (with letter from Lord Hailsham); vol. 26 (January 1983 to December 1984): Report 1953.

20 John Prevett, 'Actuaries and the Courts'. Note prepared for the Institute History Archive, 2.

21 *ibid.*, 4. Also Reports of Committees to Council, vol. 23 (January 1977 to December 1978): Report 1640. The profession was represented on the Committee by Ronald Skerman.

22 *ibid.*, 5, citing *Auty, Mills, Rogers and Popow v National Coal Board* (1985) 1 WLR 784.

23 *ibid.*, 5.

24 The actuaries who served on this committee were Gordon Bayley, Dennis Gilley, Edward Johnston and John Prevett for the Institute and Brian Reddin for the Faculty.

25 Sir Michael Ogden, *Memoirs of Sir Michael Ogden QC: Variety is the Spice of Legal Life* (2002), 182.

26 *loc. cit.*

27 *loc. cit.*

28 *Institute of Actuaries Year Book 1984–1985*, 112.

29 *loc. cit.*

30 *loc. cit.*

31 *Institute of Actuaries Year Book 1985–1986*, 113. Peter Moore was speaking at the Annual General Meeting, 24 June 1985.

32 Institute of Actuaries, *The actuarial management of a life office*, Proceedings of the 1st Actuarial Convention, 1985. F. R. Wales and C. S. S. Lyon, 'Reasonable expectations: bonus and growth illustrations', 67–75. Clause 1.4 of GN7 was amended to include the words, pertaining to the Appointed Actuary: 'If there are policies that participate in profits he should advise on the conditions in which the company could reasonably expect to be able to maintain its current rates of bonus, allowing for any changes in such rates that may be envisaged as a result of the valuation.'

33 *loc. cit.* 'Indeed, can guidance to the appointed actuary ever provide a sufficient safeguard against abuse of the discretions that are inherent in the systems of bonus distribution customarily used in this country?'

34 C. S. S. Lyon, 'Address by the President: The outlook for pensioning', 25 October 1982, *JIA* 110 (1983), 1–15.

35 *ibid.*, 4–5.

36 *loc. cit.*

37 Cited in 'The political, social and other influences on the actuarial profession in Great Britain', 'National Report', *Transactions of the 22nd International Congress of Actuaries*, Sydney, Australia, 21–27 October 1984, 89–103, 97.

38 *ibid.*, 98.

39 See 'Social Insurance and Allied Services': verbatim report of discussions of Sir William Beveridge's proposals at Staple Inn Hall on 29 January, 5 February and 12 February 1943, 46–47.

40 *Institute of Actuaries Year Book 1983–1984*, 103.

41 Nicholas Timmins, *The Five Giants: a Biography of the Welfare State*, 2nd edition (London: HarperCollins, 2001), 400.

42 *Institute of Actuaries Year Book 1983–1984*, 112–113.

43 These three documents and the discussions that followed them are reproduced in *JIA* 113 (1986) and *TFA* 39 (1987).

44 *TFA* 39 (1987), 464.

45 *loc. cit.* See also, in the Institute of Actuaries Archive, transcripts of the verbatim evidence given to the Department of Health and Social Security, Public Inquiry into Provision for Retirement, 29 February 1984: 'the advocates of personal pensions appear to think that wider personal ownership and involvement in personal wealth are more important than ensuring secure pensions in old age, and we tend to put the priorities the other way around' (14).

46 *ibid.*, 497.

47 *ibid.*, 495.

48 Timmins (2001), *loc. cit*.

49 *TFA* 39 (1987), 481.

50 Report of the Government Actuary, Cmnd 2445 (London: HMSO, 1994).

51 'National Report', *Transactions of the 22nd International Congress* (1984), 94.

52 Institute of Actuaries, AIDS Working Party, *AIDS Bulletin* 1 (August 1987), 2.

53 Institute of Actuaries, AIDS Working Party, *AIDS Bulletin* 2 (December 1987), 2.

54 Peter Johnson, 'Actuaries and General Insurance'. Note prepared for the Institute History Archive, 4 June 2001.

55 The series of a dozen monographs was produced between 1968 and 1983 under the general title 'Accident Excess of Loss'. See also F. E. Guaschi, 'Non-proportional reinsurance', *JIASS* 19 (1971), 55–71, published after presentation and discussion at a Students' Society meeting on 22 November 1968.

56 David Craighead himself felt that the standard actuarial methods of calculating reserves were not well suited to the syndicates and so devised his own models. Interview with David Craighead, 21 October 2001.

57 See Reports of Committees to Council, vol. 25 (January 1981 to December 1982): Report 1876, 12 July 1982; vol. 27 (January 1985 to December 1986): Report 2101, 12 May 1986. With reference to discussions with the DTI, see T. G. Clarke's letter to A. C. Russell of the DTI, 13 October 1989, covering a statement prepared by the General Insurance Joint Committee entitled 'Supervision of companies transacting non-life insurance. The role of professional certification'. On relations with Lloyd's, see Institute of Actuaries Council Agendas and Committee Reports (on CD-ROM) (1987 to 1994): Report 2337 (to Council of 1 December 1989) and letter from Roger Corley of the Institute to Michael Lawrence, the Chairman of Lloyd's, 3 January 1990, attached to Report 2340 (to Council of 12 January 1990).

58 The way this worked was that Lloyd's 'Names', whose participation was traditionally on a basis of unlimited liability, paid a one-off 'Equitas premium' and could then, if they wished, retire from Lloyd's with no future liabilities. The premium, subject to the exhaustion of the fund set up for the purpose, limited a Name's aggregate losses in a four-year period to no more than 80 per cent of his or her highest premium limit for that four-year period. See Colin Czapiewski, 'Lloyd's – a thundering future?', *The Actuary*, October (1992).

59 See Terry Clarke, 'A statutory role in general insurance', *Fiasco* 125, May (1990); Colin Czapiewski, 'The Lloyd's task', *The Actuary*, April (1993), and 'The biggest actuarial project of all time', *The Actuary*, May (1996); Ravi Manjrekar, 'The future of the London Market', *The Actuary*, August (1995).

60   Institute Historical Archive, Marshall Field, 'Opening Address', in Institute of Actuaries, *The actuary in pensions – a time of change*, Proceedings of the 2nd Actuarial Convention, 20–22 September 1987 (1987), 2.

CHAPTER NINE

1   See J. P. Bannon and M. D. Moule, *The Financial Services Act* (Staple Inn Actuarial Society, 1987). On 1 December 2001 the Financial Services Authority (FSA) became the single statutory regulator directly responsible for the regulation of deposit taking, insurance and investment business under the Financial Services and Management Act 2000. The rise of electronic trading and the development of advanced investment products such as derivatives exerted pressure for change upon the traditional distinction between jobbers and brokers.
2   Institute of Actuaries Council Agendas and Committee Reports (on CD-ROM) (1987 to 1994): Report 2162, 13 April 1987. The Institute sent out 1,654 letters and received 1,345 replies, of which 1,035 were in favour, 275 against and 35 non-committal. The Faculty sent out 451 letters and received 235 replies, of which 101 were in favour, 114 against and 20 non-committal.
3   *Institute of Actuaries Members' Handbook*, April 1989, H/11.
4   See Bannon and Moule (1987), 15.
5   I am indebted to Peter Tompkins, Paul Thornton and Roy Brimblecombe for their comments on these events.
6   The NAPF was particularly emphatic about the care that would be required in selling personal pensions, policing such sales, and the responsibility that the vendors should assume for the actions and promises of their sales force, whether tied or independent. It also pleaded for a longer timescale for the introduction of such a fundamental change to the pensions system, recognising that the stability achieved since 1975 through consensus was threatened by the increasingly political nature of the pensions debate.
7   Marshall Field, 'Opening Address', in Institute of Actuaries, *The actuary in pensions – a time of change*, Proceedings of the 2nd Actuarial Convention, 20–22 September 1987 (1987), 2.
8   I am indebted to Gordon Bayley and Alex McKinnell for their comments on these events.
9   Nicola Foote, 'Pensions transfers', *The Actuary*, March (1994), 25; and Jennifer Lang, 'Lessons from pension transfers', *The Actuary*, March (1994), 3.
10 Letter from L. J. Martin of the Institute to J. R. C. Young of the SIB, 9 September 1994. Report to Council 2809 (of the 18 February Group, 26 September 1994).
11 Office of Fair Trading (OFT), *Report of the Director General's Inquiry into Pensions*, vol. 1 (July 1997), clause 479, Table 4:7 'Pensions review progress statistics: period ending 31/10/97'.
12 Katie Dawson and Debra Evans, 'The personal pensions review: an insurance company perspective', *The Actuary*, August (1996), 14. Financial Services Authority Press Release, 27 June 2002.
13 The OFT Report cited above indicates that 570,129 personal pensions, or 10 per cent of those sold, had been misrepresented, and of these 420,913 were sold by product providers (that is, companies selling pensions). Some 499,496 of the pensions mis-sold were classed as 'priority cases', and of these 373,495 were sold by product providers.
14 Jonathan Seres, *Pensions: A Practical Guide*, 4th edition (1997), 406–407. It should not be forgotten that the ultimate damage to pensioners and members of the Mirror Group pension funds was essentially very limited, partly because of the government guarantees underlying guaranteed minimum pensions in contracted-out schemes, and even more so because of the successful efforts to recover moneys from City institutions and elsewhere. Unfortunately the Goode Report omitted to recommend the one measure that would have prevented the Maxwell theft – namely, independent custody of the assets, which had to await the Myners review in 2001.
15 'Pension Law Review Committee: the Actuarial Profession's Response', December 1992.
16 In future, where a fund's solvency fell below a base level of 90 per cent of the minimum solvency standard, the employer was obliged to make good the shortfall at least to the 90 per cent level within three months. Should it fall to a level between 90 and 100 per cent, the shortfall had to be made good within three years. *Pension Law Reform. Summary of the Report of the Pension Law Review Committee* (1993), 15, clauses 22 and 25.
17 Although the idea of the minimum solvency requirement was among the profession's own, the level proposed for the test in the actual Bill was far short of a solvency test. The profession protested that this terminology would mislead members of pension funds into thinking that their accrued rights were as secure as, say, in an insurance company meeting minimum solvency requirements. The Government did not want to alter the level, as it was concerned that this might exacerbate the trend away from final salary pension schemes, and so it was agreed to alter the wording instead, to Minimum Funding Requirement.
18 See the Parliamentary Ombudsman, Annual Report 2001–2002 (HC 897); the Financial Services Authority Report into Equitable Life (the Baird Report), October 2001; and the Treasury Memoranda ordered to be published by the House of Commons on 25 February 2003, which may be found on the following web page: http://www.publications.parliament.uk/pa/cm200203/cmselect/cmtreasury
19 R. H. Ranson and C. P. Headdon, 'With profits without mystery', *JIA* 116 (1989), 301–345.
20 Report of Corley Committee of Inquiry (2001), 6, clauses 22–25. Asset shares can be defined as 'the accumulation of premiums less expenses incurred, allowing for the investment return earned for a group of similar policies. In making the calculation, the asset share would normally be charged for the cost of accruing guarantees, life cover and any capital charges.' (Also M. Shelley, M. Arnold and P. D. Needleman, 'A review of policyholders' reasonable expectations', *BAJ* 8 (2002), 705–755, see clause 2.6.4.) The concept of asset share was not unique to Equitable Life.

21 Select Committee on Treasury Minutes of Evidence. Thursday 8 February 2001. Evidence of Chris Daykin. Reply to question 33.

22 The Annuity Guarantees Working Party presented its Report at the 1997 Life Convention in Brighton. See also Mike Bolton, 'Guaranteed annuity rates', *The Actuary*, September (1998), 22. An interesting comparison with GARs is provided by maturity guarantees, which had attracted the attention of the DTI and an Institute Working Party back in 1977. The DTI survey had revealed great diversity of opinion among companies about the level and approach to reserving for maturity guarantees, ranging from no reserve at all, through arbitrary bases, to elaborate procedures for calculating the required reserve. The Institute's own Maturity Guarantees Working Party appointed in the same year had suggested that out of this diversity the profession needed to agree on a common policy for reserving against guarantees. Both it and the DTI seem to have accepted that guarantees, if given, should be reserved for; the question was, how. 'Report of the Maturity Guarantees Working Party', *JIA* 107 (1980), 103–113.

23 Corley Report (2001), 12, clauses 54 and 55.

24 *ibid.*, clauses 55–57.

25 Edward Johnston, 'The Appointed Actuary', *JIA* 116 (1989), 27–100.

26 Corley Report (2001), 14, clause 67.

27 *ibid.*, 15, clause 73.

28 Select Committee on Treasury Minutes of Evidence. Evidence of Sir Howard Davies. Evidence of 30 October 2001, question 8. Concerning the Equitable's alleged lack of cooperation with the regulator, see also questions 6, 28, 81 *et seq.*; evidence of 15 February 2001, question 169; evidence of 13 November 2001, question 167.

29 *ibid.*, questions 44–83. The Appeal judgment was handed down on 21 January 2000. In February the Equitable sent out a letter to policyholders expressing the view that this judgment posed no threat to the company.

30 See House of Lords, Opinions of the Lords of Appeal for Judgment in the Cause *Equitable Life Assurance Society v. Hyman* on 20 July 2000.

31 The Guidance Notes that concern the responsibilities of the Appointed Actuary are GN1, GN2, GN7 and GN8.

32 See the extensive evidence given to the Select Committee on Treasury Minutes of Evidence concerning the Equitable, but especially that of Sir Howard Davies on Thursday 15 February 2001, Tuesday 30 October 2001, Tuesday 13 November 2001 and Thursday 14 November 2002. The evidence given by Ruth Kelly MP, Economic Secretary to the Treasury, on Tuesday 30 October 2001, may also be of interest.

33 Chris Daykin, 'The developing role of the Government Actuary's Department in the supervision of insurance in the United Kingdom', *JIA* 119 (1992), 339.

CHAPTER TEN

1 By 1990 there were 76 per cent more actuarial students, at 4,375, in the UK than in 1981 when there were 2,472; the great majority of these received their training from the Institute. The very positive 50 per cent increase in the number of Fellows during the same period, from 2,935 to 4,375, brought its own administrative burden. See 'Recent developments in the United Kingdom' in *Transactions of the 24th International Congress of Actuaries*, Montreal, Canada, 31 May to 5 June 1992 (1992), 332.

2 Hugh Scurfield, 'Address by the President: Developing a proactive role', 25 June 1990, *JIA* 118 (1991), 10. Also 'Joint education with the Faculty', a Note prepared for the Institute Historical Archive, 30 May 2001.

3 Faculty of Actuaries and Institute of Actuaries Planning Joint Committee, 'Strategy for the 1990s', *JIA* 118 (1991), 429.

4 *ibid.*, 439.

5 See *Fiasco*, May (1990), in which the move and new premises were featured. This issue also contains an article by Chris Lewin, 'John Napier (1550–1617)', page numbered 0.8451.

6 'Institute Subscription Fees from 1970–1971 to 2003', a compilation drawn from Year Books and Members' Handbooks.

7 Ralph Garden and Tim Bateman, 'National report – United Kingdom: Recent developments in the United Kingdom', *Transactions of the 25th International Congress of Actuaries*, Brussels, 10–15 September 1995 (1995), N, 192–193.

8 Duncan Ferguson, 'Address by the President: For goodness sake', *BAJ* 3 (1997), 17.

9 *ibid.*, 18.

10 Paul Thornton, 'Address by the President: Lessons from history', 14 October 1998, *BAJ* 5 (1999), 38.

11 The level of Institute activity was quite high: in 1997–98, for example, the eight sessional meetings were supplemented by thirty-six conferences and seminars. Duncan Ferguson, speech at the Annual General Meeting, 8 July 1998, *BAJ* 5 (1999), 49.

12 Garden and Bateman (1995), 194–195.

13 See Institute of Actuaries Council Agendas and Committee Reports (on CD-ROM) (1987 to 1994): Report of the Eastern Europe Sub-committee to the Education Joint Committee on 18 June 1991, and the Report of its successor, the International Educational Development Sub-committee, to the Joint Councils on 9 November and 4 December 1992.

14 'The future of the profession: a study looking out to 2005 to identify challenges for the profession', September 1995, presented 22 January 1996. See charts, 10–11. Also in *BAJ* 2 (1996), 325–397.

15 *ibid.*, 59–60.

16 Paul Thornton, 'Address by the President' (1999), 8.

17 See S. F. Whelan, D. C. Bowie and A. J. Hibbert, 'A primer in financial economics', *BAJ* 8 (2002), 28.

18 Later, the Institute of Investment Management and Research, now the United Kingdom Society of Investment Professionals.

19 W. John Bishop, 'Actuaries and Financial Economics', a Note prepared for the Institute Historical Archive.

20 Bill Abbott, 'Managing the money', in D. F. Renn (ed.), *Life, Death and Money: Actuaries and the Creation of Financial Security* (1998), 185.

21 Chris Lewin, 'Financial Economics and Actuarial Science', a Note prepared for the Institute Historical Archive.

22 Jeremy Goford, 'Address by the President: Thinking and behaviour', 17–18, *BAJ* 9, 1–34.

23 Abbott, 'Managing the money' in *Life, Death and Money* (1998), 187. An informative watch on behalf of the profession itself has been kept by John Brumwell, who supplied 'Notes on the FT–Actuaries Equity Indices' to the *JIA* from 1970 to 1999.

24 Chris Lewin, 'Investment', a Note prepared for the Institute Historical Archive. I am grateful to Chinwe Nzewi for advice on this subject.

25 Chris Lewin, 'Corporate Finance', a Note prepared for the Institute Historical Archive.

26 Paul Thornton, 'Address by the President: Lessons from history', 14 October 1998, *BAJ* 5 (1999), 15.

27 Chris Daykin, 'The future of the actuary' in *Life, Death and Money* (1998), 203.

28 Interview with Michael Clark, 12 May 2003.

29 C. D. Daykin, D. A. Akers, A. S. Macdonald, T. McGleenan, D. Paul and P. J. Turvey, 'Genetics and insurance – some social policy issues', a paper presented to the Institute of Actuaries, 17 March 2003, *BAJ* 9.

30 *ibid.*, 10.

31 See C. D. Daykin, 'The regulatory role of the actuary', *BAJ* 5 (1999), 529–574. Paper presented to the Institute of Actuaries, 22 February 1999: 'The actuarial opinion is required under Lloyd's regulations, but is effectively a statutory role because of the approval of these regulations by the Insurance Directorate of H M Treasury as part of the procedures under the Lloyd's Act 1982 for the approval of Lloyd's rules for valuing assets and liabilities.'

32 *loc. cit.*

33 'The McCrossan Group'. Notes compiled by John Henty for the Institute Historical Archive. John Henty, 'International Forum of Actuarial Associations', *The Actuary*, April (1996). Roger Corley, 'Actuaries in an International Context', a Note prepared for the Institute Historical Archive, 8 November 2001.

34 Clare Bellis, *The Future-managers: Actuaries in Australia 1853–1997* (1997), 54–55.

35 Daykin, 'Regulatory Role', 5–9.

36 Several more dining clubs were founded during the 1980s: the Waterloo, the Six and Out (for actuaries qualified less than six years), the Seven Up (to which they graduate), the Maniacs (for actuaries working 'out of the mainstream and in small operations', according to a list that appeared in *The Actuary* of July/August 1991) and the Twenty Nine (for those who became Fellows on 29 February 1988 with the abolition of the two-year experience rule). The total number of them, including the regional societies' dining clubs, is seventeen.

37 'Presentation of an Institute Finlaison Medal to Mr John Howard Webb', *BAJ* 2 (1999), 261–263.

38 Paul Thornton, 'Address by the President' (1999), 21.

39 Jeremy Goford, 'Address by the President' (2002), 11. See also Institute of Actuaries and Faculty of Actuaries, 'Vision and Values'.

40 Peter Clark, 'Address by the President: Communication, culture and companionship', *BAJ* 7 (2001), 25.

41 C. D. Sharp, *Professionalism, Vision and Values* (1999), 9. Paper presented to the SIAS, 8 June 1999.

42 Jeremy Goford, 'Address by the President' (2002), 3.

43 The idea of a control cycle involving profit testing to build up a model of a company, the monitoring and analysis of results and the refinement of assumptions used in the tests is set out in Jeremy Goford, 'The control cycle: financial control of a life assurance company', *JIASS* 28 (March 1985), 99–114. As developed and simplified into a tool applicable to a wide variety of actuarial problems by Australian actuaries, the actuarial control cycle has come to signify the feeding back into the process of improvement of the knowledge gained through monitoring the means chosen to solve an identified problem. The Education Strategy for 2005 not only includes it as topic of study, but has borrowed from it, especially in the 'Core Applications' stage in which actuarial concepts such as risk, reserving and funding are taught across a range of subject areas. See '2005 Education Strategy' (an Institute brochure published March 2003) and J. Goford and others, 'Principles of the Future Education Strategy', presented to the Faculty of Actuaries, 15 January 2001, and to the Institute of Actuaries, 22 January 2001. See also C. Bellis, J. Shepherd and R. Lyon (eds.), *Understanding Actuarial Management: the Actuarial Control Cycle*, Institute of Actuaries of Australia, 2003.

44 Goford, 'Address by the President' (2002), 7.

45 Frank Redington, 'Address by the President', 27 October 1958, *JIA* 85, 1–13. Also in *A Ramble Through the Actuarial Countryside. The Collected Papers, Essays and Speeches of Frank Mitchell Redington*, edited by Gary Chamberlin (1986), 166–167.

Presidents of the Institute of Actuaries

John FINLAISON (1783–1860)	1848–1860
Charles JELLICOE (1804–1882)	1860–1867
Samuel BROWN (1812–1875)	1867–1870
William Barwick HODGE (1802–1885)	1870–1872
Robert TUCKER (1815–1875)	1872–1875
John Hill WILLIAMS (1814–1887)	1875–1878
Arthur Hutcheson BAILEY (1823–1912)	1878–1882
Thomas Bond SPRAGUE, MA, LLD (1830–1920)	1882–1886
Archibald DAY (1830–1904)	1886–1888
William SUTTON, MA (1842–1898)	1888–1890
Benjamin NEWBATT (1834–1896)	1890–1892
Augustus HENDRIKS (1834–1905)	1892–1894
Alexander John FINLAISON, CB (1840–1900)	1894–1896
Thomas Emley YOUNG, BA, FRAS (1843–1933)	1896–1898
Henry William MANLY (1844–1914)	1898–1900
Charles Daniel HIGHAM (1849–1935)	1900–1902
William HUGHES (1839–1912)	1902–1904
Henry COCKBURN (1848–1936)	1904–1906
Frank Bertrand WYATT (1853–1929)	1906–1908
Sir George Francis HARDY, KCB (1855–1914)	1908–1910
Sir Gerald Hemmington RYAN Bt (1861–1937)	1910–1912
Frederick SCHOOLING (1851–1937)	1912–1914
Ernest WOODS (1855–1932)	1914–1916
Samuel George WARNER (1858–1928)	1916–1918
Geoffrey MARKS CBE (1865–1938)	1918–1920
Sir Alfred William WATSON, KCB (1870–1936)	1920–1922
William Peyton PHELPS, MA (1865–1942)	1922–1924
Arthur Digby BESANT, BA (1869–1960)	1924–1926
Sir Joseph BURN, KBE (1871–1950)	1926–1928
Abraham LEVINE, MA (1870–1949)	1928–1930
Harold Moltke TROUNCER, MA (1871–1948)	1930–1932
Sir William Palin ELDERTON, KBE, PhD (Oslo) (1877–1962)	1932–1934
Charles Ronald Vawdrey COUTTS (1876–1938)	1934–1936
Henry BROWN, MA (1876–1943)	1936–1938
Henry John Percy OAKLEY, MC (1878–1942)	1938–1940
William PENMAN, MBE (1880–1970)	1940–1942
Henry Edward MELVILLE (1883–1976)	1942–1944
Reginald Claud SIMMONDS (1888–1969)	1944–1946
Sir Andrew Herrick ROWELL, MA (1890–1973)	1946–1948
Sir George Henry MADDEX, KBE (1895–1982)	1948–1950
Frederick August Andrew MENZLER, CBE, BSc (1888–1968)	1950–1952
Walter Frank GARDNER, CBE (1900–1983)	1952–1954
John Farrant BUNFORD, MA (1901–1992)	1954–1956
Charles Florestan WOOD (1905–1979)	1956–1958
Frank Mitchell REDINGTON, MA (1906–1984)	1958–1960
John Henry GUNLAKE, CBE (1905–1990)	1960–1962
Kenneth Ascough USHERWOOD, CBE, MA (1904–1988)	1962–1964
Sir Herbert TETLEY, KBE, CB, MA (1908–1999)	1964–1966
Bernard BENJAMIN, PhD (1910–2002)	1966–1968

James Basil Holmes PEGLER, TD, BA (1912–1992)	1968–1970
Ronald Sidney SKERMAN, CBE, BA (1914–2002)	1970–1972
Geoffrey HEYWOOD, MBE, BA	1972–1974
Gordon Vernon BAYLEY, CBE	1974–1976
Charles Michael O'BRIEN, MA	1976–1978
Peter Edward MOODY, CBE	1978–1980
Antony Robin Napier RATCLIFF	1980–1982
Colin Stewart Sinclair LYON, MA	1982–1984
Peter Gerald MOORE, PhD, DSc	1984–1986
Marshall Hayward FIELD, CBE	1986–1988
Roger David CORLEY, CBE, BSc	1988–1990
Hugh Hedley SCURFIELD, MA	1990–1992
Leonard John MARTIN, CBE	1992–1994
Christopher David DAYKIN, CB, MA	1994–1996
Duncan George Robin FERGUSON, MA	1996–1998
Paul Noel THORNTON, MA	1998–2000
Peter Nigel Stuckey CLARK, MA	2000–2002
Jeremy GOFORD, MA	2002–2004

Chief Administrative Staff

Sydney H. Jarvis	1892–1939	Assistant Secretary from 1902
Allan D. Dale	1939–1962	Secretary from 1952
Norman J. Page	1952–1983	Secretary from 1963, Secretary-General from 1977
Clive D. A. Mackie	1975–1990	Secretary-General from 1983
Arthur G. Tait†	1991–1997	Secretary-General
Gregor B. L. Campbell†	1993–2002	Secretary-General from 1997
Caroline M. Instance†	2002–	Secretary-General

†Since 1997 the Secretary-General leads as 'Chief Executive, The Actuarial Profession' in the secretariat for the Faculty of Actuaries and Institute of Actuaries. Earlier-serving members of staff feature in R. C. Simmonds, *The Institute of Actuaries 1848–1948*.

Biographies

Ronald Abbott CVO CBE, Finlaison Medal
FIA 1946. Senior Partner, Bacon & Woodrow. A member of Council and a chairman of the Occupational Pensions Board, he has written articles on pensions funding, and is the author of a history of the Association of Consulting Actuaries (ACA).

Francis Bacon
FIA 1934. Senior Partner, Bacon & Woodrow. As an economist as well as an actuary, he had a lifelong interest in the economics of State pension schemes. A member of Council, and a chairman of the ACA.

Rodney Barnett, Finlaison Medal
FIA 1945. Founder and senior partner of Rodney Barnett & Co., later Barnett Waddingham, he was the secretary and the driving force of the Continuous Mortality Investigation Bureau (CMIB) for thirty-five years, and the author of a number of papers based on research into mortality and related matters.

Gordon Bayley CBE, Gold Medal
FIA 1946. President 1974–76. Chief Executive of the National Provident Institution. The author of seminal papers on annuity business and, with Wilfred Perks, on the relationship of investment to the bonus distribution of a life office, he was also a chairman of the Life Offices Association (LOA), and a member of the Occupational Pensions Board. He served on the Wilson Committee and on a number of other government review committees.

Bobbie Beard OBE, Silver Medal
FIA 1932. General Manager of the Pearl. A member of Council and author of many papers on actuarial science, he contributed to developments in mortality analysis, and ASTIN grew out of his interest in the application of statistical methods to general insurance. He had strong international and learned society links, and was the author of the first textbook on risk theory for insurance. He was a chairman of the Industrial Life Offices Association (ILOA).

Bernard Benjamin, Gold Medal
FIA 1941. President 1966–68. Director of Statistics at the Ministry of Health and then Director of Intelligence for the Greater London Council. A leading figure in the fields of medical and actuarial demography, he was the author of over a hundred papers on these and related subjects. He was the first Professor of Actuarial Science at City University, and the UK representative on the Population Commission of the United Nations.

Sidney Benjamin, Gold Medal
FIA 1957. Partner in Bacon & Woodrow. A member of Council and a prolific author on a very broad range of subjects, he was one of the pioneers in the use of computers in actuarial work. He was instrumental in introducing actuarial methods into general insurance. His enthusiasm for research in many areas encouraged many others, and he also fostered cross-fertilisation between the traditional actuarial approach and non-traditional fields. A Visiting Professor at City University.

Arthur Digby Besant
FIA 1895. President 1924–26. General Manager and Actuary of Clerical Medical, he gave long and varied service to the Institute. He was a founder member of the Gallio Club, of which he wrote the first history.

Roy Brimblecombe CBE
FIA 1964. The Actuary of Eagle Star and then a consultant with Aon, he was a long-standing member of Council and a chairman of many diverse committees. As founder chairman of the Wider Fields Board, he encouraged new areas of activity for actuaries, such as banking and capital projects, and was presented with a President's Award.

John Bunford
FIA 1930. President 1954–56. General Manager and Actuary of the National Provident Institution, he was President for the return to Staple Inn and the granting of the coat of arms. He was also a chairman of the LOA and of the Investment Protection Committee for the Association of British Insurers (ABI).

Peter Clark
FIA 1971. President 2000–02. Chief Actuary of Sun Life (later AXA Sun Life), he has worked in many areas within the Institute and is also the longest-serving member of the Groupe Consultatif, joining in 1982 and becoming chairman in 2002.

Sir Brian Corby, Hon DSc, City University; Hon DSc, University of Hertfordshire
FIA 1955. Chief Executive and then chairman, Prudential. A long-standing member of Council with a notable contribution to professional guidance, he was also involved with the establishment of the Groupe Consultatif.   A number of high-profile appointments included chairman of the ABI, a director of the Bank of England, president of the Confederation of British Industry and chairman of the South Bank Board.

Roger Corley CBE
FIA 1960. President 1988–90. Chief Executive of Clerical Medical. He is particularly associated with the international actuarial scene and the conversion of the International Actuarial Association (IAA) from an association of individual actuaries to one of actuarial associations (for which he was presented with a President's Award), but was also active in developments in Investment, Life Assurance and Practising Certificates.

David Craighead, Finlaison Medal
FIA 1949. A Rhodes Scholar, he worked in life insurance in South Africa until he was banned for political involvement. He moved to England, where he began working as a consultant on systems design for Lloyd's syndicates and reinsurance companies. Through the development of methods for calculating reserves he became a leading actuarial pioneer in the London Market.

Chris Daykin CB, Hon DSc, City University; Gold Medal and Finlaison Medal
FIA 1973. President 1994–96. Government Actuary since 1989. The author of many learned papers, and co-author of *Practical Risk Theory*, he chaired the profession's committees on AIDS and genetics. He also played an important part in education strategy over many years. He is closely associated with the Groupe Consultatif, has chaired the IAA, and has extended and supported the growth of the profession in central and eastern Europe and in China.

Sir William Elderton KBE, Gold Medal and Faculty Gold Medal
FIA 1901. President 1932–34. General Manager and Actuary of the Equitable. He was a founder member and first President of the Students' Society, and also helped to establish the CMIB and to promote statistical studies. A prolific author who cast an innovative eye upon many classical actuarial subjects, he fostered international exchanges.

Duncan Ferguson
FIA 1970. President 1996–98. Senior Partner, Bacon & Woodrow. He has provided actuarial advice in thirty-seven countries. The International Congress of Actuaries in Birmingham took place during his presidency.

Marshall Field CBE
FIA 1957. President 1986–88. Chief Executive, Phoenix Assurance, then consultant, Bacon & Woodrow. He was a chairman of the LOA and a vice-president of the IAA. He served on the Fowler Enquiry into Provision for Retirement and chaired the 'Group of 18 organisations' which made recommendations for the regulation of the marketing of financial services. He has been the chairman of five different actuarial dining clubs.

Dennis Gilley
FIA 1950. Pensions consultant and partner, R.Watson & Son. His long service on Council, with chairmanship of many committees, was marked for his ability to cut through to the heart of a problem and by his concern that all should maintain the very highest standards in their professional lives.

Jeremy Goford
FIA 1971. President 2002–04. A Principal, Tillinghast Towers Perrin, with a strong interest in actuarial education who, with Lis Goodwin, designed the 2005 syllabus, widening it to be relevant to the UK, North American and Australian associations.

Frank Guaschi
FIA 1961. Mercantile & General Reinsurance and then a general insurance consultant, he was a pioneer amongst actuaries working in non-life insurance. As a member of Council, he was particularly involved with general insurance and, internationally, with ASTIN.

John Gunlake CBE
FIA 1933. President 1960–62. Senior Partner, R Watson & Sons. A chairman of the ACA and a member of many governmental commissions, he was a statistician as well as an actuary, and he wrote the standard textbook *Premiums for Life Assurance and Annuities*.

Steven Haberman
FIA 1975. Professor of Actuarial Science and Deputy Dean, Cass Business School, City University. A member of Council particularly concerned with continuous professional development, research and education, he is a prize-winning author of many papers and three books, which include the monumental *History of Actuarial Science* (with Trevor Sibbett).

Bert Haycocks, Silver Medal
FIA 1932. Tutor and Secretary of the Actuarial Tuition Service. He spent his whole career, except for a war interlude in operational research, instructing students and writing textbooks and courses for them, and was a lecturer at the London School of Economics to the first actuarial students to be university trained in the UK. He worked with Jack Plymen to develop the FT–Actuaries Index.

Brian Hey
FIA 1966. He qualified as an actuary after successful careers in computing and banking, and then worked with the Co-operative Insurance Society. He became an outstanding tutor and examiner, and was active in ASTIN and the General Insurance Study Group, and especially its Solvency Working Party. He was also the editor of the *GIRO Bulletin*.

Geoffrey Heywood MBE
FFA 1939, FIA 1946. President 1972–74. Senior Partner, Duncan C. Fraser. He was a co-founder of the ACA, the founder chairman of the International Association of Consulting Actuaries and the founder Master of the Worshipful Company of Actuaries. He has written on pensions and investments, notably on the valuation of equities in pension funds on a discounted cash flow basis, a practice that was followed for many years.

Sir Edward Johnston KBE, Finlaison Medal
FIA 1957. Government Actuary, he was very influential in the introduction of the Appointed Actuary system, which several other countries have copied. He was much involved with State pension schemes, but was also known for his work on occupational schemes, including the development of the Occupational Pensions Board. A long-term member of Council, he introduced a wide range of seminars and conventions for the continuing development of actuaries.

Bob Kirton CBE, Silver Medal
FIA 1930. General Manager of the Equity & Law, and a member of Council with strong interests in actuarial education, hospital administration and national pensions, he was a chairman of the LOA. With Trevor Haynes, he devised the basis on which the national PAYE tax system operates.

Max Lander
FIA and FFA 1946. Partner, Duncan C. Fraser. A strong early supporter of equity investment for pension funds, and of international links between consultants, he was the founder president of the International Employee Benefit Association and a chairman of the National Association of Pension Funds.

Sir Ernest Lever
FIA 1913. Prudential, after exceptionally distinguished war service. Involved with reorganisation and amalgamation of various steel companies in South Wales, he formed and became chairman of the Steel Company of Wales and later, president of the British Iron & Steel Federation. He was also active within the Institute.

Chris Lewin, Finlaison Medal
FIA 1964. A pensions manager, latterly with Unilever. Chairman of a joint committee with the civil engineers which, in 1998, published RAMP, a successful framework for project risk management, he has also written extensively on the history of the profession and is the author of *Pensions and Insurance before 1800 – a social history*.

Stewart Lyon, Gold Medal
FIA 1954. President 1982–84. Group Chief Actuary, Legal & General. A member of the Occupational Pensions Board and of the Fowler Inquiry, he has written notable papers on the role of State and occupational benefits in pensions and disability. He is a Fellow of the Society of Antiquaries and has been awarded the gold medal of the British Numismatic Society.

Sir George Maddex KBE
FIA 1920. President 1948–50. Government Actuary. He took a prominent part in the post-1945 remodelling of the national social security system and health service. He was a member of a number of official inquiries and public bodies, including the Statistics Committee of the Royal Commission on Population.

John Martin CBE, Finlaison Medal
FIA 1954. President 1992–94. Senior Partner, R.Watson & Son. He was a founder member, and later chairman, of the Groupe Consultatif. With the Institute he has been strongly associated with international education, and was a chairman of the ACA.

Reginald Maudling
FIA 1909. An early protagonist of widening the scope of the actuarial profession, he headed R. Watson & Son for over forty years. A member of Council and a member of a departmental committee advising the Royal Commission on National Health Insurance.

Fred Menzler CBE
FIA 1919. President 1950–52. Chief Development Research Officer, London Transport. Early training in the Government Actuary's Department (GAD) fostered an interest in statistics and demography, and the conviction that actuarial profession's destiny lay in 'wider fields'. He was a member of many departmental committees and Royal Commissions.

Peter Moody CBE
FIA 1947. President 1978–80. Group Chief Investment Manager of the Prudential. A respected and powerful voice in the City, he raised the profile of the profession in the fields of investment analysis and management. On ceasing active management of investments, he became a highly regarded director of some substantial companies.

Peter Moore TD
FIA 1956. President 1984–86. Principal of the London Business School, having been a founding professor. His books reflect a strong interest in operational research and risk analysis and include *Reason by Numbers* and *Basic Operational Research*.

Peter Nowell
FIA 1973. Fund manager and then Group Chief Actuary of the Prudential, he became a consultant, seconded to Equitable Life. A member of Council, chairing the Life and the Finance and Investment Boards, he has also chaired working parties on 'The Future of the Profession' and 'Financial Services in a Low Inflation Environment'.

Mike O'Brien
FIA 1949. President 1976–78. General Manager and Actuary of the Royal National Pension Fund for Nurses. His service whilst a member of Council included chairing recruitment and education committees, and he was chairman of the committee responsible for writing the first guidance note (GN1).

Maurice Ogborn, Silver Medal
FIA 1932. General Manager and Actuary of the Equitable. Author of *Equitable Assurances*, the history of the first two hundred years of his company and, coincidentally, of scientific life assurance. A long-standing member of Council.

Jim Pegler
FIA 1939. President 1968–70. General Manager and Actuary of Clerical Medical and later Professor of Actuarial Science at City University. He was the author of an influential paper on life office investment, the main propositions of which became known as 'Pegler's Principles'. He was a chairman of the LOA and of the Life Working Group of the Comité Européen des Assurances.

Gordon Pepper CBE, Finlaison Medal
FIA 1961. A stockbroker, specialising in bonds, who revolutionised statistical techniques and then developed monetary economics. He was the principal author of the internationally acclaimed Greenwell's *Monetary Bulletin*. A member of the Economic and Social Research Council and chairman of the Macroeconomic Modelling Consortium, he became an unofficial adviser to Margaret Thatcher and various Chancellors of the Exchequer. A Professor and Honorary Professor at City University, he is the author of five books.

Wilfred Perks, Gold Medal
FIA 1923. Actuary of the Pearl. A member of Council and the author of distinguished papers, and (with H. W. Haycocks) of the textbook *Mortality and other Investigations*.

William Phillips OBE, Gold Medal
FIA 1913. Called to the Bar in 1928, he practised as a barrister after his retirement from Manufacturers Life. His *Binary Calculation* (1936) was the first advance towards computer development since Babbage. A versatile innovator who expanded the horizons of the profession, he was the author of many papers and of *Pension Scheme Precedents*.

Jack Plymen
FIA 1937. A partner in the stockbroking firm of Greenwell, his contribution to the profession's literature on various aspects of equity investment is both substantial and impressive. His most notable paper, with Robert Clarkson FFA, claimed that rigorous investment analysis produced superior results where modern portfolio theory failed.

Mike Pomery
FIA 1970. A Principal Consultant and Partner with Hewitt, Bacon & Woodrow, he was chairman of the Pensions Board at the time of discussions on the replacement of the Minimum Funding Requirement for final salary occupational pension schemes. His work was acknowledged by the then Secretary of State for Social Security and by a President's Award.

John Prevett OBE, Finlaison Medal
FIA 1955. Partner, Bacon & Woodrow. He had a career-long special (and eventually successful) interest in persuading the courts to accept the application of actuarial methods in the assessment of damages. The first discussion of this subject within the Institute was based on his 1968 paper. He was a chairman of the ACA.

Tony Ratcliff, HonDLitt, City University
FIA 1953. President 1980–82. Chief Executive of Eagle Star, he was active in the ABI and a vice-president of the Geneva Association. Within the Institute his responsibilities included commissioning publishable papers for many sessional meetings, and he became an active Visiting Professor of City University Business School.

Harold Raynes
FIA 1909. Working in the Legal & General, he was an early proponent of investment in ordinary shares for life assurance and annuity funds. He served for many years as a tutor and examiner and was the first actuary to qualify as a Fellow of the Chartered Insurance Institute. He was also involved with London County Council, the London School of Economics and the LOA and was the author of books on company investment, social security and British insurance history.

Frank Redington Gold Medal
FIA 1934. President 1958–60. Chief Actuary of the Prudential, he developed the with-profits contract for pensions and terminal bonuses for life assurance policies, and he introduced the concept of 'immunization' of a fund against the valuation instability caused by rises and falls in interest rates. As chairman of the LOA he addressed the effect of nationalisation of life insurance in India, and as President he led the profession in its response to the change in State pensions. A book of his writings, published in 1986, captures the eloquence, good humour and good sense of a much revered actuary.

George Ross Goobey
FIA 1941. Manager, Imperial Tobacco Company Pension Fund. He was a champion of high-yielding equity investments, and later of property investment, for pension funds. He was a president of the National Association of Pension Funds and, as an early Master of the Worshipful Company of Actuaries, he fostered the profession's links with the City; for his pioneering investment work he received the Worshipful Company's first Award of Honour.

Sir Andrew Rowell
FIA 1922. President 1946–48. General Manager and Actuary of Clerical Medical. He was a pioneer of using life insurance funds to finance property development, and of deposit administration pension funding, and was instrumental in founding the British United Provident Association (BUPA) and the Nuffield Nursing Homes Trust. He was President for the centenary celebrations.

Hugh Scurfield
FIA 1963. President 1990–92. General Manager and Actuary of the Norwich Union, he was the founder chairman of the General Insurance Study Group. A reforming President, he was co-chairman of the first joint meeting of the Institute and Faculty Councils. He also chaired the organising committee for the 1998 International Congress and was President of that Congress.

Clifford Sharp
FIA 1940. After an extensive career in life assurance in the UK and Australia, he joined Noble Lowndes. He was a member of the first Occupational Pensions Board and has written papers on mortality and on ethics.

Reginald Simmonds
FIA 1911. President 1944–46. Actuary and Life Manager of the Alliance. Active in the Actuarial Tuition Service, he had a lifelong concern for the welfare of widows and the elderly, expressed through his work on pensions and annuities. He gave much time to the Institute, including writing its history for the centenary year, and to the LOA, and he served on the Government Committee to review the Tax Treatment of Superannuation Schemes.

Ronald Skerman CBE, Gold Medal
FIA 1940. President 1970–72. Chief Actuary of the Prudential. He was a chairman of the LOA, of the British Insurers' European Committee and of the Common Market Working Group of the Comité Européen des Assurances. His paper for the German Actuarial Society on solvency embraced 'Skerman's Six Principles' which, although at first regarded as controversial, were eventually adopted as the basis of the European Union directive covering this subject. Within the Institute he strongly supported setting practice standards and this led to the publication of guidance notes.

Frank Spratling
FIA 1932. He followed Menzler into the wider fields and became Chief Establishment Officer for London Transport. He gained respect for the profession in industrial contexts, and he co-authored (with Dr Leslie Norman) *Health in Industry*. A member of Council, he chaired many committees and drafted the original Memorandum of Professional Guidance and Practice.

Colin Stewart CB
FIA 1953. Directing Actuary, GAD, he was a long-standing member of Council and of the Council of the IAA. He submitted a paper on the financing of social security schemes and, with David McLeish, on prioritising accrued benefits on wind-up in the assessment of funding levels for occupational pension schemes.

Sir Herbert Tetley KBE
FIA 1934. President 1964–66. Government Actuary. He was a member of several public commissions in a period of great importance to national pensions and was the author of two actuarial textbooks on statistics.

Paul Thornton
FIA 1975. President 1998–2000. Senior Partner, Watson Wyatt LLP. Chairman of both the Pensions Committee of the Groupe Consultatif and the Employee Benefits Committee of the IAA, he has written papers on occupational pensions, and chaired the ACA.

Kenneth Usherwood CBE
FIA 1925. President 1962–64. Chief Executive of the Prudential. Having completed the actuarial examinations whilst a Cambridge undergraduate, he remained a mathematician with a wide-ranging interest in the applications of operational research, technology and computing. He was a chairman of the ILOA.

Howard Webb CBE, Finlaison Medal
FIA 1960. Actuary, Commercial Union. Long-serving member of Council, chairing many committees, including the Professional Affairs Board. He has made a significant contribution to the development of professional conduct standards, and these have been adopted as the international standard.

David Wilkie CBE, Gold Medal and Faculty Gold Medal, Finlaison Medal; Hon DSc, City University
FFA 1959, FIA 1961. A partner of Watson Wyatt and a Visiting Professor and Research Consultant of Heriot-Watt University, he was a member of both the Institute and the Faculty Councils, of the CMI Bureau and of the FT–Actuaries Index Committee. A prolific author, his contributions have been mainly in the fields of investment modelling, the construction of mortality tables and indices, and the modelling of AIDS and genetics.

Andrew Wise
FIA 1974. Pensions consultant and partner, Watson Wyatt LLP. He has written many papers on theoretical and practical aspects of investment for, and valuation of, pension funds and was one of the first actuaries to promote the relevance of financial economics to actuarial assessments.

Membership of the Institute of Actuaries

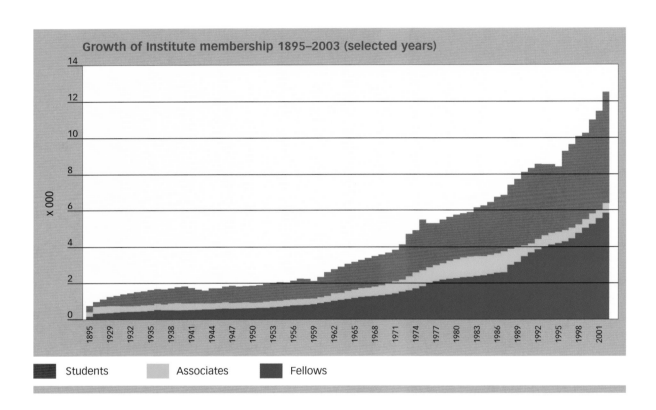

Growth of Institute membership 1895–2003 (selected years)

■ Students   ■ Associates   ■ Fellows

Source: Membership analyses in Institute of Actuaries *Yearbook* and *Handbook* for respective years unless otherwise stated.

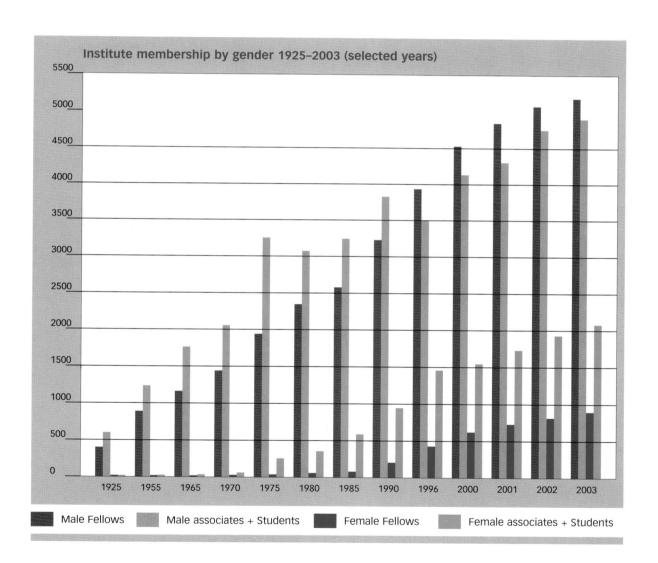

Institute membership by gender 1925–2003 (selected years)

Male Fellows   Male associates + Students   Female Fellows   Female associates + Students

MIND OVER DATA

AN ACTUARIAL HISTORY

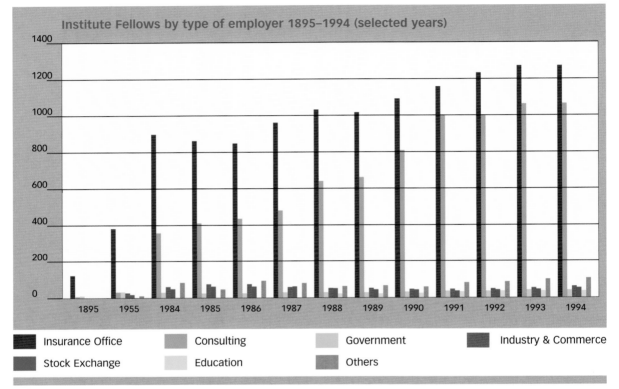

Institute Fellows by type of employer 1895–1994 (selected years)

Insurance Office   Consulting   Government   Industry & Commerce

Stock Exchange   Education   Others

Source: *Future of the profession: a study looking out to 2005*. 1995.

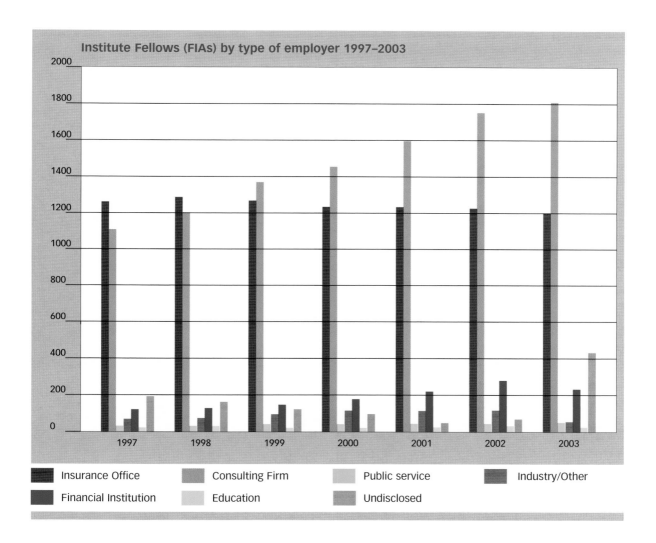

Institute Fellows: employment by country 2002

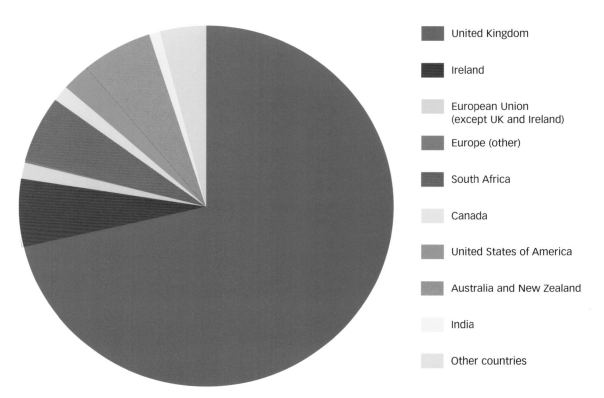

- United Kingdom
- Ireland
- European Union (except UK and Ireland)
- Europe (other)
- South Africa
- Canada
- United States of America
- Australia and New Zealand
- India
- Other countries

UK Institute Fellows: predominant area of work of those in consultancies as at June 2003

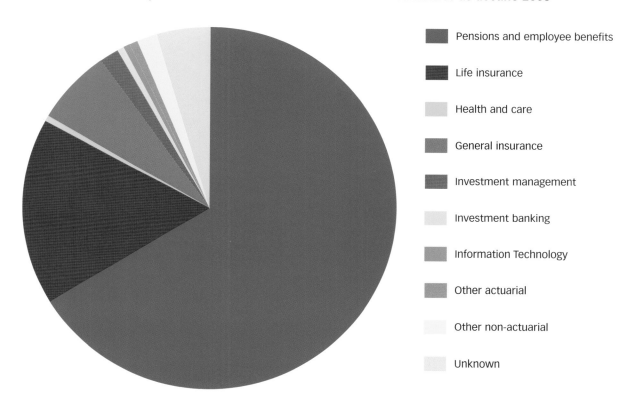

- Pensions and employee benefits
- Life insurance
- Health and care
- General insurance
- Investment management
- Investment banking
- Information Technology
- Other actuarial
- Other non-actuarial
- Unknown

Bibliography

PRIMARY SOURCES

Institute of Actuaries

Council Minutes Books 1943–2000
Reports of Committees to Council, numbered in series in bound volumes until 1986
Council meeting agendas and papers 1994–2000 (on CD-ROM, including minutes and numbered Reports of
 Committees to Institute Council)

'Miscellaneous [Committee] Minute Books' 1945–2000

Institute Business – Special Anniversaries (Anniversaries)
(archive files relating to celebrations in 1948, 1973 and 1998, as well as the 'Return to Staple Inn' in 1955)

Institute of Actuaries *Year Book* (years 1943/44 to 1986)
(These contain, among other material, the full text of the Bye-laws, annual Reports of Council, the minutes of the
 annual general meetings and record of ordinary general (termed 'sessional') meetings.)

Institute of Actuaries *Members Handbook* (years 1987–2002)
Institute of Actuaries Annual Report and Accounts (years 1989/90 to 2001/02)
Memorandum on Professional Conduct 1965–
Advice on Professional Conduct
Guidance Notes (as cited by number in the text)
(The Actuarial Profession libraries hold 'variorum' sets of each Guidance Note issued and subsequent revised
 versions.)

Life Offices Association (held by Guildhall Library)

MS28376 (scrapbooks containing agendas, minutes, reports, circulars etc., supplied to members); volumes 43 to 54
 cover the period 1942–50.

SECONDARY SOURCES

Abbreviations: see Notes.

Abbott, R. W. (1955). Pension schemes, aims and achievements. *The Accountant,* 29 January, 115.
— (1960). Growth of state pensions and their effect on occupational schemes. *The Accountant,* 4 June, 688.
— (1991). *A short history of the Association of Consulting Actuaries.* London: ACA.
Alborn, T. L. (1994). A calculating profession: Victorian actuaries among the statisticians, *Science in Context* 7,
 433–468.
Anonymous (1861). Memoir of the late John Finlaison, Esq, Actuary of the National Debt, government calculator, and
 President of the Institute of Actuaries. *JIA* 10, 147–169.
Anonymous (1862). *Memoir of the public services of the late John Finlaison Esq, Actuary of the National Debt,
 Government Calculator and President of the Institute of Actuaries.* London.
The Argonauts (dining club) (1980). *The Argonauts.* London.

Bacon, F. W., Elphinstone, M. D. W. and Benjamin, B. (1954). The growth of pension rights and their impact on the
 national economy: report. *JIA* 80, 141–265; Memorandum of evidence submitted by the Councils of the Institute
 and Faculty to the 'Phillips Committee' on the economic and financial problems for the provision for old age. *JIA*
 80, 266–283; Statistics of privately administered schemes. *JIA* 80, 284–288.

Bailey, A. H. (1861–1863). On the principles on which the funds of life assurance societies should be invested. *JIA* 10, 142–147.

Bannon, J. P. and Moule, M. D. (1987). *The Financial Services Act*. London: Staple Inn Actuarial Society.

Barley, R. G. (1957). The Institute coat of arms. *JIA* 83, 1–4.

Barlow, T. (1855). Memoir of the late Griffith Davies, Esq, FRS. *JIA* 5, 337–348.

Barnard, W. T. L. (1965). Some changes in actuarial methods arising from the use of a small computer in a medium-sized office. *JIA* 91, 108–146.

Barnett, H. A. R. (1991). CMI reminiscences. *The Actuary*, January, 12–14.

Barrow, G. E. (1976). Actuaries and long-term insurance business: introductory notes. *JIA* 103, 137–166.

Bayley, G. V. and Perks, W. (1953). A consistent system of investment and bonus distribution for a life office. *JIA* 79, 14–73.

Bellis, C. S. (1997). *The future-managers: actuaries in Australia 1853–1997*. Sydney: Institute of Actuaries of Australia.

— (1998). The self-taught actuaries. *The Actuary,* May, 22–23.

Bellis, C. S., Shepherd, J. A. and Lyon, J. A. (2003). *Understanding Actuarial Management: the actuarial control cycle*. Sydney: Institute of Actuaries of Australia.

Benjamin, B., Cox, P. R. and Menzler, F. A. A. (1956). Modern population trends and problems. *JIA* 82, 279–332.

Bennett, M. C., Berry, P. K., Brown, G. A., Farrington, G. W., and Hey, G. B. (1974). An approach to the use of computers in actuarial work. *JIA* 101, 299–351.

Benz, N. (1960). Some notes on bonus distributions by life offices. *JIA* 86, 1–29.

Besant, A. D. (1953). *The Gallio Club, 1903–1953*. London: The Gallio Club.

Beveridge, W. H. (1942). *Social insurance and allied services: Report*. Cmd 6404. London: HMSO.

Bolton, M. J. (1998). Guaranteed annuity rates. *The Actuary*, September, 22.

Bolton, M. J. *et al.* (1997). *Reserving for annuity guarantees*. Report of the Annuity Guarantees Working Party. 1997.

Boyle, J. (1992). Association of Consulting Actuaries. *The Actuary,* June, 34.

Bunford, J. F. (1991). Interview: John Bunford. *The Actuary,* September, 38–39.

Carr-Saunders, A. M. and Wilson, P. A. (1933). *The professions*. London: Frank Cass.

Clark, P. N. S. (2001). Address by the President of the Institute of Actuaries: Communication, culture and companionship. *BAJ* 7 (2001), 1–32. Address of 25 September 2000.

Clarke, T. G. (1990). A statutory role in general insurance. *Fiasco*, 126 May, page numbered 1.2788.

Cockerell, H. A. L. and Green, E. (1976). *The British insurance business 1547–1970: an introduction and guide to the historical records in the United Kingdom*. London: Heinemann.

Cooper, D. R. (1998). Life's little difficulties. *The Actuary,* November, 29.

Corby, F. B. (1980). Actuaries and professional conduct. *JIA* 107, 441–486.

Corley, R. D.; Corley Committee of Inquiry (2001). *Report of the Corley Committee of Inquiry regarding the Equitable Life Assurance Society* [The 'Corley Report']. Faculty of Actuaries and Institute of Actuaries.

Cox, P. R and Storr-Best, R. H. (1962). *Surplus in British life assurance*. Cambridge University Press.

— (1963). Surplus: two hundred years of actuarial advance. *JIA* 89, 19–60.

Cumming, O. D. and Purchase, H. F. (1969). Correspondence about the meaning of 'Actuaria'.

Czapiewski, C. J. W. (1992). Lloyd's – a thundering future? *The Actuary,* October, 24–25.

— (1993). The Lloyd's task. *The Actuary,* April, 8–9.

— (1996). The biggest actuarial project of all time. *The Actuary,* May, 22.

Davidson, A. R. (1956). *The history of the Faculty of Actuaries in Scotland 1856–1956*. Edinburgh: Faculty of Actuaries.

Davidson, I. H. (1985). Do actuaries need standards? *JIASS* 28, 43–52.

Dawson, K. and Evans, D. (1996). The personal pensions review: an insurance company perspective. *The Actuary,* August, 14.

Daykin, C. D. (1987). The 75th anniversary of the Students' Society. *JIASS* 30, 217–219.

— (1992). The developing role of the Government Actuary's Department in the supervision of insurance in the United Kingdom. *JIA* 119, 313–343.

— (1995). Address by the President: Turning promises into reality. *BAJ* 1, 5–36. Address of 27 June 1994.

— (1999). The regulatory role of the actuary. *BAJ* 5, 529–574.

Daykin, C. D. *et al.* (2003). Genetics and insurance – some social policy issues. *BAJ* 9.

Dennett, L. (1998). *A sense of security: 150 years of Prudential*. Cambridge: Granta Editions.

Deuchar, D. (1901). *Early actuarial and managerial associations*. Edinburgh, 1901.

Devine, H. [and Abbott, R. W.] (2001). *50 years on: a history of the Association of Consulting Actuaries* [with] *Annual Review 2001*. London: ACA. This book draws on Abbott, R. W. (1991) above.

Equitable Life Assurance Society [Society for Equitable Assurances] (1962). *The bi-centenary of scientific life assurance. Catalogue of an exhibition of portraits, documents, models, maps and items of historical interest concerning life assurance and the City of London through 200 years, held at Grocers Hall, Princes Street, London EC2 in September 1962*. London, Equitable Life.

Evans, J. V. and Kelly, K. P. (1984). From death to immortality. *Transactions of the 22nd International Congress of Actuaries* 4, 271–279.

Faculty of Actuaries Council and Institute of Actuaries Council (1959). *National pensions: an appeal to statesmanship.* Issued by the Council of the Faculty of Actuaries and Council of the Institute of Actuaries, May 1959.

Faculty of Actuaries and Institute of Actuaries (1973). *Continuous Mortality Investigation Report* 1. Institute of Actuaries and Faculty of Actuaries.

Faculty of Actuaries and Institute of Actuaries (1975–1988). *GIRO Bulletin* 1–47, 1975–1988.

Faculty of Actuaries and Institute of Actuaries (1976). National report: The diversification of insurance products in recent years and anticipated future development in Great Britain. *Transactions of the 20th International Congress of Actuaries* 1, 149–169.

Faculty of Actuaries and Institute of Actuaries, Maturity Guarantees Working Party (chairman A. Ford) (1980). Report of the Maturity Guarantees Working Party. *JIA* 107, 101–212.

Faculty of Actuaries and Institute of Actuaries (1984). National report: The political, social and other influences on the actuarial profession in Great Britain. *Transactions of the 22nd International Congress of Actuaries* N, 89–103.

Faculty of Actuaries and Institute of Actuaries Committee (chairman S. P. L. Kennedy) (1984). Report of the Committee to review the Structure for Education and Training. 1984. [The 'Kennedy Education Report']

Faculty of Actuaries and Institute of Actuaries (1984). [Responses to Government: 'Inquiry into Provision for Retirement' dated 30 January, 30 March, 16 July 1984] in Pensions issues: a discussion. *TFA* 39 (1985), 427–500. Discussion held at the Faculty of Actuaries, 18 February 1985.

Faculty of Actuaries and Institute of Actuaries, Planning Joint Committee (1991). Strategy for the 1990s. *JIA* 118, 429–452.

Faculty of Actuaries and Institute of Actuaries, Education Board (chairman J. F. Hylands) (1997). Development of Education and Continuing Professional Development strategy. 1997. *BAJ* 3, 785–834.

Faculty of Actuaries and Institute of Actuaries (1998). *Modelling the future: a celebration of the UK actuarial profession: catalogue of the exhibition*. London: Faculty of Actuaries and Institute of Actuaries.

Faculty of Actuaries, Institute of Actuaries and Association of Consulting Actuaries (2002). *Response to the consultation by the Lord Chancellor's Department on 'Damages for future loss: giving the courts the power to order periodical payments for future loss and care costs in personal injury cases'.*

Fellowship Club (1961). *Account of the Fellowship Club*. London.

Ferguson, D. G. R. (1997). Address by the President: For goodness sake, *BAJ* 3, 1–26. Address of 7 October 1996.

Field, M. H. (1986). Opening address in Institute of Actuaries, *Proceedings of the second actuarial convention, 20–22 September 1987: The actuary in pensions – a time of change.*

Financial Times (1973). The actuary: Financial Times survey. *Financial Times,* 2 July.

Financial Times. (1998). Actuarial services: Financial Times survey. *Financial Times*, 14 October.

Finelli, J. J. (1960). Installing electronic procedures – a progress report. *JIA* 86, 161–214.

Foote, N. (1994) Pension transfers. *The Actuary*, March, 25.

Forfar, D. O. (1998). History of the development of the actuarial profession and of actuarial thought in Scotland. *Transactions of the 26th International Congress of Actuaries* 2, 451–479.

Francis, J. (1853). *Annals, anecdotes and legends: a chronicle of life assurance.* London: Longman, Brown, Green, and Longmans.

Garden, R. and Bateman, T. J. (1995). National report: Recent developments in the United Kingdom. *Transactions of the 25th International Congress of Actuaries* 1, 191–211.

Gardner, W. F. (1953). Address by the President. *JIA* 79, 1–13. Address of 27 October 1952.

Gilbert, M. J. (2001). A very great pity. *The Actuary*, August, 30–31.

Gilley, D. F. (1972). The dissolution of a pension fund. *JIA* 98, 179–232.

— (1973). The past and future development of the consulting actuary's work. *JIA* 100, 71–107.

— (1987). *How to be a happy pension fund trustee: an eye-opener for the newcomer.* Reigate: Ringley Communications.

Goddard, P. R. (1979). The education and examination of actuaries. *JIA* 106, 201–206.

Goford, J. (2003). Address by the President of the Institute of Actuaries. *BAJ* 9, 1–34. Address of 1 July 2002.

Gosden, P. H. J. H. (1961). *The friendly societies in England 1815–1875*. Manchester University Press, 1961.

Gould, A. H. (1960). Operational research, its methods and application: a review and prospect. *JIA* 86, 109–160.

Grace, P. H. (1997). Presidential address [to the Faculty of Actuaries]. *BAJ* 3, 29–49. Address of 14 October 1996.

Great Britain and Ireland (1820). *Laws respecting friendly societies; including the substance of all the Acts now in force; with an abstract of the Act passed in the year 1819*. London: printed by J. Briscoe.

Guaschi, F. E. (1994). The Old Staple Inn. *The Actuary,* September, 30.

Gunlake, J. H. (1967). The Medals and Prizes book. *JIA* 93, 1–5.

— (1969). Memoir: Frederick August Andrew Menzler. *JIA* 95, 177–181.

Haberman, S. (1995). 'The history of actuarial science' in Haberman, S. and Sibbett, T. A. (editors), *History of actuarial science: Volume I. Life tables and survival model, part 1*. London: William Pickering, 1995.

Hall, L. G. (2001). *Stock's as good as money*. Private publication of memoirs.

Hannah, L. (1986). *Inventing retirement: the development of occupational pensions in Britain*. Cambridge University Press.

Harris, J. (1977). *William Beveridge: a biography*. Oxford: Clarendon Press.

Harrod, R. F. *et al.* (1952). Savings and inflation. *JIA* 78, 3–26. Abstract of the discussion held at the Institute of Actuaries, 29 October 1951.

Haycocks, H. W. and Plymen, J. (1964). The design, application and future development of the Financial Times–Actuaries index. *JIA* 90, 267–324.

Haynes, A. T. and Kirton, R. J. (1953). The financial structure of a life office. *TFA* 21, 141–218.

Heywood, G. (1999). George Henry Ross Goobey. *The Actuary,* July, 20.

Heywood, G. and Lander, M. (1961). Pension fund valuations in modern conditions. *JIA* 87, 314–370.

Higham, C. D. (1929). *Notes as to the Actuaries' Club, the Institute of Actuaries Club and the Life Offices' Association, especially with regard to their early history*. London.

Honey, F. J. C. (1937). The estimated population of Great Britain 1941–1971. *JIA* 68, 323–368.

Horton, J. and Macve, R. (1992). *The development of accounting regulation in the UK: the history of life assurance 1583–1991*. (*Working Papers in Accounting and Finance*; 29/1). Aberystwyth: University of Wales Department of Accounting.

— (1994). The development of life assurance accounting and regulation in the UK: reflections on recent proposals for accounting change. *Accounting, Business and Financial History,* 4, 295–320.

Institute of Actuaries (1928–1985). *Institute of Actuaries Year Book*. (Annual for years 1928–1929 to 1985–1986)

Institute of Actuaries (1943). '*Social insurance and allied services': verbatim report of discussions of Sir William Beveridge's proposals at Staple Inn Hall on 29 January, 5 February and 12 February 1943*. Cambridge University Press.

Institute of Actuaries (1948). *Centenary Assembly 1948: exhibition catalogue*.

Institute of Actuaries (1950). *Proceedings of the Institute of Actuaries Centenary Assembly 1948*. Cambridge University Press.

Institute of Actuaries (1955). The taxation treatment of provisions for retirement. Report of discussion of House of Commons Committee Report (Cmd 9063) held at Institute sessional meeting on 22 November 1954. *JIA* 81, 15–50.

Institute of Actuaries (1955). *Return to Staple Inn*. London.

Institute of Actuaries (1960). Jenkins Committee on Company Law: Memorandum of evidence submitted by the Council of the Institute. *JIA* 86, 215–220.

Institute of Actuaries (1972). State and occupational pension provision. *JIA* 98, 1–16. Discussion of Government White Paper *Strategy for pensions* (Cmd. 4755) held on 25 October 1971.

Institute of Actuaries (1973). *125th anniversary assembly: exhibition catalogue*. London.

Institute of Actuaries (1975). State and occupational pension provision. *JIA* 102, 17–33. Discussion of Government White Paper *Better pensions* (Cmd 5713) and on consultative document *Partnership with occupational pension schemes* held on 25 November 1974.

Institute of Actuaries (1985). *Proceedings of the First Actuarial Convention, September 1985: The Actuarial Management of a Life Office*.

Institute of Actuaries (1985). *Some landmarks in actuarial science*. London: Canada Life.

Institute of Actuaries (1987). *Proceedings of the Second Actuarial Convention, 20–22 September 1987: The Actuary in Pensions – A Time of Change*.

Institute of Actuaries, AIDS Working Party (1987–1991). *AIDS Bulletin*, 1–5. 1987–1991.

Institute of Actuaries Education Committee (Chairman K. A. Usherwood) (1958). Report of the Education Committee. 1958.

Institute of Actuaries Education Committee (Chairman R. S. Skerman) (1967). Report of Committee to review tuition and examinations. 1967. [The 'Skerman Education Report, 1975']

Institute of Actuaries Education Committee (Chairman C. J. Cornwall) (1975). First report of the Committee to review the education and training of actuaries. 1975. [The 'Cornwall Education Report, 1975']

Institute of Actuaries Education Committee (Chairman C. J. Cornwall) (1976). Second report of the Committee to review the education and training of actuaries. 1976. [The 'Cornwall Education Report, 1976']

Institute of Actuaries Examination Sub-Committee (Chairman E. H. Lever) (1946). The report of the Examination Sub-Committee on the Institute's examination system. 1946. [The 'Lever Report, 1946']

Institute of Actuaries Futures Committee. Education Working Party (Chairman C. D. Daykin) (1987). Educating actuaries for an uncertain future. Report of the Education Working Party of the Futures Committee. 1987.

Institute of Actuaries and Associated Examining Board (Francis, J. C.) (1990). Examination reform: a review of current practice and recommendations for future action. 1990.

See also Faculty of Actuaries and Institute of Actuaries for joint publications and documents.

Institute of Actuaries Students' Society (1945). *Report by the Committee on the Future of the Profession*. Institute of Actuaries. 1945.

Insurance Institute of London, Historic Records Working Party (1969). *The history of individual annuity contracts*. Report HR 12. London: Insurance Institute of London.

International Actuarial Association (1970). *75th anniversary of the First International Congress*. *JIA* 96, 401.

Johnson, P. D. and Hey, G. B. (1971). Statistical studies in motor insurance. *JIA* 97, 199–249.

Johnston, E. A. (1989). The appointed actuary. *JIA* 116, 27–100.

Jolliffe, J. A. (1972). Review: Report of the Tribunal appointed to inquire into certain issues in relation to the circumstances leading up to the cessation of trading by the Vehicle and General Insurance Company Limited. *JIA* 98, 276–278.

King, G. (1921). Memoir of Thomas Bond Sprague, MA, LLD. *JIA* 52, 241–259.

Kingston, T. D. (2001). Address by the President of the Faculty of Actuaries: A learning profession. *BAJ* 7, 51–73. Address of 2 October 2000.

Lang, J. (1993). Attracting women to the profession: editorial. *The Actuary,* September, 3.

— (1994). Lessons from pension transfers: editorial. *The Actuary,* March, 3.

— (1995). Women in the profession: editorial. *The Actuary,* March, 3.

Lewin, C. G. (1988). 1848 and all that. *Fiasco,* 105 July, 7–8.

— (1988). 1848 and all that. *Fiasco,* 106 August, 6–7.

— (1990). John Napier 1550–1617. *Fiasco,* 126 May, [7–10].

— (1998). Breaking into wider fields. *The Actuary*, September, 32–33.

Lewin, C. G., Carne, S. A., De Rivaz, N. F. C., Hall, R. E. G., Mckelvey, K. J. and Wilkie, A. D. (1995). Capital projects. *BAJ* 1, 155–249 (discussion, 294–330).

Lidstone, G. J. (1915). Memoir: Sir George Francis Hardy, KCB. *JIA* 49, 1–14; 178–180.

Lloyd, T. O. (1993). *Empire, welfare state, Europe: English history 1906–1992.* 4th ed. Oxford University Press.

Lloyd, F. J. (1997). Air Force actuary. *The Actuary,* November, 24–25.

Loades, D. H. (1993). Sir William Beveridge: a tide in the affairs of men. *The Actuary*, March, 14–16.

London Market Actuaries Group; Hart, D. M. (editor) (1989). *An actuarial view of Lloyd's and the London reinsurance market.* London: Institute of Actuaries.

Lyon, C. S. S. (1968). Social security and occupational pension schemes. *JIA* 94, 173–253.

— (1983). Address by the President: The outlook for pensioning. *JIA* 110, 1–15. Address of 25 October 1982.

MacNicol, J. (1998). *The politics of retirement in Britain, 1878–1948.* Cambridge University Press.

Maddex, G. H. (1949). Address by the President. *JIA* 75, 1–11. Address of 25 October 1948.

— (1954). The Government Actuary's Department. *TFA* 22, 146–152.

Manjrekar, R. (1995). The future of the London Market. *The Actuary,* August, 22.

Marks, G. (1919). Opening address by the President. *JIA* 51, 185–210. Address of 16 December 1918.

Martin, L. J. (1993). Address by the President: Actuarial highways. *JIA* 120, 1–16. Address of 29 June 1992.

Melchior, P. (1984). Demands on actuaries caused by development in computer technology. *Transactions of the 22nd International Congress of Actuaries* 4, 17–20.

Melville, G. L. (1970). The unit-linked approach to life insurance. *JIA* 96, 311–367.

Menzler, F. A. A. (1926). Proposed extension of professional scope. *JIA* 57, 88–126.

— (1960). *The Institute of Actuaries Students' Society: the first fifty years 1910–1960: an appreciation.* London.

Merchant, H. M. (1989). Arms and actuaries. *Fiasco,* 112 February, 4–5; 113 March, 4–5.

Michaelson, R. L. (1953). Large-scale electronic digital computing machines. *JIA* 79, 274–322.

Millerson, G. (1964). *The qualifying associations: a study in professionalization.* London: Routledge Kegan & Paul.

Moore, P. G. (1970). The theory of risk. *JIA* 96, 369–377.

Moorhead, E. J. (1989). *Our yesterdays: the history of the actuarial profession in North America 1808–1979.* Schaumburg: Society of Actuaries.

Morpeth, D. (1984). Alfred Watson Memorial Lecture: The outlook for the liberal professions. *JIA* 111, 1–14.

Murray, G. M. (1995). Presidential address [to the Faculty of Actuaries]. *BAJ* 1, 41–59. Address of 3 October 1994.

Office of Fair Trading (1997). *Report of the Director General's inquiry into pensions.* London.

Ogborn, M. E. (1956). The professional name of actuary. *JIA* 82, 233–246.

— (1962). *Equitable assurances: the story of life assurance in the experience of the Equitable Life Assurance Society 1762–1962.* London: Equitable Life Assurance Society.

— (1964). *Staple Inn.* London: Institute of Actuaries, 1964, reprinted 1980.

— (1973). *The Actuaries Club 1948–1973: sequel to 'The Actuaries Club 1848–1948' by G. H. Recknell.* London: Actuaries Club.

Ogborn, M. E. and Wallas, G. E. (1955). Deferred annuities with participation in profits. *JIA* 81, 261–299.

Ogden, M. (2002). *Memoirs of Sir Michael Ogden QC: variety is the spice of legal life.* Lewes: Book Guild.

Pegler, J. B. H. (1948). The actuarial principles of investment. *JIA* 74, 179–211.

Pegrum, J. (1993). Women in the profession. *The Actuary,* November, 28–29.

Pension Law Review Committee (chairman Roy M. Goode) (1993). *Pension law reform. Volume 1: Report; Volume 2: Research* [and] *Summary.* London: HMSO, 1993. [The 'Goode Report']

Phillips, E. W. (1927). The actuary in commerce and industry. *JIA* 58, 160–195.

— (1936). Binary calculation. *JIA* 67, 187–221.

— (1964). Private pension scheme developments since 1944. *Transactions of the 17th International Congress of Actuaries* 2, 713–723.

Plymen, J. (1950). Operational research. *Proceedings of the Institute of Actuaries Centenary Assembly 1948* 3, 313–328.

Post Magazine (1990). *150 years of insurance publishing.* London: Post Magazine.

Prevett, J. H. (1988). Actuarial assessment of damages. *JIA* 94, 293–343.

— (1999). The actuary as expert witness. *The Actuary,* December, 22–23.

Purchase, D. E. (1984). Seven years hard – a review of the examinations of the Institute of Actuaries. *JIASS* 27, 31–66.

Ranson, R. H. and Headdon, C. P. (1989). With profits without mystery. *JIA* 116, 301–345.

Ratcliff, A. R. N. (1963). State and private pension schemes in the European Economic Community and the United Kingdom. *JIA* 89, 157–225.

— (1981). Address by the President. *JIA* 108, 9–18. Address of 27 October 1980.

Raynes, H. E. (1928). The place of ordinary stocks and shares (as distinct from fixed interest bearing securities) in the investment of life assurance funds. *JIA* 59, 21–50.

— (1937). Equities and fixed interest stocks during twenty-five years. *JIA* 68, 483–507.

— (1964). *A history of British insurance*. 2nd ed. London: Sir Isaac Pitman.

Raynes, H. E. and Clay, H. P. (1935). Factors controlling the rate of interest on long-term investments. *JIA* 66, 167–197.

Reader, W. J. (1966). *Professional men: the rise of the professional classes in nineteenth-century England*. London: Weidenfeld & Nicolson.

Recknell, G. H. (1948). *The Actuaries' Club 1848–1948*. London: The Actuaries Club.

— (1950). Insurance against inflation. *TFA* 19, 17–46.

Redington, F. M. (1952). Review of the principles of life-office valuations. *JIA* 78, 286–340.

— (1959). Address by the President. *JIA* 85, 1–13. Address of 27 October 1958.

Redington, F. M.; Chamberlin, G. F. (editor) (1986). *A ramble through the actuarial countryside. The collected papers, essays and speeches of Frank Mitchell Redington*. London: Institute of Actuaries Students' Society.

Renn, D. F. (1984). The road to Windsor: centenary of the Royal Charter of 1884. *JIA* 111, 223–227.

Renn, D. F. (editor) (1998). *Life, death and money: actuaries and the creation of financial security*. Oxford: Blackwell.

Rowell, A. H. (1947). Address by the President. *JIA* 73, 1–19. Address of 28 October 1946.

Royal Statistical Society (1934). *Annals 1834–1934*. London.

Sampson, A. (1962). *Anatomy of Britain*. London: Hodder & Stoughton.

Scurfield, H. H. (1991). Address by the President: Developing a proactive role. *JIA* 118, 1–15. Address of 25 June 1990.

Seres, J. S. D. (1997). *Pensions: a practical guide*. 4th ed. London: FT Law & Tax.

Sharp, C. D. (1999). Vintage years. *The Actuary*, November, 26.

— (1999). *Professionalism, vision and values: are we behaving properly as a profession? A follow-up on the issues raised in the 'Vision and values' discussions*. London: Staple Inn Actuarial Society.

Shedden, A. D. (1986). Presidential address [to the Faculty of Actuaries]. *TFA* 39, 1–18. Address of 17 October 1983.

Shelley, M., Arnold, M. and Needleman, P. D. (2002). A review of policyholders' reasonable expectations. *BAJ* 8, 705–755.

Short, E. and Pain, R. H. (1992). The Index comes of age. *The Actuary,* October, 8–9.

Simmonds, R. C. (1933). The work of George King. *JIA* 64, 241–263.

— (1936). Twenty-five years. *JIASS* 4, 269–273.

— (1948). *The Institute of Actuaries 1848–1948: an account of the Institute of Actuaries during its first one hundred years*. Cambridge University Press.

Sked, A. and Cook, C. (1993). *Post-war Britain: a political history*. 4th ed. Harmondsworth: Penguin.

Skerman, R. S. (1968). The assessment and distribution of profits from life business. *JIA* 94, 53–100.

— (1973). The work of a life office actuary in the United Kingdom: recent developments and a look into the future. *JIA* 100, 35–69.

Smith, A. D. (1996). How actuaries can use financial economics. *BAJ* 2, 1057–1193.

Sprague, A. E. (1911). *A treatise on insurance companies' accounts being a second edition of 'A treatise on life insurance accounts', originally written by Thomas B. Sprague.* London.

Stewart, C. M. (1985). *The Students' Society Log 1960–1985: twenty-five years of enterprise*. London: Institute of Actuaries Students' Society.

Supple, B. (1970). *The Royal Exchange Assurance: a history of British insurance 1720–1970*. Cambridge University Press.

Suttie, T. R. (1946). The treatment of appreciation or depreciation in the assets of a life assurance fund. *JIA* 72, 203–228.

— (1947). Equity in bonus distribution. *JIA* 73, 37–65.

Sverdrup, E. (1954). *Scientific requirements in the actuarial profession*. Norway: Norwegian Society of Actuaries.

Tait, A. (2001). *A story of Staple Inn on Holborn Hill*. London: Institute of Actuaries, 2001.

Tappenden, H. J. (1962). Memoir: Sir William Palin Elderton, KBE, PhD (Oslo). *JIA* 88, 245–251.

Thornton, P. N. (1998). National report for the UK: an historical perspective. *Transactions of the 26th International Congress of Actuaries* 2, 497–511.

— (1999). Address by the President of the Institute of Actuaries: Lessons from history. *BAJ* 5, 27–48. Address of 14 October 1998.

The Times (1964). Supplement on 'The Actuary's Profession'. *The Times,* 25 May.

Timmins, N. (2001). *The five giants: a biography of the welfare state*. 2nd ed. London: HarperCollins, 2001.

Townsend, S. S. (1989). Old men remember. *Fiasco*, 119 October, 10–11.

— (1990). More of the same. *Fiasco*, 122 January, 8–9.

— (1990). Interlude in Whitehall. *Fiasco*, 127 June, 11–13.

— (1993). Examination echoes. *The Actuary*, August, 22–23.

— (1994). *Year Book* memories. *The Actuary*, May, 32–33.

United Kingdom. Department of Health and Social Security (1974). *Better pensions: fully protected against inflation. Proposals for a new pensions scheme*. London: HMSO.

Usherwood, K. A. (1963). Address by the President. *JIA* 89, 1–18. Address of 22 October 1962.

Wales, F. R. and Lyon, C. S. S. (1985). Reasonable expectations: bonus and growth illustrations. *Proceedings of the First Actuarial Convention, September 1985: The Actuarial Management of a Life Office*, 67–75.

Walford, C. (1871–1980). *The Insurance Cyclopaedia: being a dictionary of the definition of terms used in connection with the theory and practice of insurance in all its branches; a biographical summary, a bibliographical repertory, an historical treasury, and an account of the rise and progress of insurance in Europe and America.* London: Charles and Edwin Layton.

Warner, F. (1988). Alfred Watson Memorial Lecture: Public and professional attitudes to risk. *JIA* 115, 155–168.

Weaver, D. (1950). Notes on the changing background of institutional investment in the United Kingdom. *Proceedings of the Institute of Actuaries Centenary Assembly 1948* 3, 119–130.

Webb, S. and Webb, B. (1917). Special supplement on professional associations. *The New Statesman*, 21, 28 April.

Westall, O. (editor) (1984). *The historian and the business of insurance.* Manchester University Press.

Whelan, S. F., Bowie, D. C. and Hibbert, A. J. (2002). A primer in financial economics. *BAJ* 8, 27–74.

Wilkie, A. D. (1986). A stochastic investment model for actuarial use. *TFA* 39, 341–403.

— (1998). Four British Congresses. *Transactions of the 26th International Congress of Actuaries* 9, 315–322.

Wood, C. F. (1957). Address by the President. *JIA* 83, 5–17. Address of 22 October 1956.

Young, T. E. (1898). Presidential address: The origin and development of scientific and professional societies, with their bearing upon the Institute of Actuaries and its associated profession. *JIA* 33, 453–485. Address of 29 November 1897.

Published obituaries on members are the main source for the author's biographical profiles of late Institute Fellows. A reference list by name of these memoirs may be found on the Actuarial Profession website:
http://www.actuaries.org.uk/link/library/obituaries.html

An on-line archive of articles from the *Journal of the Institute of Actuaries* and *Transactions of the Faculty of Actuaries* is in progress at: *http://www.actuaries.org.uk/link/library/JIA-TFAvolumes.html*

INDEX